THE LONDON MISCELLANY

H. M. B.

from

J. W. P. A.

April
1938

STATE BED

Prepared especially for the Great Exhibition by Messrs. Faudel & Phillips of Newgate Street. In this exquisite specimen of needlework thirty young Englishwomen were employed for upwards of ten months, and it is highly creditable to the proprietors as a good specimen of the present state of fancy needlework and embroidery in England – a specimen which may well compete with the most finished productions of ancient or modern days.

THE UNIVERSAL EXHIBITOR, 1851

COMPILED BY ROBERT HARLING

THE LONDON MISCELLANY

A NINETEENTH CENTURY SCRAPBOOK

LONDON AND TORONTO

WILLIAM HEINEMANN LTD

1937

FIRST PUBLISHED DECEMBER 1937

PRINTED IN ENGLAND FOR WM HEINEMANN LTD
BY THE SHENVAL PRESS LONDON AND HERTFORD

LIST OF

CONTENTS

OF THE LONDON MISCELLANY

LIST OF

PLATES

IN THE LONDON MISCELLANY

The reproductions on the endpapers are as follows:

Front left: The Colosseum, Regent's Park
right: Blackwall Tunnel

Back left: The Philharmonic Rooms, Hanover Square
right: Tattersalls'

PROLOGUE

TO THE LONDON MISCELLANY

I COULD NOT HOPE to vie with those felicitous phrases with which Mr. Charles Knight introduced his London *Weekly* sheets to a waiting world in 1842. I do therefore that which is most proper to a scissors and paste practitioner, and borrow phrases from Mr. Knight's persuasive prose.

It will be neither a 'Survey' nor a 'History' of London claimed Mr. Knight for his many volumes, and I can at least say that. Those who look in these pages for a chronological record of London during the nineteenth century should now close these pages; those who look for an actuarial report upon the growth of the great wen will look in vain for many maps and statistics. Rather, the compiler of this miscellany has the same modest object as Mr. Knight himself: to combine information with amusement. To do this in two hundred and fifty-odd pages is certainly possible to the scrapbook maker, but what of the scrapbook browser? He or she will probably have other ideas concerning information and amusement. There is, then, only one possible course: to compile your own nineteenth century scrapbook – if London and that strange period hold you as intriguingly as they hold me.

After all, a scrapbook is a personal affair. But others are usually unusually interested in its inconsequential scrappiness. Others have been interested in these records. They incline towards what, I suppose, the Georgians and Victorians regarded as factual, circumstantial narrative. Because they did not strive for big effects and bright colours, so now, at this later date, they seem to have achieved them.

Looking through the pages again I find that my interest in newspapers, the magnificent efforts of Mr. Nash, the oddities of industrial design and the career of Lord Beaconsfield is shown fairly

9

strongly, but why not? The critic's job is to find omissions and we are all critics of compilations of this character. Indeed, it is probable that the one sure test of a London anthology is the right of the reader to claim, 'My God, he's left out Ackermann's description of this, *The Times* report of that.' There may even be suggestions that I should have altered the spelling or punctuation, brought them up-to-date . . .

So I leave the London Miscellany to critics kind and captious. Some of the quotations are likely to be known to the general reader, but not too many. I learn from booksellers that sets of Knight's LONDON remain in their shelves for longer than they can reason why. Other quotations are scarcely likely to be known outside the sphere of the specialist historian's activities. George Smalley's letters to the *New York Herald*, for instance, now out of print, deserve some publisher's keen attention. That correspondent's incisive comments on London personalities at the end of the century, would, with our current reawakening of interest in *Victoria Regina* and her times, be worth a re-examination. But enough . . . an anthologist's job is to get out of the picture as soon as possible and let his scissors and paste build up that pattern most pleasing to himself. R.H.

My thanks are due to the Editors of 'The Times', 'The New York Herald-Tribune', 'The Illustrated London News', 'Wisden's Cricketer's Almanack', and 'The Star', for permission to use extracts from those publications. Also to the Salvation Army for permission to quote from General Booth's book 'In Darkest England and the Way Out'. Also to Mary MacCarthy and to Secker & Warburg for permission to reprint an extract from 'A Victorian Childhood'. My thanks must also go to J. H. McMillan of William Heinemann, to S. L. Righyni of the 'New York Herald-Tribune', London, to William Littlewood and to James Shand of the Shenval Press and to my Secretary, Helen Mann.

THE LONDON

VISITOR

DURING THE NINETEENTH CENTURY

SELECTED FROM
CONTEMPORARY SOURCES
AND INCLUDING

AN ALMANAC OF THE AMUSEMENTS OF LONDON
INDICATING ALL THE OBJECTS
DESERVING NOTICE THROUGHOUT THE YEAR
FROM 'THE MIRROR OF LONDON,' 1804

A 'CAMERA OBSCURA' VIEW OF THE METROPOLIS
WITH THE LIGHT AND SHADE ATTACHED TO 'SEEING LIFE'
FROM PIERCE EGAN'S 'LIFE IN LONDON,' 1821

DIRECTIONS FOR STRANGERS
CONCERNING INNS, LODGINGS, CARRIAGES, ETC
AND A WEEK'S PERAMBULATION OF THE METROPOLIS
FROM WHITTOCK'S 'PICTURE OF LONDON,' 1836

A VISIT TO THE PRINTING OFFICE OF 'THE TIMES'
BY RALPH WALDO EMERSON, 1847

SOME NOTES UPON THE SMITHFIELD CLUB AND ADVICE TO
VISITORS, BY J. C. PLATT, 'KNIGHT'S LONDON,' 1842

TOGETHER WITH
OTHER BRIEFER REFERENCES
AND NOTICES

MR. HEAVYSIDE, *of Hanover Square*

Has a Friday evening meeting, every week during the winter and spring, of gentlemen of the medical profession and others, in his noble museum of anatomy and natural history. A respectable stranger known to any of his friends, may easily obtain access to this very agreeable and instructive assembly.

Richard Phillips, MIRROR OF LONDON, 1804

OF THE

AMUSEMENTS OF LONDON:

INDICATING ALL

THE OBJECTS DESERVING NOTICE THROUGHOUT THE YEAR

*** *The † after the day of the Month, denotes that the particular Day is not absolutely fixed.*

JANUARY

6 TWELFTH-DAY; the Bishop of London makes an offering of gold, frankincense, and myrrh, at the Chapel Royal, St. James's.

Confectioners and Pastry-cooks shops furnish an interesting spectacle, especially in the evening.

18 The Queen's birth-day kept – A grand gala at court at noon – Ode for the New Year performed – And in the evening a superb ball, at St. James's – Illuminations of public places, and the houses of the royal tradesmen.

20† The lectures commence at the Royal Institution – Dr. Young on Natural Philosophy, and Mr. Davy on Chemistry, Galvanism, &c.

22† Masquerade and Supper at Ranelagh, in honor of the Queen's birth-day.

N.B. In the course of this and the ensuing five months, masquerades are occasionally held at Ranelagh, the Opera-house, and the Pantheon, always previously advertised in the newspapers, admission 10s. 6d., 1l. 1s. and 2l. 2s. and dresses may be hired at the masquerade warehouses, from 5s. to 2l. 2s. each.

On the First Thursday after the Queen's birth-day, the PIC NIC amusements commence.

N.B. The Pic Nic society has now published their new plan, of which the following is a summary: – First meeting, the Thursday after the Queen's birth-day, and to continue every alternate Thursday till June – Every fourth week an harmonic dinner – Once in the season a dress ball, and once a masquerade. None but subscribers to the club can take out tickets for these, and the numbers to be limited to 500. – The dramatic performances to consist of two new French, and two new English pieces, with farces, played by amateurs nine times in the course of the season. – The Club to consist of 200 original gentlemen members, each of whom may recommend a lady or gentleman to be a member of the club, who must be named and approved of by the committee. – Six concerts during the season, under the direction of Mr. Salomon. – Subscription for gentlemen 13 guineas, ladies 7 guineas.

23 Hilary Term begins. On this, and the first day of every term, the Judges breakfast with the Lord Chancellor, at his house in Russel-square, and thence go in grand procession to Westminster-hall, to open the courts. This is a sight worthy of notice, particularly when the Judges arrive at the hall, where strangers should be about twelve o'clock.

First Sunday in term, the Judges go in state to St. Paul's.

The Gresham Lectures are daily, during the terms, delivered over the Royal Exchange, at noon in Latin, and one o'clock in English; open to the public gratis.

30 King Charles's Martyrdom; the House of Lords go in procession to Westminster-abbey, to attend divine service; the Commons to St. Margaret's church.

Every Sunday evening, from Christmas to Easter, the boys at Christ-church Hospital sing an anthem, and sup in public at six o'clock. Tickets to this interesting sight may be had of any of the numerous governors.

Every Sunday, during the year, service is performed at the Magdalen, and at a quarter past eleven, in the morning, and a quarter past six in the evening; at the Asylum. These places are much frequented, and highly interesting to strangers, both from the celebrity of the preachers, and the sweetness of the music.

In time of frost, the Canal in St. James's-park, and the Serpentine River in Hyde-park, are covered with skaiters; here a stranger will find much amusement.

FEBRUARY

1† CONCERT of Ancient Music commences in the Great Room, in the King's Theatre, Haymarket.

6† Anniversary of the Society for discharging Persons confined for Small Debts, Craven-street, Strand.

7† Concert for the Benefit of the Choral Fund, Theatre-Royal, Haymarket.

8† Subscription Concert, King's Theatre, Haymarket.

12† Hilary Term ends; after which, as at the end of every term,

RECREATIONS ON THE ICE

The good tidings that the ice on St. James's water or on the Serpentine is strong enough to bear (its safety is another matter) circulates far and wide, and the scene becomes ere long as animated as any that London has to display. Groups of warmly-clad ladies and children are gradually drawn to the scenes of action to watch the sport, and by their presence and encouragement to add gaiety to the scene. The less confident aspirants are encouraged to essay a venture for the sake of the bright eyes that look on; and the heroes of the day redouble their exertions to astonish and gratify the spectators, by vigorous efforts and intrepid feats of skill. Some few are to be seen, so well instructed by art, or gifted by nature, as to tread the slippery floor with as much decision and grace as would be exhibited by the most finished dancer in a drawing-room, and would half inspire the belief that they had never trodden rougher ground in their lives, or had been shod otherwise than with the narrow strip of steel which now supports them. Skating has one advantage over many other amusements, that it is free alike to the rich and poor. THE ILLUSTRATED LONDON ALMANACK, 1853

15

the *sittings* commence for the trial of causes, the first day at Westminster-hall, the next at Guildhall, in the city, then return to Westminster, and sit till the business is over, and afterwards go back to Guildhall, and continue till the business is finished.

22† Mr. Fuseli's Lectures on Painting commence at the Royal Academy, Somerset-place; admission gratis, by tickets to be had of the Academicians.

During Lent, on Wednesday and Friday evenings, Oratorios are performed at Covent-garden Theatre.

At the Hay-market Theatre, on Wednesday and Friday evenings, has generally been exhibited by Mr. Walker, the Eidouraneon, or Grand Transparent Orrery.

During the winter season, there are generally a variety of occasional exhibitions, particularly at the Lyceum in the Strand, as Phillipstall's Phantasmagoria, and Cartwright's Philosophical Glasses.

MARCH

1 SAINT David's-day, Anniversary of the Welch Charity. After service at St. Andrew's church, Holborn, dine at the Crown and Anchor.

4† Anniversary of the Marine Society, at the London Tavern.

17 Anniversary of the Benevolent Society of St. Patrick, at the Crown and Anchor.

N.B. Most of the public Anniversary Dinners are either on the same day, or the previous Sunday, preceded by a sermon, by some eminent preacher, and announced in the newspapers. The admission to the dinners is by tickets to be had of the stewards, or at the bar of the tavern, usually at 10s. 6d. a head.

Maunday Thursday, His Majesty's bounty is distributed to the poor at Whitehall-chapel, by His Majesty's Almoner.

Towards the end of this month, and during most of the spring and summer, are to be seen reviews, and other military spectacles, in Hyde Park, generally two or three mornings in the week. Notice of these may be had at the offices of the Commander-in-Chief, or of the Adjutant-general, at the Horse-guards, Whitehall.

Every morning a pleasing spectacle is displayed on the Parade, behind the Horse-guards, about ten o'clock, where the stranger will likewise be entertained with a charming concert of martial music.

16

LIFE IN THE PARKS

The few green enclosures which have been preserved from the encroachments of brick and mortar, acquire a value in our eyes to which it is to be feared their intrinsic merits give them but slender claim. They are the only refreshing spots in the great wilderness of smoke and dirt. If the trees be somewhat bare and stunted, and the grass present a somewhat arid and dusty appearance, they are trees and it is grass notwithstanding; and if the air be wanting somewhat in the pure inspiring oxygen that invigorates us in the country, it is heaven itself to the hot and smoky atmosphere of the neighbouring streets. The Londoner, therefore prizes his Parks as though they were fresh and fair as Arcadia itself.

They serve him with a hint
That Nature lives. That sight-refreshing green
Is still the livery she delights to wear,
Though sickly sample of the exuberant whole.

THE ILLUSTRATED LONDON ALMANACK, 1853

APRIL

1† ANNIVERSARY Dinner of the Literary Fund for the relief of authors in distress, at Willis's Rooms, St. James's.

5† Anniversary of the Freemasons' Charity, for educating Female Children, at the Crown and Anchor.

6† Anniversary of the Royal Humane Society, at the London Tavern. After dinner is a most interesting procession of persons who have been restored to life.

10† Anniversary of the Institution at Bermondsey, for the Education of the Deaf and Dumb, where they are taught to speak and read articulately, write, &c. held at the London Tavern. This meeting vies with the meetings of a similar kind at Paris.

Easter Monday, The Lord-mayor, Aldermen, &c. go in state to Christ-church, and attend divine service; after which a grand dinner at the Mansion-house, and a ball in the evening. Tickets given by the Lord-mayor, and with his permission, by the sheriffs.

Easter Monday, the following Summer Theatres open;
Sadler's Wells.
Amphitheatre of Arts (Astley's).
The Royal Circus.

Easter Monday and Tuesday, days of great frolic and revelry, in Greenwich-park, and deserving of notice.

Easter Monday, the City Hunt at Epping Forest, where the equestrian feats of the Cockneys will furnish a rich treat to a stranger.

Easter Term begins the third Wednesday after Easter Sunday, and lasts twenty-six days.

In this month, and during the summer, every day, but particularly on Sunday, from two o'clock till five, Hyde Park is a great resort of persons on foot, on horse-back, and in carriages. Kensington-gardens form also, during the same time, a great fashionable promenade.

MAY

MAY-DAY, The Chimney Sweepers parade the streets, drest in fantastic finery, and form very whimsical groups.

1† Clerical Levees commence at Lambeth Palace, every Saturday.

3† The Annual Exhibition of the Royal Academy commences at Somerset Place.

† The Anniversary Meeting of the Royal Institution.

6† The Anniversary of the Sons of the Clergy is held at St.

PRIVATE VIEW AT THE ROYAL ACADEMY

The most noticeable men among the artists in the palmy days of Private Views were the courtly Lawrence, the impersonation of graceful adulation, and old-world courtesies; Turner, our English Claude, with the manners, dress, gait, and physiognomy of the steward of a Margate steamer; Howard, the polished gentleman of the old school, with that suavity of manner, and blandness of courtesy, which were his characteristics; Constable, lavish of caustic criticism on his neighbours' pictures, but sensitive to a fault of any unfavourable remark upon his own; Flaxman and Stothard, simple-hearted old men with flowing silver locks; Etty, coarse-visaged and plebeian-looking, and strikingly awkward in his gait; Uwins, grave, sententious, and venerable beyond his years; Shee, poet-painter, polished and exuberant in his courtesies; Wilkie, with his slouching walk, and Doric simplicity, stealing now and then an exulting glance at the bulkhead picture (so called because it occupies the seat of honour at the head of the room, and used in those doys to be defended from too close a pressure of its admirers by a brass rail); Calcott, with an air of aristocratical assumption; Landseer, leading about the room some lady of high birth, and indicating to her what she is to admire. ILLUSTRATED LONDON ALMANACK, 1855

19

Paul's, where is performed a fine concert of sacred music and afterwards there is a dinner at Merchant Taylor's Hall. Tickets to be had of Mr. Robson, bookseller, Bond-street; Messrs. Rivingtons, St. Paul's Church-yard; John Bacon, Esq., First Fruits Office, Temple; and the Rev. Dr. Pearce, Lambeth Terrace, gratis.

7† Anniversary of the Magdalen Charity.

12† Ditto of the Foundling Hospital.

12† Ditto of the Asylum.

19† Annual Benefit Concert of the Royal Society of Musicians, at the King's Theatre.

25† On the last Tuesday of this month, the medals and rewards are distributed to successful candidates, by the Society of Arts, at their grand room in the Adelphi, and the sight is one of the most pleasing afforded by the metropolis. Any member can introduce his friends; or admission may be obtained, on application to Mr. Taylor, the secretary.

26† Anniversary Dinner of the Philanthropic Society, Crown and Anchor.

Whit-Monday and Tuesday the revels at Greenwich are repeated as at Easter, and are equally interesting.

Trinity term commences the first Friday after Trinity Sunday, and lasts three weeks.

JUNE

THE Thursday before Whitsunday, the Charity Children of the metropolis unite and attend divine service at St. Paul's Church, to the number of about 6,000, and form the grandest and most interesting sight which is to be seen in the whole world.

2† Anniversary Dinner of the Naval Asylum for the Support and Education of the Orphans and Children of British Sailors and Marines, London Tavern.

3† Vauxhall opens.

3† Anniversary of the Friends of the indigent Blind.

4 His Majesty's Birth-day. Grand drawing-room at St. James's. Birth-day ode performed. In the evening illuminations of his majesty's tradesmen and public places. At five in the afternoon the Mail-coaches form a very fine procession from the Post-office to St. James's and back. This should be a busy day to the curious stranger.

12† The Royal Academy Exhibition closes.

15† Astley's Annual Prize Wherry rowed for at Westminster-bridge, about four in the afternoon, in honor of his majesty's birth-day.

17† Regatta and rowing match at Ranelagh on the same occasion.

18† The Theatres of Drury-lane and Covent-garden close, and the Haymarket opens.

During this and other summer months are a variety of Cricket Matches at Lord's ground, Mary-le-bone, and Montpelier-gardens, Walworth. Admission 6d. or 1s.

Besides the rowing and sailing matches, mentioned in this and the subsequent months, there are a variety of occasional ones, which may be heard of at Searle's boat-yard, or the Mitre, Stangate.

During the summer there are also Launches of large Ships at Deptford, &c. which, if they are of consequence, are generally mentioned in the newspapers.

JULY

3† SILVER CUP and Cover, given by the Proprietors of Vauxhall Gardens, sailed for by gentlemen's pleasure boats.

6† Regatta and Annual Rowing Match at Bermondsey Spa, Kew Gardens opened to the public on Sundays.

17† A Silver Cup run for at Spa Gardens, Bermondsey, by gentlemen's ponies.

21† The Opera House closes.

30† Wherry rowed for, given by the Proprietors of Vauxhall.

31† The British Museum shuts for two months.

In this month the parliament is generally prorogued by his majesty. The procession from St. James's to Palace-yard and back, and the delivery of his majesty's speech in the House of Lords, both now and at the opening of parliament, are objects of proper curiosity.

AUGUST

1 COAT and Badge, bequeathed by Dogget, a player, annually rowed for by six watermen, in the first year after serving their apprenticeship.

2 The State Lottery begins drawing at the Scotch Corporation hall, in Crane-court, Fleet-street, instead of Guildhall, as formerly, and continues every Monday and Thursday for four weeks.

N.B. The lottery of 1802 was the first of three lotteries of 100,000 tickets, each to be drawn in eight days, being four weeks twice in the week. This consists of 24,000 tickets; the second, of 36,000 tickets, the commissioners have appointed to commence drawing the 29th Nov. and the third, of 40,000 tickets, to be drawn in the month of April.

12 Prince of Wales's Birth-day. This is the principal gala night of the season at Vauxhall.

18 Camberwell Fair.

21 Peckham Fair.
In this dull season for amusement, these two fairs afford great diversion to all descriptions of persons.

30† Vauxhall closes.

SEPTEMBER

2 BARTHOLOMEW Fair begins, and is a favourite popular spectacle for three days.

13 Drury-lane and Covent-garden Theatres open. For about three weeks they perform alternately each three nights a-week, then for some time each four nights, then each five nights, till at about the end of six weeks they play every night.

15 The Haymarket Theatre closes.

16† Annual Rowing Match at Deptford.

21 The Lord-mayor and Aldermen attend a sermon at Christ Church, after which at Christ's Hospital two orations are delivered in the hall, between one and two o'clock. The hall is open to every person.

23† Annual Rowing Match at Greenwich.

29 The Lord-mayor elected.

OCTOBER

1 THE British Museum opens, and may be seen *gratis* by applying at the gate for tickets.

5† The Circus, the Amphitheatre of Arts, and Sadler's Wells, close. The Royalty Theatre opens.

10 Anniversary Dinner of Mr. Fox's first election for Westminster; it is held at the Shakespeare Tavern, Covent-garden; and is attended by the friends of freedom from all parts of the kingdom. Tickets 10s. 6d.

NOVEMBER

6 MICHAELMAS Term begins.

7† Mr. Sheldon's Lectures on Anatomy at the Royal Academy begin, and are delivered every Monday. Tickets may be obtained gratis from the Academicians.

22

THE FIREPROOF LADY

AT BARTHOLOMEW FAIR, 1814

A famous person in the Fair was the Fireproof Lady, Madame Giradelli. This lady put melted lead into her mouth and spat it out marked with her teeth, passed red-hot iron over her body and limbs, her tongue and her hair, thrust her arm into fire, and washed her hands, not only in boiling lead but also in boiling oil and aquafortis. HISTORY OF BARTHOLOMEW FAIR

9   Lord Mayor's Day. A grand procession from the Mansion-
house to the Old Swan stairs, and thence by water, in the
state barges, to Westminster-hall, where his lordship is
sworn in before the Lord Chief Baron. After which the procession returns to Blackfriars-bridge, and passes up Lud-
gate-hill to Guildhall. A grand dinner succeeds at Guildhall,
to which admission is to be had by tickets from the Lord
Mayor and Sheriffs. The different city companies have also
dinners at their respective halls.

28 Michaelmas Term ends.

30 Royal Society's Anniversary meeting.
Anniversary of the Scotch Corporation for the relief of
Indigent Scotchmen; at the London Tavern.

DECEMBER

4† ANNIVERSARY of the society for promoting Religious Knowledge; at the London Tavern.

9† One of Terence's comedies performed at Westminster School.

20† The Annual Shew of Prize Cattle, Sheep, &c. at Smithfield,
with dinners at the Crown and Anchor, which are attended
by the principal Agriculturists from every part of the
united kingdom.

N. Phillips, MIRROR OF LONDON, 1804

LITERARY ASSEMBLIES OPEN TO EMINENT STRANGERS

IN LONDON several regular and known meetings are held of
literary characters, who converse upon philosophical subjects, new
discoveries, &c. One of the chief of them takes place between the
hours of seven and nine every Thursday evening, during the meetings of the Royal and Antiquarian Societies, in an outer room of
the apartments in Somerset-house, appropriated for their reception, and is exceedingly interesting to every intelligent stranger,
who feels any degree of scientific and literary curiosity. About
seven those gentlemen drop in who mean to assist at the meeting
of the Society of Antiquaries. The members of the Royal Society
enter at eight, when the conversations, turning chiefly on philosophical subjects, are renewed and prolonged till nine. A stranger
may be introduced to these conversations by any member of either
of the two societies. He will not elsewhere obtain so advantageous
an idea of the union of politeness, scientific intelligence, and talents
for conversation, in the English character.

N. Phillips, MIRROR OF LONDON, 1804

LONDON! thou comprehensive word,
What joys thy streets and squares afford!
And think not thy admirer rallies
If he should add thy *lanes* and *alleys*.
Thy INDEPENDENCE let me share
Though clogged with smoke and foggy air;
Though I'm obliged my doors to make fast;
Though I can get no cream for breakfast;
Though knaves, within thee, cheat and plunder,
And fires can scarcely be kept under;
And many a rook finds many a pigeon
In LAW, and *physic*, and *religion*,
Eager to help a thriving trade on,
And proud and happy to be preyed on;
What signify such paltry blots?
The glorious sun himself has spots.

IT SEEMS ONLY IN LONDON are the finishing touches of *character* to be obtained. To acquire 'excellence' in the Metropolis is a circumstance so 'devoutly to be wished,' that it is the genuine passport throughout all the provinces in England; nay more, it is wafted across the briny deep, and this sort of 'greatness' is acknowledged, admired, and sought after in all parts of the world.

LONDON is the looking-glass for TALENT – it is the faithful emporium of the enterprising, the bold, the timid, and the bashful individual, and where all can view themselves at full length, affording innumerable opportunities either to push forward, to retreat, to improve, or to decide. In no other place can FORTUNE be so successfully wooed as in London; and in no other place does she distribute her favours with so liberal a hand.

It is in LONDON too, that, almost at every step, TALENT will be found jostling against TALENT, – and greatness continually meeting with greatness, – where ABILITY stares ABILITY full in the face – and where *learning*, however extensive and refined, is opposed by *learning* equally erudite and classical. *Intellect* also meets with a formidable opponent in *intellect*. *Independence* likewise challenges *independence* to its post. And where *superiority* on the one side always operates as a check upon *superiority* on the other, that *self-importance* may be humbled, and *egotism* pulled down and exposed.

25

In order to give weight to these remarks, let us state, that it was the opinion of Dr. Johnson, 'that in London a man stored his mind better than any where else; and that in remote situations a *man's body* might be *feasted*, but his MIND was *starved* and his FACULTIES *apt to degenerate from want of exercise and competition*.' 'No place,' he said, 'cured a man's vanity or arrogance so well as London; for as no man was either great or good, *per se*, but as compared with others not so good or great, he was sure to find in the Metropolis many his equals and some his superiors.'

> Such London *is*, by taste and wealth proclaim'd
> The fairest CAPITAL of all the world,
> By riot and incontinence the worst.

The EXTREMES, in every point of view, are daily to be met with in the Metropolis; from the most rigid, persevering, never-tiring industry, down to laziness, which, in its consequences, frequently operates far worse than idleness. The greatest love of and contempt for money are equally conspicuous; and in no place are pleasure and business so much united as in London. The highest veneration for and practice of religion distinguishes the Metropolis, contrasted with the most horrid commission of crimes; and the *experience* of the oldest inhabitant scarcely renders him safe against the specious plans and artifices continually laid to entrap the most vigilant. The next-door neighbour of a man in London is generally as great a stranger to him as if he lived at the distance of York. And it is in the Metropolis that *prostitution* is so profitable a business, and conducted so openly, that hundreds of persons keep houses of ill-fame, for the reception of girls not more than *twelve* and *thirteen* years of age, without a blush upon their cheeks, and mix with society heedless of stigma or reproach; yet honour, integrity, and independence of soul that nothing can remove from its basis, are to be found in every street in London. Hundreds of persons are always going to bed in the morning, besotted with dissipation and gaming, while thousands of his Majesty's liege subjects are quitting their pillows to pursue their useful occupations. The most bare-faced villains, swindlers, and thieves walk about the streets in the day-time, committing their various depredations, with as much confidence as men of unblemished reputation and honesty. In short, the most vicious and abandoned wretches, who are lost to every friendly tie that binds man to man, are to be found in swarms in the Metropolis; and so depraved are they in principle, as to be considered, from their uncalled-for outrages upon the inhabitants, a *waste of wickedness*, operating as a complete terror, in spite of the *activity* of the police. Yet, notwithstanding this dark and melancholy part of the picture, there are some of the worthiest, most tender-hearted, liberal minds, and charitable dispositions, which ornament London, and render it the delight and happiness of society.

Indeed, the Metropolis is a complete CYCLOPÆDIA, where every man of the most religious or moral habits, attached to any sect, may find something to please his palate, regulate his taste, suit his pocket, enlarge his mind, and make him happy and comfortable. If places of worship give any sort of character to the *goodness* of the Metropolis, between four and five hundred are opened for religious purposes on Sundays. In fact, every SQUARE in the Metropolis is a sort of *map* well worthy of exploring, if riches and titles operate as a source of curiosity to the visitor. There is not a *street* also in London, but what may be compared to a large or small volume of intelligence, abounding with anecdote, incident, and peculiarities. A *court* or *alley* must be obscure indeed, if it does not afford some remarks; and even the *poorest* cellar contains some *trait* or other, in unison with the manners and feelings of this great city, that may be put down in the note-book, and reviewed, at an after period, with much pleasure and satisfaction.

'*Seeing Life*' will be found to have its advantages; and upon this calculation, whether an evening is spent over a bottle of champagne, at *Long's*, or in taking a '*third of a daffy*'[1] at *Tom Belcher's*, if the MIND does not decide it *barren*, then the purposes are gained. Equally so, in *waltzing* with the *angelics* at my *Lady* FUBBS'S assembly, at Almack's, or *sporting a toe* at Mrs. SNOOKS'S *hop* at St. Kit's, among the pretty *straw* damsels and *dashing* chippers, if a *knowledge* of 'Life,' an acquaintance with *character*, and the importance of *comparison*, are the ultimate results.

A *blow out* may likewise be found as *savory* and as *high scented* at Mother O'Shaughnessy's, in the *back settlements* of the *Holy Land*, by the hungry *cut-away* Paddy Mulroony, as the *Mulligatawny soup* may be swallowed with peculiar *gout* by one of the fastidious, squeamish, screwed-up descendants of the OGELBY train at Grillion's hotel. A morning at TATTERSALL'S, among the *top-of-the-tree* heroes in society, *legs* and *levanters;* or an hour *en passant* at Smithfield, on a Friday afternoon, among 'I's Yorkshire' and the *copers*, may also have its effect.

Rubbing against the CORINTHIANS in the circle of Hyde Park on Sundays, and breathing the air of nobility, contrasted with the aping, behind-the-counter, *soi-disant* gentry, supported by their

[1] Third part of a quartern of gin.

helegant tender creatures, decked out in all the made-up para-
phernalia of Cranbourne-Alley; and carrying the contrast still
further, of the various modes of disposing of time, practised by the
rude unsophisticated residents in the purlieus of St. Giles's, down
to the vulgar inmates of St. Catherine's, Wapping, – if, duly
appreciated, the *tout ensemble* is one of the finest pictures of 'LIFE
IN LONDON.'

Paying a visit to the *Fives Court*, to view the NONPAREIL and
Turner exhibit, or in taking a turn in the evening, to listen to,
Coleridge, Fuseli, Flaxman, and Soane, is the MIND make a *hit*,
and some *striking* impressions are implanted upon the memory
then the advantages resulting from the *varieties* of 'LIFE' must here
again be acknowledged.

The ITALIAN OPERA (this luxurious wardrobe of the great, this
jeweller's shop of the nation, this *scent* and *perfume* repository of
the world, and Arabian Nights' spectacle of Fortunatus's cap) is
one of the most *brilliant* collection of portraits of LIFE IN LONDON.
It possesses such fascinations, and the *spell* is so powerful, that to
be '*seen there*' is quite enough, the performances being mere *dumb
show* to most of its visitors; and however the languishing 'die
away' strains of Ambroghetti's *Don Giovanni* may almost cause an
earthquake in the ear of the tasteful critic, and call forth 'Bravo!'

> Vivan le femine,
> Viva il buon vino,
> Sostegno e gloria,
> D'umanita.
>
> ATTO II. SCENA 14.

yet, how strange it is, that the *Italian Opera*, to the great majority
of JOHN BULL's descendants, is positively worse than *physic*, and
who prefer being almost squeezed to suffocation, amidst clouds of
smoke, the fumes of porter, and the strong smell of *Deady's Fluid*,
at a Free and Easy Club, to hear TOM OWEN's '*Rum Ould Mog*,'
and, from the richness of its slang, pronounce it 'fine!' Such is the
diversity of LIFE IN LONDON.

RUM OULD MOG was a *leary flash* MOT,[1] and she was round and fat,
With *twangs* in her shoes, a wheel-barrow too, and an oil-skin
    round her hat,
A blue bird's-eye deck'd her *dairy*[2] fine, as she *mizzled* through
    Temple-bar,
Of vhich side of the vay, I cannot tell, but she *bon'd*[4] it from a Tar!
    Singing – Fol-lol-lol, de rol-lol-lol, de rol-lol-lol de lido!

[1] A knowing Cyprian.   [2] Bosom.   [3] Stole.

Again, while many prefer attending to hear the elevated judgements delivered by the LORD CHANCELLOR; others listening to the wit and eloquence of CANNING, and to the solid oratory and comprehensive mind of BROUGHAM; thousands in the Metropolis are to be seen setting at defiance wind, weather, and even property, enjoying beyond description the humour and antics of CALEB BALDWIN's *bull* upon Tothil Downs.

It should seem, then, that TASTE is everything in 'this *here* LIFE!' but it is also observed to be of so meretricious a nature to its admirers, that it is as perplexing to fix a decisive hold upon 'good taste,' as to take into custody the 'will-o'-the-wisp' that plays such whimsical tricks with the benighted traveller: and, perhaps, after all our researches and anxiety to obtain this desideratum of character, it matters but little to the mass of society in London, whether the *relish* for this chameleon sort of article is obtained over a quartern of *three outs* of Hodge's *full proof*, to complete a bargain of 'lively soals' at Billingsgate, before peep of day, by *Poll Fry*, so that happiness is the result; or, whether it is realized with all qualities of a barometer by Mr. HAZLITT, in the evening lolling at his ease upon one of *Ben Medley's*[1] elegant couches, enjoying the reviving comforts of a good *tinney*,[2] smacking his *chaffer*[3] over a glass of old hock, and topping his *glim*[4] to a *classic* nicety, in order to throw a *new light* upon the elegant leaves of ROSCOE's Life of Lorenzo de' Medici, as a *composition* for a NEW LECTURE at the Surrey Institution. This is also LIFE IN LONDON.

A *peep* at Bow-street Office – a *stroll* through Westminster Abbey – a *lounge* at the Royal Academy – an hour passed with the Eccentrics – a *strut* through the lobbies of the Theatres, and a *trot* on Sundays in Rotten-row, in calculation, have all turned to good account. Even, if out of wind, and compelled to make a *stand still* over the Elgin marbles at the British Museum, it will be found the time has not been misapplied. Washing the *ivory* with a prime *screw*[5] under the *spikes*[6] in Saint George's Fields, or in tossing off, on the sly, some *tape*[7] with a *pal* undergoing a *three months' preparation*[8] to come out as a new member of society, is a scene that developes a great deal of the human heart.

Again, hundreds of individuals in the Metropolis think it no loss

---

[1] A well-known hero in the Sporting World.
[2] Fire. [3] The tongue. [4] A candle. [5] A turnkey.
[6] Belonging to the King's Bench, formerly called ELLENBOROUGH's *teeth;* but later ABBOTT's.
[7] Gin. But spirituous liquors not being admitted into any prison, they were disguised under various appellations.
[8] *Whitewashing;* an old phrase now obsolete.

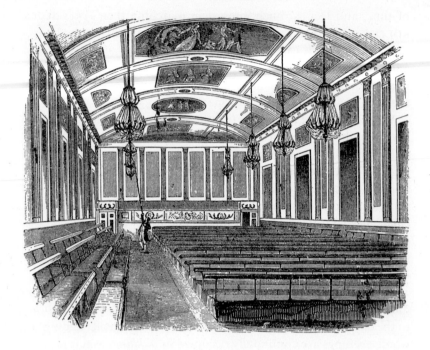

THE PHILHARMONIC ROOMS

HANOVER SQUARE

It was something in a lifetime to remember that first visit to the old Hanover Square Rooms, on one of the eight Philharmonic nights. The works of Mozart and Haydn, Beethoven, Weber, and Spohr, were rendered there in a more masterly style perhaps than anywhere else, unless it be at the representations of their operas by their own countrymen, when they occasionally visit us.

KNIGHT'S LONDON, 1877 edition

of time, and feel as much interest in matching their *tykes* at JEM ROLFE'S amphitheatre for a *quid* or two; or in drawing the badger at HARLEQUIN BILLY'S menagerie, and boasting of the goodness and breed of their dogs, as My Lord CARE-FOR-NOTHING does in relating the pedigree of his high-mettled cattle, and talking with the *touters* and jockeys at Newmarket.

While the entire happiness of others, it should seem, consists in diving night after night into the *Cellar*[1] to hear a good *chaunt*, although emitting volumes of smoke like a furnace, and crowded together like the Black Hole in Calcutta, yet no inconvenience appears to be felt, (and who, like their betters at routes, prefer rooms crowded to suffocation, than to experience what is termed *ennui*, arising from ease and comfort) and many of the singers who from their '*good-fellow*' traits have brought themselves into the last stage of a consumption, acting up to an old saying – 'a short life and a merry one!'

There are also numbers of individuals in London who feel as much (indeed more) interest in the *election* of a *Most Noble Grand* to the chair, than the return of a member to Parliament; and whose whole evenings are continually occupied in *toddling*, as it is termed, from one lodge to another.

From the many *tricks* and *fancies* the inhabitants of this great Metropolis are subject to, it seems some poet has humorously described *London* as '*the Devil!*' The contrasts are so fine and delightful – so marked with light and shade – and, upon the whole, offer such an extensive volume of intelligence, that the peruser must be ignorant indeed if something of importance does not fasten upon his mind, and which may, at some future period, be applied with success. However, it is not from hearing the amateurs cry out '*bravo*' and '*encore*,' at the Hanover-Square Concert-Rooms, that a knowledge of music is to be acquired; and it is not in witnessing great numbers of society swallow *blue ruin* like water, at the *gin-spinners*,[2] that the whole of the lower orders in the Metropolis are to be libelled and traduced; neither is it from beholding that description of *bon vivants*, whose peculiar enjoyment consist in *flooring* the watchmen at midnight, that 'seeing Life' can be said to have its advantages.

No. Life in London is intended to show that individuals ought not to be too confident, or too precise; but, above all, it affords them the opportunity of appreciating the advantages that experience holds forth, not to look down upon their fellow-creatures with contempt.

[1] Spring Gardens.   [2] Wine-vaults.

LIFE IN LONDON is also to admire the good and to avoid the vicious; but never to entertain an idea, that however bad and depraved some individuals may appear to be, that they are past any attempt to reclaim them from their evil ways; and likewise to bear in mind, that 'it is never too late to mend.'

To get 'out into the world,' or 'seeing Life,' is not merely an empty phrase upon every person's tongue, but it is an actual object in view. The father urges its necessity to his son, – the uncle talks of its value to his nephew, – and the aunt mentions it to her niece as an object worthy of the highest consideration; and, in short, it is a paramount idea with all persons who have under their care, and who feel anxiously towards the promotion of youth. It is, however, not absolutely necessary to a man's salvation, or as the only road to make his fortune, that he should pay a visit to London, like the Mahometans, who are compelled to undertake a pilgrimage once in their lives to do homage before the tomb of Mahomet, at Mecca; any more than the assertion proves correct, that a man, born in England, who does not visit London during his existence, dies 'a fool.'

Pierce Egan, LIFE IN LONDON, 1821

DIRECTIONS FOR STRANGERS

CONCERNING INNS, BOARDING-HOUSES, ETC;

AND A JOURNAL OF A WEEK'S PERAMBULATION

OF THE METROPOLIS

POINTING OUT ALL THAT CAN BE SEEN IN THAT TIME

THE STRANGER WHO is induced to visit London, from motives of curiosity, and only intends devoting a short time for this purpose, will find that the proper selection of a lodging, as a temporary home, during his sojourn in the metropolis, will greatly facilitate his progress and contribute to his enjoyments.

We must suppose that the stranger, on his arrival in London, either sojourns at an inn, or has apartments for a few days. If he is alone, it is probable that he will find himself most comfortable at a quiet, respectable inn – not a coach inn, where he will be sure to be disturbed every hour of the night – but, at the numerous inns or taverns to be found in the streets leading from the principal thoroughfares of London. If his business, for instance, is in the city, the traveller would prefer the quietude and convenience of the Axe Inn, Aldermanbury; where, in a well-aired, lofty apartment, he would, though in the very centre of the city, be as free from noise as in a secluded village: the same may be said of the Guildhall Coffee-house, in King Street, and many others similarly situated. The charges at most of the inns are about the same as at the commercial inns throughout the kingdom. If the visitor has no particular business in the city, he will find it most convenient and pleasant to take up his abode westward; he will be nearer the theatres and principal exhibitions. The inns and hotels in the vicinity of the Strand will afford him excellent accommodation; or, if he prefers apartments, he may procure them, for any number of days, in most of the streets leading from the Strand to the Thames, which are principally inhabited by persons who keep boarding-houses, or that let apartments to visitors to the metropolis. The visitor of every sphere of life may be accommodated according to his circumstances; if he wishes splendid apartments and first-rate attendance, the hotels in the Adelphi, Covent Garden, or Leicester Square will be found equal to his wishes; if he only requires cleanliness, comfort, and security, he may obtain them at the taverns and lodging-houses in the respectable cross streets; but if he would sleep at night, let him most carefully avoid the coach inns, or the inns in the leading streets. Visitors that intend staying two or three weeks, particularly if there are three or four in the party, would find lodgings much more comfortable and economical than living at an inn. It is impossible to fix any general scale of terms, as the prices of boarding-houses vary from two to five guineas per week; and private lodgings, with attendance, from fifteen shillings to two pounds per week. The visitor whose time is limited, will find it better to have lodgings without board, as he can take his meals at any time or place, according to his own convenience.

The visitor to the metropolis, that has no particular friends to greet him on his arrival, and whose business will only allow him to devote a few days, to the survey of the architectural beauties and splendid exhibitions which surround him on all sides, on his arrival in London, will feel the necessity of so regulating his time, that he may see the various objects that are contiguous to each other on the same day; and, supposing him to have only a week that he can spare for this purpose, we will endeavour to point out the best mode of regulating his hours, so that he may have an opportunity of seeing the greatest number of objects within that time.

We will therefore suppose the visitor to have taken apartments near Charing Cross, and to commence his perambulation of the metropolis on *Monday* morning, at half-past nine o'clock. He will have ample time to see Whitehall, the statue of King James behind it, the Horse Guards, and the Admiralty. Walk into St. James's Park, stand a few minutes to observe the military parade, which always takes place at ten o'clock; walk through the Park to Storey's Gate; thence, down Princes Street, and he will see Westminster Abbey, and the New Westminster Hospital, to the greatest advantage. Passing through St. Margaret's churchyard, he will observe the beautiful entrance to the north transept of the Abbey. The next object that will present itself, is the chapel of Henry VII, and he will arrive at Poet's Corner at about half-past ten o'clock: the entrance to the Abbey will be open, and he will have an opportunity of hearing the cathedral service performed, and likewise of seeing the beautiful choir of the Abbey; the service is ended about eleven o'clock, and he can then survey every part of this venerable pile, which will occupy about an hour. On leaving the Abbey, at half-past twelve, the stranger may cross the road, to the Houses of Lords and Commons, and Westminster Hall, see the interior of them, and at one o'clock find himself on Westminster Bridge, surveying the buildings on the banks of the Thames. If this survey should engender historical reminiscences, the stranger would probably wish to visit the scene of Wolsey's greatness, and the residence of the primate of England, Lambeth Palace; should he do so, he will find his time occupied till two o'clock. On leaving the palace, if he continues down Canterbury Place, he will, in a short time, arrive at Bethlem Hospital; to some, the interior is interesting, if so, it will occupy half an hour. Near the same spot, is the Asylum for the Deaf and Dumb, the Philanthropic Asylum, and other charitable foundations, the whole of which may be visited, and the party return home over Waterloo Bridge, observe the grand front of Somerset House, and arrive at their lodgings by half-past four o'clock, dine, and finish the day by visiting Drury Lane Theatre.

Tuesday. Starting at half-past nine, proceed eastward, enter Somerset House; see King's College; turn down Arundel Street, to the Temple; see the Fountain, Ancient Hall, and the church of the Inner Temple, which is frequently open in the morning. On leaving the Temple, enter Fleet Street, onwards to Ludgate Hill, to the north entrance of St. Paul's. There is morning service at St. Paul's, which occupies about three-quarters of an hour, during which time the cathedral cannot be shown; the party, in this case, if they do not wish to hear the service sung, may proceed to the Post Office, and Goldsmiths' Hall, then return to St. Paul's, which it is always best to view in the morning: St. Paul's may be seen in an hour. Next visit the Bank; observe the Pay Office, the Rotunda, and some of the offices, you need not go through them all, as they are nearly alike. See the Auction Mart, and Royal Exchange. By way of rest and refreshment, take a basin of soup at Birch's, or any of the coffee-houses about the Exchange. Proceed down King William Street, to London Bridge, thence to the Tower, and the Mint; survey St. Katherine's Dock; then take a boat from the Tower, and you will see the Custom House, London, Southwark, and Waterloo Bridges, with the buildings on either side of the river; and return to dine in your own apartments at five o'clock; when, by seven o'clock, the party will be sufficiently rested to enjoy the play at Covent Garden Theatre.

Wednesday. Visit the Adelaide Gallery; the British Museum; ride to the Regent's Park, see the Diorama, the Colosseum, Swiss Cottage, &c.; return home down Regent Street, dine, and in the evening visit Astley's Amphitheatre.

Thursday. Get into the omnibus or coach that goes to Blackwall, see the East and West India Docks; a short walk thence will take you to the Ferry-House; on crossing the Thames, see Greenwich Hospital; ride on the Railroad as far as Bermondsey; walk to Rotherhithe, devote an hour to the examination of the Tunnel; dine at Rotherhithe, and afterwards ride to the Surrey Zoological Gardens. Towards the evening return to dress, and at eight o'clock go by water to Vauxhall.

Friday. West end: walk to St. James's; see the Palace, Clubhouses, and British Gallery, if open; walk through the Park, see the New Palace, and York House; walk through the Green Park to Hyde Park; see the Triumphal Arch, and Statue of Achilles. At Oxford Street Gate, ride to the Zoological Gardens, spend two hours, return by Portland Place to Oxford Street; visit the Bazaars, return home, dine, and in the evening, visit *Braham's New Theatre*, recently erected in King Street, St. James's Square. This theatre is the last erected, and is certainly the most beautiful minor theatre in the metropolis; it is opened under a licence from the lord chamberlain, granted to this favoured votary of Apollo, who has been the leading singer, not only of England, but of Europe, upwards of thirty years. The exterior is plain, but the interior is superb. The boxes are supported by cariatydes, and the ornaments are of the most gorgeous description, in the style used in France during the reign of Louis XIV. The performances are operas and farces; Braham frequently appears in both, and being seconded by an excellent company, it would be a matter of surprise if the theatre was not fashionably and numerously attended. The prices of admission are, to the boxes, five shillings; pit, three shillings; gallery, one shilling and sixpence: the half-price commences at nine o'clock.

Saturday. Visit Covent Garden Market, before breakfast; return, go over Hungerford Market, take a boat at the stairs, to Chelsea; see Westminster Bridge, the Speaker's House, the Penitentiary, Vauxhall Bridge, the Royal Hospital, at Chelsea; walk to the Duke of York's School, thence to the Pantechnicon, through Belgrave Square. Ride home, and in the evening go to the Opera House.

Sunday. Attend divine service in the morning, at the Foundling Hospital; then ride in the omnibus to the Edgeware Road, promenade in Hyde Park, dine at home, and in the evening, attend divine service at the Magdalen Hospital.

The week has now terminated, and the stranger that has visited all the places, in the order laid down for him, will have seen every part of the metropolis, and all the principal objects. He will find that ample time has been allowed for a cursory view of most of the curiosities.

In the foregoing directions, it is supposed that the party is in the middle rank of life; the same route would be pointed out to those who kept a carriage, but they would, in consequence, be enabled to visit more objects in the same time, from the facility of conveyance from one place to another.

The reader will observe that in the various excursions during the week, he will frequently be obliged to ride, and for cheap and expeditious means of conveyance, no place can be superior to London. In nearly every leading street, are stands for hackney coaches, chariots, and cabriolets; either of these conveyances can be hired, either by the hour or per mile; every carriage is numbered on a conspicuous part, and a stranger, hiring one of these vehicles, should be particularly careful in noticing the number. The fares are regulated according to the distance, but gross impositions are frequently practised upon strangers, by the drivers of the various carriages. To avoid any altercation about the charge, it will always be advisable for the stranger to inquire the fare before he hires the vehicle; if he thinks the demand is too much, he can refuse to give the amount, and it is most probable that another driver will offer to take him for less; at any rate, if he agrees to give the fare demanded, it saves all disagreeable altercation at the end of the journey. Should such an occurrence take place, if the stranger thinks he is charged too much, he had better place the amount demanded in his hand, and holding it before the coachman, desire him to take his fare and no more. If he takes more, he can be sum-

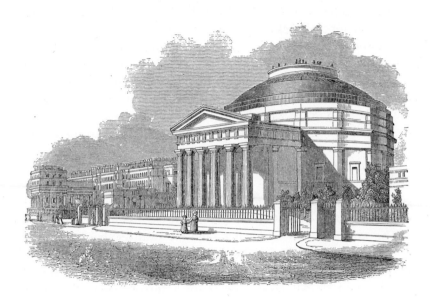

THE COLOSSEUM, REGENT'S PARK

The building bearing this name, in the Regent's Park, is a polygon of sixteen faces, each twenty-five feet in length, making the outer circuit of the building four hundred feet: the front is adorned with a noble Doric portico of six columns, supporting an entablature and pediment; the entablature is continued round the building, supported at each angle by pilasters. Above the entablature is an attic, from which rises the dome, surmounted by a parapet, which forms the front of a gallery, where the spectators ascend to view the surrounding country. This vast structure was erected in three years, from designs by Decimus Burton, Esq.

The origin of this edifice is singularly curious. Mr. Horner, a meritorious and indefatigable artist, and as it should seem a man of great force of character, undertook, at the time of the repair of the ball and cross of St. Paul's, to make a series of panoramic sketches of London, from that giddy elevation. That he might overcome the difficulties which the smoke of the vast city ordinarily presented, he invariably commenced his labours immediately after sun-rise, before the lighting of the innumerable fires which pour out their dark and sullen clouds during the day, and spread a mantle over this wide congregation of the dwellings of men, which only midnight can remove. On a fine summer morning, about four o'clock, London presents an extraordinary spectacle. The brilliancy of the atmosphere – the almost perfect stillness of the streets, except in the neighbourhood of the great markets – the few living beings that pass along those lines which in the day are crowded like some vast mart, such as the traveller hurrying to his distant starting-place, or the labourer creeping to his early work – all these circumstances make up a picture which forcibly impresses the imagination.

What the artist who sketched this panorama saw only in the earliest hours of a brilliant morning, the visitor of the Colosseum may behold in all seasons, and all hours of the day.   N. Whittock, PICTURE OF LONDON, 1836 moned before a magistrate, when a summary conviction takes place, and he will not only have to refund the extra fare, but will also be fined for the offence. Well knowing this, a driver will seldom risk taking more than the amount he can prove to be due to him. Omnibusses now run through the leading thoroughfares; their charge is generally stated on the outside of the carriage. At the present time it is as cheap as the most rigid economist could desire; as a person can ride in a handsome vehicle from the Bank to Paddington, a distance of four miles, for sixpence; the charges in other directions are equally reasonable. The stranger, in London, cannot see the bridges and other objects near the river without taking a boat. There are a great number of watermen standing at the foot of the bridges, or other places leading to the river, plying for passengers, and no mode of conveyance can be more agreeable on a fine day. But it will be particularly necessary to make a bargain with the waterman, to prevent altercation, as he seldom thinks of regulating his demand according to the proper fare.

Persons desirous of visiting Windsor, Richmond, or other places, a short distance from the metropolis, will find a quick and easy conveyance by stage coaches that leave London at different hours in the day. The places where they start from may be known by inquiring at any of the coach offices.

N. Whittock, PICTURE OF LONDON, 1836

AN ACCOUNT BY RALPH WALDO EMERSON

OF A VISIT TO

THE OFFICE OF 'THE TIMES' IN 1847

I WENT ONE DAY with a good friend to *The Times* office, which was entered through a pretty garden-yard, in Printing-House Square. We walked with some circumspection, as if we were entering a powder-mill; but the door was opened by a mild old woman, and, by dint of some transmission of cards, we were at last conducted into the parlour of Mr. Morris, a very gentle person, with no hostile appearances. The statistics are now quite out of date, but I remember he told us that the daily printing was then 35,000 copies; that on 1 March, 1848, the greatest number ever printed – 54,000 – were issued; that, since February, the daily circulation had increased by 8,000 copies. The old press they were then using printed five or six thousand sheets per hour; the new machine, for which they were then building an engine, would print twelve thousand per hour. Our entertainer confided us to a courteous

assistant to show us the establishment, in which, I think, they employed a hundred and twenty men. I remember I saw the reporters'
room, in which they redact their hasty stenographs, but the editor's
room, and who is in it, I did not see, though I shared the curiosity
of mankind respecting it.

The staff of *The Times* has always been made up of able men.
Old Walter, Sterling, Bacon, Barnes, Alsager, Horace Twiss, Jones
Loyd, John Oxenford, Mr. Mosely, Mr. Bailey, have contributed
to its renown in their special departments. But it has never wanted
the first pens for occasional assistance. Its private information is
inexplicable, and recalls the stories of Fouché's police, whose
omniscience made it believed that the Empress Josephine must be
in his pay. It has mercantile and political correspondents in every
foreign city; and its expresses outrun the despatches of the government. One hears anecdotes of the rise of its servants, as of the
functionaries of the India House. I was told of the dexterity of one
of its reporters, who, finding himself, on one occasion, where the
magistrates had strictly forbidden reporters, put his hands into his
coat-pocket, and with pencil in one hand, and tablet in the other,
did his work.

The influence of this journal is a recognized power in Europe,
and, of course, none is more conscious of it than its conductors.
The tone of its articles has often been the occasion of comment
from the official organs of the continental courts, and sometimes
the ground of diplomatic complaint. What would *The Times* say?
is a terror in Paris, in Berlin, in Vienna, in Copenhagen, and in
Nepaul. Its consummate discretion and success exhibit the English
skill of combination. The daily paper is the work of many hands,
chiefly, it is said, of young men recently from the University, and
perhaps reading law in chambers in London. Hence the academic
elegance, and classic allusion, which adorn its columns. Hence, too,
the heat and gallantry of its onset. But the steadiness of the aim
suggests the belief that this fire is directed and fed by older
engineers; as if persons of exact information, and with settled views
of policy, supplied the writers with the basis of fact, and the object
to be attained, and availed themselves of their younger energy and
eloquence to plead the cause. Both the council and the executive
departments gain by this division. Of two men of equal ability, the
one who does not write, but keeps his eye on the course of public
affairs, will have the higher judicial wisdom. But the parts are kept
in concert; all the articles appear to proceed from a single will.
The Times never disapproves of what itself has said, or cripples
itself by apology for the absence of the editor, or the indiscretion

of him who held the pen. It speaks out bluff and bold, and sticks to what it says. It draws from any number of learned and skilful contributors: but a more learned and skilful person supervises, corrects, and co-ordinates. Of this closet, the secret does not transpire. No writer is suffered to claim the authorship of any paper; everything good, from whatever quarter, comes out editorially; and thus, by making the paper everything, and those who write it nothing, the character and the awe of the journal gain.

The English like it for its complete information. A statement of fact in *The Times* is as reliable as a citation from Hansard. Then, they like its independence – they do not know, when they take it up, what their paper is going to say; but, above all, for the nationality and confidence of its tone. It thinks for them all; it is their understanding and day's ideal daguerreotyped. When I see them reading its columns, they seem to me becoming every moment more British. It has the national courage, not rash and petulant, but considerate and determined. No dignity or wealth is a shield from its assault. It attacks a duke as readily as a policeman, and with the most provoking airs of condescension. It makes rude work with the Board of Admiralty. The Bench of Bishops is still less safe. One bishop fares badly for his rapacity, and another for his bigotry, and a third for his courtliness. It addresses occasionally a hint to Majesty itself, and sometimes a hint which is taken. There is an air of freedom even in their advertising columns, which speaks well for England to a foreigner. On the days when I arrived in London in 1847, I read among the daily announcements, one offering a reward of fifty pounds to any person who would put a nobleman, described by name and title, late a member of Parliament, into any county gaol in England, he having been convicted of obtaining money under false pretences.

Was ever such arrogancy as the tone of this paper. Every slip of an Oxonian or Cantabrigian who writes his first leader, assumes that we subdued the earth before we sat down to write this particular *Times*. One would think the world was on its knees to *The Times* Office for its daily breakfast. But this arrogance is calculated. Who would care for it, if it 'surmised,' or 'dared to confess,' or 'ventured to predict,' &c. No; *it is so*, and so it shall be.

The morality and patriotism of *The Times* claims only to be representative, and by no means ideal. It gives the argument, not of the majority, but of the commanding class. Its editors know better than to defend Russia, or Austria, or English vested rights, on abstract grounds. But they give a voice to the class who, at the moment, take the lead; and they have an instinct for finding where

40

the power now lies which is eternally shifting its banks. Sympathiz-
ing with, and speaking for the class that rules the hour, yet being
apprised of every ground-swell, every Chartist resolution, every
Church squabble, every strike in the mills, they detect the first
tremblings of change. They watch the hard and bitter struggles of
the authors of each liberal movement, year by year – watching
them only to taunt and obstruct them – until, at last, when they
see that these have established their fact, that power is on the point
of passing to them – they strike in, with the voice of a monarch,
astonish those whom they succour as much as those whom they
desert, and make victory sure. Of course, the aspirants see that
The Times is one of the goods of fortune, not to be won but by
winning their cause.

The Times, like every important institution, shows the way to a
better. It is a living index of the colossal British power. Its existence
honours the people who dare to print all they know, dare to know
all the facts, and do not wish to be flattered by hiding the extent of
the public disaster. There is always safety in valour. I wish I could
add, that this journal aspired to deserve the power it wields by
guidance of the public sentiment to the right. It is usually pre-
tended, in Parliament and elsewhere, that the English press has a
high tone – which it has not. It has an imperial tone, as of a
powerful and independent nation. But, as with other empires, its
tone is prone to be official, and even officinal. *The Times* shares all
the limitations of the governing classes, and wishes never to be in a
minority. If only it dared to cleave to the right, to show the right
to be the only expedient, and feed its batteries from the central
heart of humanity, it might not have so many men of rank among
its contributors, but genius would be its cordial and invincible ally;
it might now and then bear the brunt of formidable combinations,
but no journal is ruined by wise courage. It would be the natural
leader of British reform; its proud function, that of being the voice
of Europe, the defender of the exile and patriot against despots,
would be more effectually discharged; it would have the authority
which is claimed for that dream of good men not yet come to pass,
an International Congress; and the least of its victories would be
to give to England a new millennium of beneficent power.

R. W. Emerson, ENGLISH TRAITS

ARISTOCRATIC VISITORS

THE ARISTOCRACY have often no residence in London, and only
go thither a short time, during the season, to see the opera.

R. W. Emerson, ENGLISH TRAITS

CLOSELY CONNECTED WITH the interests of Smithfield Market
is the annual competition of fat cattle for the prizes awarded by
the Smithfield Club. This club, which consists of noblemen and
gentlemen of extensive landed possessions, was established at the
close of the last century, when the improvement of the rural arts
was looked upon as a patriotic duty. The annual show of the prize-
cattle, sheep, pigs, &c., is one of the 'sights' of London. For the
last two or three years the exhibition has taken place at the Horse
Bazaar, King-street, Portman-square, which, though not quite so
eligible as could be wished, is superior to the former exhibition-
yard in Aldersgate-street. The show always takes place in December, about a week or ten days before Christmas-day, and after the
prizes have been adjudged the public are admitted on payment of
one shilling, during the remainder of the week. In December, 1841,
there were exhibited fifty-seven oxen, nineteen cows, fifty-four
sheep, and nineteen pigs, the animals of each species being the
most perfect specimens of their kind which the united judgment
and experience of breeders and graziers can produce. The Scotch
oxen had, in some cases, been brought by steam-boats a distance
exceeding five hundred miles; and in nearly every case the railways
were made use of for the conveyance of both cattle and sheep from
all parts of England. Formerly the animals were brought to
London in vans, at a great expense, as the rate of travelling was
necessarily slow.

The interest of the show is, as may be expected, chiefly confined
to certain classes. On entering the place the visitor at once perceives that the company consists chiefly of country gentlemen,
cattle-breeders, graziers, cattle-salesmen, and butchers, with a
sprinkling of townsmen, who have a relish, imbibed in early life,
for country pursuits. But the sight is one of rational interest to any
man. Here he sees the result of exertions, principally carried on
during the last eighty years, to unite and bring to perfection the
most desirable points in the various breeds of domestic animals
which were once peculiar to different parts of Great Britain but
are now spread, in their improved form, over every part of the
country. In the gallery, a portion of which overlooks the show-
yard, are to be seen agricultural implements and machinery of the
latest and most improved construction; roots and plants adapted
to our climate, but which are as yet comparatively unknown;

samples of artificial manures; and specimens of the soil of districts differing from each other in their geological formation. In spite of all the advances which agriculture has made during the present century, how slowly do improvements extend beyond the intelligent circle in which they are first adopted! And it is one of the great advantages of institutions such as the Smithfield Club to spread them more rapidly and over a wider surface, by drawing the agriculturist from the secluded scenes amid which he carries on his occupations, and bring them before him in the manner best calculated to demonstrate their utility.

The prize oxen or sheep which we see at this exhibition are fatter than is required for the ordinary market; and hence it is often supposed that the stimulus of prizes for bringing an animal into a state of unnecessary fatness is altogether a work of supererogation. But the power of reaching this point is simply a test, showing the capacity of the breed for acquiring, at the least expense of food and at the earliest age, such a useful marketable condition as the public demand requires. This course has been perfectly successful; and to show that it has been so, we need only advert to the period when improved breeds of cattle were less common than they are now. Culley, who was himself a great improver of cattle, and wrote a work on the subject at the commencement of the century, speaks of a kind of oxen which had not then become extinct, that were 'more like an ill-made black horse than an ox or a cow'; and the flesh (for he says it did not deserve to be called beef) was 'as black and coarse-grained as horse-flesh'; and yet such an animal was less profitable than an ox of the present improved breeds. After feeding on the best pastures for a whole summer, it was scarcely fatter or in better condition than at the commencement, as the food which it consumed went to the support of 'offal.' There were breeds of sheep which equally stood in need of improvement. But what is the case now? A sheep can be fattened for the market in two years, which formerly required three years, or even a longer period, the saving to the consumer from this cause alone being above thirty per cent.; and in cattle, the small-boned, true-proportioned animal of the improved breeds has in the same way been rendered above twenty-five per cent. more profitable. The meat thus obtained at a less expense of food, and in a shorter space of time, is far superior in quantity and quality to the carcass of the old breeds. When Davenant stated that the average weight of cattle sold in Smithfield was 370 lbs., and sheep and lambs, averaged together, only weighed 28 lbs., we can show, as will have been seen from a previous estimate, that the former average 640 lbs., while

43

the average weight of the Teeswater sheep is 28 lbs. per quarter; of the Leicester, 22 lbs. per quarter; and of the Southdown, 18 lbs. per quarter. Culley states (and the work of improvement has been carried to a higher point, as well as very widely diffused, since his time) that the difference between the coarse and fine, or between the best and worst parts of beef, when cut up, was formerly not less than one hundred per cent.; but in the improved breeds the quality of the coarse parts has been made very much better, and the quantity of bone is also diminished. These are no trifling advantages to the poorest class of consumers. In mutton, the difference between one part and another has also gradually become less and less. In this useful object of agricultural zeal the Smithfield Club has rendered great services; and the London butchers, who purchase the prize cattle and sheep as a means of enhancing the reputation of their shops, have equally promoted the same end; and by combination of purpose and competition between cattle-breeders, graziers, and others, the average standard of quality in meat has been raised to an extent which may be compared with the still more important step of converting a whole population into consumers of wheaten bread instead of that made from oats, barley, or other inferior grain. The cattle-breeder looks no farther for his reward than to the grazier; the grazier expects encouragement from the butcher; and the butcher calculates upon the support of a 'discerning public,' who must in all cases either communicate the stimulus to improvement, or support it when once its career has commenced.

J. C. Platt, KNIGHT'S LONDON, 1842

THE LONDON

VISTA

DURING THE NINETEENTH CENTURY

SELECTED FROM

VARIOUS CONTEMPORARY SOURCES

AND INCLUDING

A REVIEW OF THE MOST RECENT AND PROJECTED

IMPROVEMENTS IN AND ABOUT THE METROPOLIS

WITH OBSERVATIONS

ON THE MODERN STATE OF ARCHITECTURE.

FROM DAVID HUGHSON'S 'WALKS THROUGH LONDON,' 1817

DESCRIPTIONS OF CERTAIN LONDON STATUES

WITH PARTICULAR REFERENCE

TO THE WORK OF MR WESTMACOTT.

FROM CHARLES KNIGHT'S 'LONDON,' 1842

AN ACCOUNT OF THE ARCHITECTURAL AMENITIES

OF THE RECENTLY ERECTED

SAVOY HOTEL IN THE STRAND.

FROM 'THE ILLUSTRATED LONDON NEWS,' 1889

NOTES UPON

LONDON THUNDERSTORMS AND FOGS

TOGETHER WITH

OTHER BRIEFER REFERENCES

AND NOTICES

We shall soon be utterly without a lane or an alley throughout the whole of London; while as to architecture, the old brick and the order will be utterly superseded by the modern stuccoite. It is all very well to enlarge the streets if we can enlarge the means of the people sufficiently to enable them to live in them; but if the habitations of the poor are superseded by palaces, while pauperism still remains, we would simply ask what on earth is to become of it?

PUNCH, 1845

A REVIEW

OF THE MOST RECENT AND PROJECTED IMPROVEMENTS
IN AND ABOUT THE METROPOLIS
WITH OBSERVATIONS
ON THE MODERN STATE OF ARCHITECTURE

IN ORDER TO POINT OUT the improvements which have grown with the growth, and strengthened with the strength of this great city, it may only be necessary to refer to a minute account of the progress of the new buildings. To all the attractions of external splendour, it is not too much to say that every internal convenience has been added.

The whole neighbourhood of Tottenham Court Road, and from thence to the Regent's Park and Paddington, presents a new and increasing suburb to the city. On the western side of Tottenham Court Road, nearly in the angle formed by the end of this, and part of the new road, is *Fitzroy-Square*, not yet completed. The houses are faced with stone, and have a greater proportion of architectural embellishments than most others in the metropolis: they were designed by the Messrs. Adams.

In this neighbourhood, in Tottenham-Street, Tottenham Court Road, is the *Regency Theatre*, distinguished by its elegant portico, formed by a range of square stone pillars. The whole extent of this edifice, which appears in the street, the entrance excepted, is blank, but embellished with pilasters, &c. At present it is principally used for astronomical and mechanical exhibitions, and thus partakes of that desertion which has more or less affected all the theatres in the metropolis since the late peace.

Portland-Place is one of the finest streets in Europe. It was intended to form the opening to the new street next to the *Regent's Park* and *Mary-la-bone Park*. The north end of this street is terminated by an iron railing and a gate, which separated it from a field, extending to the New Road. That field is now a garden and a shrubbery, enclosed on all sides by handsome railing, corresponding with that which encloses the Regent's Park on the other side of the road. The new part of the street commences with a crescent on each side of the way, which is not finished, and the works have been so long in this half-built state, that grass has grown on the top of the walls, reaching, in some places, not higher than the kitchen windows. The houses nearest to Portland Place are entirely raised and covered in, but since the peace, are fast returning to their pristine mould, as the wood work is rapidly decaying, from exposure to the weather: the fronts, as far as completed, have a very neat colonade of double Ionic pillars, with a balustrade and a balcony. Many of the houses on this spot have pediments; and those with this addition face each other all the way on both sides of the street: the intermediate houses, without pediments or pilasters, are Tuscan or Doric. The new parish church of *St. Mary la Bonne*, near this spot, now completed, and opened for divine service, is beyond all doubt one of the handsomest structures of the kind. The north front is extremely rich and elegant, and consists of a noble portico of the Composite order, supported by eight rich pillars, and two pilasters, with a handsome balustrade, extending round the whole of the church. The steeple is of exquisite workmanship; a square rustic tower supports a beautiful cupola, raised on Corinthian pillars, on the capitals of which are eight angels, supporting another cupola: on its summit is a small openwork tower and vane. The inside of this edifice is superb. The roof of the church is just visible above the balustrade: the body is brick, covered with Roman cement; the steeple and portico of stone. The north-east and west corners have each two composite columns and pilasters; between these pilasters are niches, and above them an architrave and cornice.

Mary la Bonne Church was consecrated, in the year 1817, by the Bishop of London, in the presence of a great number of persons of distinction. The organ is placed at the back of the altar, and in the centre of the organ is an open arch, in which is placed a very fine picture, painted by Benjamin West, Esq., President of the Royal Academy: the subject is, the Angel of the Lord appearing to the Shepherds.

The *Regent's Park* is very extensive, and though it is not likely to receive a speedy completion, it is one of the greatest Sunday promenades about town. An immense sewer, extending from hence to the river Thames, is in great forwardness. A new chapel, at the northern extremity of this park, is a very elegant building. The canal adds considerably to the beauty and verdure of this delightful place.

With the showy improvements, or rather, the alterations that were intended to connect the communication between Carlton House and the Regent's Park, some extravagant ideas were evidently connected; '*Circusses* were to be made where the new connecting street was to cross Piccadilly and Oxford-Road.' The reason given for which by Mr. Nash, the surveyor, was, 'that it would avoid the sensation of passing Oxford-Street, and insensibly unite the two divisions of the city.' The given estimate of the expense of this intended street was 300,000*l.*; but there was no doubt that it would cost a great deal more. The imperious necessity of retrenchment, however, has altered this plan, and the new street therefore is to be no farther proceeded in than Piccadilly: it will be continued so far with façades of Ionic columns in plaster, corresponding with those in the square opposite Carlton House. The two lodges will be erected on the east and west of the Regent's Palace. The screening colonade of the latter will be taken down, and some light description of railing or balustrade be substituted in its place.

On the 15th of July, 1816, orders were positively issued to stop the improvements north of Piccadilly. The perspective from Carlton House, is to extend only to the intended crescent in Piccadilly. St. James's Market and the houses in Jermyn-Street, which intersect the view, are to be removed. The new United Service Club House will be built on an extensive scale.

The name of Waterloo-place has been given to the opening in front of Carlton House. The buildings here have been stuccoed, instead of being faced with Bath Stone, and are already of the shades between white and black, the smoky, and the dirty grey. Whether that side of Pall-Mall shall be a good thoroughfare, will depend upon the mode of paving this place. To afford safety to walkers, it has been proposed, that the foot pavement should be so continued as to leave a space for carriages not wider than the breadth of Pall-Mall, and that to mark the distinction between the two pavements, lamps should be placed on stone pedestals.

It is still understood that Oxford-Road will be continued as far as Bayswater Brook, making it the longest street in Europe. When the new Post Office is finished the western mails are to go direct along Holborn, instead of passing Charing Cross and Piccadilly; and a short cut is also to be made into the other western road angular from Shepherds Bush to Hammersmith.

The old wall of Kensington Gardens on the Bayswater Road, has lately been repaired and lighted, the ditches drained, and an open gateway designed to be made, opposite the broad walk in Kensington Gardens, to give passengers a slight view of the beautiful grounds.

But the absolute amelioration of a whole neighbourhood, must be admitted in the change which took place on the site of Bedford Square and the adjacent new streets north of Broad St. Giles', by new and elegant erections, encroaching upon the vicinity of the still wretched *Dyot, or George-Street, Bainbridge-Street, Rats Castle, &c.*, and a large space eastward of them, which, within the

RIVER FRONT OF HUNGERFORD MARKET

An Act was obtained in 1830, incorporating a company of proprietors for the re-establishment of 'Hungerford Market.' The site of the old market has been purchased, together with the surrounding houses, those in Hungerford-street, and some few in the Strand, in order to ensure a proper frontage and secure a convenient access to that thoroughfare. Many of these buildings are pulled down. The architect of the New Market is Mr. C. Fowler. The front to the river is completed externally, and forms a very elegant structure, as represented in the above view. The basement of the centre next the river constitutes the Fish-Market. The wings are intended for taverns, connected by a colonnade with a terrace which occupies the entire front. From the Fish-Market the ascent is by a spacious flight of steps in the centre externally, and two staircases within, at the extremities of the portico, which is separated from the hall by a screen of arches. The hall, exclusive of the porticoes, is 157 feet long by 123 feet wide, consisting of a nave and two aisles, besides ranges of shops against the side walls, with galleries over. THE PENNY MAGAZINE, 1832 last threescore years, was most appropriately styled *the Ruins of St. Giles;* at that time mostly an open space, which had been occupied by a number of decayed dwellings.

In Broad-street, vulgarly Broad St. Giles's, it should have been observed, stands the parish church of St. Giles in the Fields. The outside of the church has a rustic basement, and the windows of the galleries have semi-circular heads, and over them, a modillion cornice. The steeple is one hundred and sixty-five feet high, and consists of a rustic pedestal, supporting a Doric order of pilasters; and over the clock is an octangular tower, with three quarter Ionic columns, supporting a balustrade, with vases, on which stands the spire, which is also octangular and belted. The interior is chaste and beautiful; the ornamental ceiling being one of the best in the metropolis.

Among other accommodations in agitation for the benefit of this part of the metropolis, it is proposed to build a new fish-market, on the bank of the Thames, west of Old Hungerford Market, now nearly fallen into disuse.

Another material improvement is exhibited in Black Friars Road or Great Surrey-Street, near the corner of Holland-Street, in the application of *iron* in lieu of stone, as a substitute for pavement in the streets of this metropolis. This succedaneum consists of square pieces of cast iron suitably shaped, roughed and dove-tailed. This experiment, made in the summer of 1816, has succeeded so far, that it has been resolved to pave some streets in the city in this manner, and to begin with Wood-Street, Cheapside. It is computed that an iron pavement well adjusted will endure twenty years in a great thoroughfare; whereas, it is too well known, that a stone pavement very frequently requires repairs, and a new adjustment. The pieces already laid down resemble a batch of eight or nine rolls, and are united like the parts of a dissected map, without interstices or even palpable joints. From their sustaining every kind of load, and the roughest of usage, there is no doubt of the ultimate success of this invention.

This vicinity will probably receive considerable benefit from the erection of the *New Cobourg Theatre*, in the centre of the New Cut, in the direct line of Waterloo Bridge, and distant from it about a quarter of a mile. On the exterior surface of the foundation the following inscription was cut: 'The first stone of the Royal Cobourg Theatre was laid Sept. 14, 1816, by his Serene Highness the Prince of Saxe Cobourg, and her Royal Highness the Princess Charlotte of Wales, by their Serene Highnesses' proxy, Alderman Goodbehere.'

51

Extending our views down the river, we find the improvements still more promising. An embankment in front of the New Custom House, in consequence of a fair adjustment between the City and the Government, through the medium of the Lord Mayor, has taken place. This is intended to increase the wharfage there, and render more commodious the shipping, landing, and stowage of goods, and also the carriage way. Part of Billingsgate dock is to be taken in, and yet leave room enough for the fishing vessels, the fish-market is to be widened, and the landing stairs separated at the wharf, so as to render the facility of passengers taking boat more safe and comfortable than it has hitherto been.

East of London, a new iron bridge is to form a communication between the Essex, and Kent roads. This bridge is to cross the Thames from New Gravel-Lane to Rotherhithe.

Directing our attention again to the city, we observe the old north wall of London running behind the site of Old Bethlem Hospital, entirely taken down, which has thrown open to public view the area of the new square, enclosed with handsome iron railing. The wall was found uncommonly thick, and the bricks double the size of those now used. The centre had been filled in with large loose stones, &c.; the line of wall now removed is partly the last vestige of that which remained of a circumference of three miles and two hundred and five yards.

The increase of new buildings in the eastern extremity of the metropolis, from Bethnal Green towards Bow and Stratford, is nearly equal to that of the western in point of extent. The formation of the East and West India Docks has, in some measure, rendered this increase necessary here, as well as in the environs of Stepney, Limehouse, and Poplar.

The rage for building has also suggested a new increase, which is intended to be made on the site of Spa Fields; this is understood to consist of several new streets, which are designed to cover the whole, or the greatest part of that salubrious spot, commonly known by the name of the *Pipe Fields*, having Sadler's Wells on the east, Bagnigge Wells on the west, the new road on the north, and part of Clerkenwell on the south. The substitution of large iron pipes for those of wood, it is said, will enable the proprietors of this verdant and diversified tract, the last remains of the *Rus in Urbe*, to cover it with houses.

Before quitting the subject of our new buildings, we must observe, that the late taste exhibited in the suburbs has employed the wit of Mr. Colman, in his *Eccentricities*, under the title of *London Rurality*.

Stretching, round England's chief Emporium, far,
(No rage for Building quench'd by raging War,)
What would-be Villas, rang'd in dapper pride,
Usurp the fields, and choke the highway side!
Peace to each swain, who rural rapture owns,
As soon as past a toll, or off the stones!
Whose joy, if buildings solid bliss bestow,
Cannot, for miles, an interruption know:
Save when a gap, of some half dozen feet,
Just breaks the continuity of street;
Where the prig Architect, with 'style' in view,
Has dol'd his houses forth, in two by two;
And rear'd a Row upon the plan, no doubt,
Of old mens' jaws, with every third tooth out.
Or where, still greater lengths of taste to go,
He warps his tenements into a bow;
Nails a scant canvas, propt on slight deal sticks,
Nick-nam'd 'Veranda,' to the first-floor bricks;
Before the whole, in one snug segment drawn,
Claps half a rood of turf he calls a lawn;
Then chuckling at his lath-and-plaster bubble,
Dubs it the Crescent, – and the rents are double.

As utility must be admitted to be superior to shew and embellishment, the completion of Southwark-Bridge will be hailed as an excellent and substantial improvement. The greatest part of the iron-work is now delivered in London, and the remainder will be ready for putting up in the course of the summer. The middle arch is two hundred and forty feet span, and the two side arches will be two hundred and ten feet each; the width of the road-way and foot paths between the parapets will be forty-two feet, the same as Black Friar's Bridge. The south abutment, with the land arch over Bank side, is nearly completed, and ready to receive the iron for that side arch, which will be the first put up. One of the two piers is completed up to above high water mark, and the other is finished to above low water.

Among the benefits attending this undertaking are the following. It will greatly facilitate the commerce both of the London and Surrey side of the river, by dividing and lessening the superabundant traffic over London and Blackfriars Bridges, and prevent the occurrence of those injurious stoppages so frequent in the avenues near London-Bridge.

It will cause a handsome street to be formed from Bankside to St. George's Church, seventy feet wide and half a mile long, and thereby open a commodious passage from Kent and Surrey into the heart of London. It will add to the Borough a neighbourhood of respectability in the room of that of an inferior kind, which must be removed. By the proximity of the new street to the heart of the city, the Bank, Royal Exchange, Stock Exchange, Excise Office, Guildhall, &c., this part of Southwark may become a convenient residence for merchants, wholesale dealers, &c. This bridge is also admirably suited to the situation, as it will tend to remove the irregularity of shallows in this part of the river, by dividing the stream, and thereby directing the current into three regular channels, and consequently clear them of many of those sand-banks which now injure the navigation; and this it will effect in a greater degree, whenever London-Bridge, which caused these impediments, may be rebuilt or altered.

However, that London is yet inferior to most capitals in architectural embellishments, is a remark made by many, besides a classical writer of our own country, who has expressed a hope, 'that the British nation ere long will triumph over every obstacle, inspire artists with genius, and teach even brick to emulate marble.' Free stone is now most ardently recommended; and it is observed, that the restoration of the exterior ornaments of Westminster Abbey has been commenced with Bath stone; and a colonade at the Regent's Circus, near Portland Place, and another before the Opera House, on the side of Pall Mall, have been erected with freestone from Somersetshire.

It is sincerely hoped that the erection of the *New Post Office*, near St. Martin's Le Grand, will be made subservient to a better display of the Cathedral of St. Paul's. 'If both purposes can be accomplished by the same alteration, and the splendid effect given to that noble edifice, which space would confer, the value of the improvement would be doubled.'

Nothing, it must be acknowledged, can more sensibly evince the present state of improvement than the contrast which may still be made between our ancient and the more modern structures in various parts of this metropolis. To pass over the exceeding rude dwellings of our early forefathers, the buildings of the middle ages, with stories projecting beyond each other as they ascended, still remind us of the slow march of improvement during several ages. A few of them which exhibit a specimen of old London, remain about Bishopsgate and Leadenhall Streets, and particularly in Holywell-Street, in the Strand. However, it is probable that another half century will obliterate the remembrance of them from almost every testimony but the works of those artists whose taste, skill, and indefatigable research have preserved many rare and valuable representations of the remains of antiquity, no longer visible.

Here we do not allude altogether to the houses of the common people, though, speaking of these, a writer upon architecture ob-

BANK OF ENGLAND

SHOWING THE IMPROVEMENTS BY

MR SOANE

The entrance on the Lothbury side exhibits a singular, yet interesting display of architectural designs, after some of the best specimens of Greece and Rome. From the return on the west side, in Princes'-Street, to the east, in Bartholomew-Lane, the architectural masses are of similar character; both the order and the forms having been copied from the Temple of the Sybils, at Tivoli. Strength and security were the first objects to be obtained; but at the same time, the monotonous insipidity of an immense line of wall has been judiciously relieved by projecting entrances, blank windows, &c.; the former being under lofty archways, and ornamented by Corinthian columns fluted, with an entablature and turrets above. The grand portico, at the north-west angle, consists of a raised basement and eight fluted columns disposed semicircularly, and supporting a very highly-enriched frieze and attic with a turret above; the whole having the appearance of a temple. Mr. Soane has been the architect of all the principal improvements in and about the Bank, from the year 1788 to the present time.

David Hughson, WALKS THROUGH LONDON, 1817

55

served, several years since, 'When I compare the modern English way of building with the old way, I cannot but wonder at the genius of old times. Nothing is, or can be more delightful and convenient than light, and nothing more agreeable to health than free air. And yet of old they used to dwell in houses, most of them with a blind stair-case, low ceilings, and dark windows; the rooms built at random, without any convenience, and often with steps from one to another. So that one would think the people of former ages were afraid of light, or loved to play at hide and seek. Whereas the taste of our times is altogether for light stair-cases, fine sash windows, and lofty ceilings.'

Objects of utility have not escaped the attention of the people at large. The Committee of the House of Commons, who have been engaged in the enquiry respecting the education of the poor, have reported that the National Society have built or added to, erected or enlarged, one hundred and twenty-two schools; and that the most useful application of public money, to promote the national education, will be in erecting school-rooms, &c., in various parts of the kingdom. The great Penitentiary on Millbank, described in the course of these Walks, has had the addition of a burial-ground, and the chapel here has lately been consecrated by the Bishop of London. The whole sum expended upon this building is 250,000*l.*; the foundation being laid upon swampy ground, having inevitably occasioned an excessive charge. Thus, whether we look to the extent of this great capital, the number and opulence of its inhabitants, or to the magnitude of the undertakings and improvements in which they engage, we may still claim the distinction of 'the *Great London*'; an appellation which a native of the German Continent, who had witnessed our prosperity, did not hesitate to bestow upon us more than a century ago.

David Hughson, WALKS THROUGH LONDON, 1817

OBSERVATIONS OF A RUSSIAN VISITOR

UPON THE STATE OF ARCHITECTURE

IN LONDON

AT PARIS, OR ST. PETERSBURGH, you will see in one hour more edifices closely following the Grecian forms than is contained in London; and even the few they have to present to us are sadly deficient in agreement of the proportions, or want of keeping in the minor parts. With the well-turned pillars of one order, you shall find squab windows of another; or a pediment approaching to the triangular shape, supported by Tuscan or Doric shafts.

A well-constructed column, which commemorates the destruction of the city a hundred and fifty years ago, is placed in the lowest situation, only visible from the water-side among the spires of surrounding churches, and is nearly lost in the distant view.

The reason for placing the column here is that only which ought not to be adduced, namely, that here began the fire; whereas sound reason would have pointed out the spot where the destructive element was conquered, where its ravages ceased, and where the affrighted people were suffered to repose. Their most splendid edifices are radically defective. St. Paul's Church cannot be seen; Somerset House is unfinished; St. Stephen's, Walbrook, is only perfect inside; the beautiful porch of St. Martin's Church is unsupported by other parts of the edifice; Carlton House is disgraced by its curtain. No; England is not the country for fine architecture; at least if we are to judge from its capital. Nothing there is grand in the design, or striking in the effect: the approach at St. Paul's is spoiled, or does not exist; at Westminster Hall it is ample, only you have nothing to approach.

What is wanting in accuracy of design in church architecture of long standing, is compensated by a solemn gloom; built in barbarous times, they are designated by the barbarians who suffered them to be reared. Germany, as well as France and England, abounds in these *Gothic* churches. Many of the builders too, brought from the most southern extremity of Europe, being enemies to our faith, indulged in sportive designs, intended to ridicule their employers and to scoff at their worship.

However, if England be not the country of stupendous buildings, it is indisputably that in which comfort is studied with complete effect. You cannot well imagine a ground plan better adapted to the purposes of domestic ease than that of Mr. B.'s house; situated in the vicinity of a number of other squares, it commands a distant view of the country, besides having a fine piece of ground laid out in the centre of the square in which it forms a part. With stabling behind, a court-yard in front, and a superb railing, many of these houses might vie with palaces, were the *material* of that only which a correct taste tells us ought to be used.

An Englishman's house being his castle, how would he enjoy that, or the freedom of his person, if he was hourly annoyed by a beggar descending from the *attic*, or abashed by the splendid equipage of a Count or a General on the ground-floor? A fine prospect of the Parisian *Boulevards*, or a *Rue Grenelle*, would counterpoise nothing in his estimation.

Translated from the original manuscripts of Oloff Napea, circa 1826

57

DESCRIPTION OF A THUNDERSTORM
IN LONDON DURING THE NINETEENTH CENTURY

A LONDON THUNDERSTORM is a great thing. Clouds, like feather-beds, lie piled thick and heavy upon the horizon; darkness is precipitated upon the earth; a chilliness, with depression, comes over the mind; the body languishes under the calm, unmoving, sultry atmosphere; a blink of sunshine streams now and then, as if to show the menacing blackness overhead; lambent lightnings play at short and rapidly-decreasing intervals; crushing, crashing, brattling thunder shakes the ground on which we tread.

Now elderly, bald-headed gentlemen, with bland, benevolent expression of face, smile placidly upon houseless wayfarers, drenched to the skin, and standing close up to the hall-door over the way, in the attitude of policemen at 'attention'; ladies, nestling in like manner, their holiday-finery bedraggled beyond repair, and their visages mournfully expressive of the irreparable fate of dress.

Now strikes upon the ear the frequent rattle of long-unemployed cabs; happy may be his dole who sits snugly ensconced within! Now omnibus 'cads,' *more* than full inside, 'have the advantage of you,' and regard you with a derisive air of independence, as, from your doorway shelter, raising your hand, you implore the favour of a seat. Now does the passenger, misled by morning sunbeams, 'wise in his own conceit,' sigh after his homely but trusty friend and protector, his cotton umbrella; now, who does not regret his folly, parted from his excellent acquaintance, Macintosh?

Thunderstorms in London do not endanger human life so frequently as we might suppose; we have ere now walked unharmed through an atmosphere, we might call it, of lambent lightning. Nor are they without salutary influences, no less in restoring the proper elemental equilibrium than in supplying the defects of the scavengers, when these gentry, as is too frequently the case, postpone their detergent operations. The streets are cleansed in an instant; the macadamized roads looking as if they had been holy-stoned, and the wood-pavement as if it had been french-polished. Of accumulated filth, egg and oyster shells, broken delf, and cabbage-stalks, the gutters are gutted: your thunderstorm is the greatest of detergents – admirable abstersive! How its torrents sweep the delining streets, scattering, like snipe-shot, the isolated stones and wandering pebbles.

John Fisher Murray, BENTLEY'S MISCELLANY, 1844

IT MIGHT BE supposed that Westmacott had really obtained a commission of the extensive character sought by Bacon, so large is his proportion of the statues erected in the present century. Whilst the other sculptors whose talents have been in requisition, have given us but few specimens of their skill, as Chantrey in the colossal bronze statue of William Pitt, in Hanover Square, an equestrian statue of George IV in Trafalgar Square, and one of the Duke of Wellington in front of the Royal Exchange; Wyatt, in the bronze equestrian statue of George III, erected in Pall Mall East in 1836, and in that of the Duke of Wellington at Hyde Park Corner ten years later; Gahagan, in the Duke of Kent's statue, also in bronze, at the top of Portland Place, erected by public subscription as a tribute to his public and private virtues; and Mr. Clarke, of Birmingham, in the bronze seated figure of Major Cartwright, in Burton Crescent, where the venerable reformer long resided; the sculptor in question alone has given us more than all his brother artists put together. Before we notice these, we must add a few words on the statue just mentioned of him who, according to Canning, was 'the old heart in London from which the veins of sedition in the country were supplied.' The honest and indefatigable Major Cartwright, whose zeal for what he believed to be the public good must be honoured even by those who disapprove of the means by which he pursued it, can afford even to have the attack recorded without the slightest apprehension of injury to his memory. A striking evidence of the purity of his intentions was given on his being brought up for judgment, in 1821, on the verdict of guilty of sedition, &c., when 'the learned judge spoke with so much respect of the character and motives of Major Cartwright that it was afterwards humourously remarked by that gentleman that he thought he was going to offer him a reward instead of inflicting a fine.'[1]

Westmacott's public statues, taking them in the order of their execution, are those of the Duke of Bedford, Fox, the Achilles or Wellington at Hyde Park Corner, the statue of the Duke of York on the pillar overlooking St. James Park from Carlton Terrace, and Canning's statue in New Palace Yard. The Bedford and Fox statues are noble works, and most happily situated, facing each other; the one on the south side of Russell Square, the other on the

[1] Life, by his niece, F. C. Cartwright.

north side of Bloomsbury Square, the opening of Bedford Place forming a fine avenue, as it were, between them. The Duke rests one arm on a plough, whilst the hand of the other grasps the gift of Ceres; and the characteristics thus expressed are continued and still further developed by the children, representative of the seasons, at the four corners, and by the interesting bas-reliefs that adorn two of the sides; in one we see preparations making for the dinner of the rustic labourer, his wife is busy on her knees, a youth is blowing the horn, and two countrymen and a team of oxen complete the group; in the other the business of reaping and gleaning is shadowed forth, one of the figures, a young woman in the centre, of graceful form and sweet features, is evidently the village belle. The statue has only this inscription: Francis, Duke of Bedford, erected 1809. It is of bronze, and about twenty-seven feet in height. The statue of Fox represents the statesman seated, arrayed in a consular robe, and full of dignity. The likeness is said to be 'perfect.' This inscription, also, is noticeable for its simplicity – 'Charles James Fox. Erected MDCCCXVI.' Thus should it always be! When a people are not sufficiently acquainted with the merits of its public men, to appreciate the honour done them in the erection of public statues, by all means let us wait till they are. Greater advantages even than the waiters anticipate would flow, not unfrequently, from such a rule. 'It was a strange piece of tyranny,' observes a writer in the *Quarterly Review*,[1] in allusion to the Achilles, 'to press it into our service; but in our service it cannot abide; remove the inscription, and the Greek is a Greek again.' Although the time was that one could not take up a newspaper but to read attacks or defences of this 'best abused' of statues, or pass a print-shop without a laugh at some new caricature of the ladies' work, and when, of course, the whole subject became most wearisomely familiar, it may be useful now to some of our readers to have it stated that it is copied from one of two splendid specimens of ancient art, standing in front of the Papal palace at Rome. Each consists of a figure in the act of reining a fiery steed; and the two have been supposed to represent Castor and Pollux. They are attributed to no less an artist than Phidias. As to their history, it is believed that they were conveyed from Alexandria by Constantine the Great, to adorn his baths in Rome, among the ruins of which they were found. To add to the doubts that envelope the whole subject, the horses were discovered some distance from the human figures, and may therefore never have belonged to them. It was certainly a daring idea to take one of these figures and stamp it

[1] Vol. xxxiv, p. 131.

decidedly Achilles, which, however, it may in reality be, though the presumption is sadly against it; and then, by a kind of mental process, which every one of course was expected to perform for himself, to transform Achilles into Wellington. But the event itself was unique, the subscription of the ladies of England for a statue to a great warrior; and we suppose it was therefore deemed advisable to commemorate it in a equally unique manner. The inscription runs thus, 'To Arthur, Duke of Wellington, and his brave companions in arms, this statue of Achilles, cast from cannon taken in the battles of Salamanca, Vittoria, Toulouse, and Waterloo, is inscribed by their countrywomen.' The cannon here referred to consisted of twelve 24 pounders. The statue is about eighteen feet high, on a basement of granite, of about the same elevation. It was placed on the latter on the anniversary day of the battle of Waterloo, in 1822; and the records of the period tell us of a curious coincidence that marked the occasion. A writer in the *Gentleman's Magazine* observes, 'In ancient Greece the honoured victors of the Olympic games, on returning crowned to their native cities, were not permitted to enter them by the common way and gate; to distinguish them above all their co-patriots, a breach was made in the wall, by which they were borne home in triumph. By one of those accidents which seem to be fate, the Ladies' statue to the Duke of Wellington, when brought to its destination, was found to be too mighty for the gates by which it should have entered, and it became necessary to breach the wall for the admission of the trophy.' The statue of Canning and the Duke of York column require no particular mention; the former was set up in its place opposite New Palace Yard, in 1832; and the latter completed in 1836. This consists of a colossal bronze statue of the 'Soldier's friend,' on the top of one of the ugliest columns perhaps that the wit of sculptor ever yet devised, of pale red granite, 150 feet high. The best thing about the whole is the view from the summit: what the Monument is for the east the Duke of York's pillar forms for the west of London.

Besides the statues of the various sovereigns mentioned above, we have one of Richard Cœur de Lion, by Baron Marochetti, in Palace Yard, Westminster; one of Elizabeth, formerly at Ludgate, but now set up in a niche in front of St. Dunstan's Church, in Fleet Street; no less than three of Queen Anne – one before St. Paul's Cathedral, one in Queen Square, Westminster, and one in Queen Square, Bloomsbury; William IV, by Nixon, stands near the foot of London Bridge. Her Majesty Queen Victoria is represented in the Royal Exchange by a marble statue from the chisel of the late

Mr. Lough, and also by a marble statue in the new St. Thomas's Hospital, at Lambeth. A statue of the late Prince Consort appears in the grounds of the Royal Horticultural Society at South Kensington; it was the work of Mr. Durham, and is commemorative of the Great Exhibition of 1851, and of its royal founder. The Prince, too, is represented by a colossal gilt statue, seated in a chair of state, and surmounted by a lofty Gothic canopy, richly gilt and adorned with glittering gems. This latter is the National Albert Memorial in Hyde Park, and stands as near as possible on the site of the Great Exhibition of 1851. The memorial, which is 176 feet in height, took upwards of twenty years before it was completed, and cost upwards of 130,000*l.*; it was erected from the designs of Sir Gilbert Scott.

Among the additions to our public statuary of late years we may mention the Nelson Monument in Trafalgar Square, which was completed, with the exception of the four colossal lions at its base, in 1843. It consists of a fluted Corinthian column, upwards of 170 feet high, surmounted by a bronze statue of the hero of the Nile and Trafalgar, executed by Mr. E. H. Baily. The four sides of the pedestal contain, in basso-relievo, representations of Nelson's four great battles, cast in the gun metal taken in his fights from the enemy. The four gigantic lions at the angles of the base were excuted by the late Sir Edwin Landseer, but were not forthcoming and in their place till upwards of twenty years after the completion of the column. In Trafalgar Square we have likewise the counterfeit presentment of another naval hero, – Sir Charles Napier; the Army being represented by Behne's bronze statue of the gallant Havelock, whilst General Outram looks down upon the Thames from a pedestal on the Victoria Embankment. In Waterloo Place, Pall Mall, we have Bell's Memorial to the Guards who fell during the war with Russia in 1854–56; and opposite the western entrance of Westminster Abbey, a column with statuary, designed by Sir Gilbert Scott, in memory of Lord Raglan and other officers educated at Westminster School, who fell during the Russian and Indian wars (1854–59). Lord Clyde and Sir John Franklin are both represented in Waterloo Place; whilst Dr. Jenner, the introducer of vaccination, is represented by a sitting figure of bronze in Kensington Gardens; Robert Stephenson, the engineer, by a standing statue in Euston Square; Sir Hugh Myddelton by a marble statue in Islington Green; Richard Cobden by one in the High Street at Camden Town; George Peabody by a bronze seated figure close by the Royal Exchange, and Sir Robert Peel by a standing statue in bronze at the end of Cheapside; Captain Coram,

STATUE OF CHARLES I

WITH THE UNFINISHED NELSON TESTIMONIAL, 1842

At the end of Parliament Street, is 'Charing Cross', so called from a cross having been erected upon this spot, the resting place of the body of the 'Chere Reyne', or dearly beloved Queen of Edward I. This cross was either taken down, or removed, about the year 1633, to make way for the statue of Charles I, executed by Le Sieur. A cross was erected at some distance from it, which was destroyed by the populace, previous to the death of Charles. The equestrian statue was afterwards condemned, and ordered to be broken to pieces by the Rump Parliament, and it was sold to a brazier, named John River. The brazier having more taste, or more loyalty than the parliament, buried it, unmutilated, and showed the officers of parliament some pieces of brass, as part of the broken figure. At the restoration of Charles II, the statue was disinterred, and placed upon an elegant pedestal, as it now appears. Charles is most admirably represented in armour, with his head uncovered. The horse is a noble figure.

N. Whittock, PICTURE OF LONDON, 1836

the founder of the Foundling Hospital, is represented by a statue in front of that institution, by W. Calder Marshall. Lord Palmerston and Lord Derby are fittingly commemorated by statues near the scene of their great senatorial triumphs, in New Palace Yard. In Leicester Square, in place of the equestrian statue of George I, we have now a marble statue of Shakespeare, the base of the pedestal serving as a drinking fountain, whilst in the four corners of the enclosure are busts of four noted individuals whose names are associated with Leicester Square, namely, Hogarth, Newton, John Hunter, and Reynolds.

Charles Knight, LONDON, 1842
with additions by E. Walford, 1877

A LONDON FOG

A LONDON FOG is a sad thing, as every inhabitant of London knows full well: dingy, dusky, dirty, damp; an atmosphere black as smoke and wet as steam, that wraps round you like a blanket; a cloud reaching from earth to heaven; a 'palpable obscure,' which not only turns day into night, but threatens to extinguish the lamps and lanthorns with which the poor street-wanderers strive to illumine their darkness, dimming and paling the 'ineffectual fires,' until the volume of gas at a shop door cuts no better figure than a hedge glow-worm, and a duchess's flambeau would veil its glories to a will-o'-th'-wisp. A London fog is, not to speak profanely, a sort of renewal and reversal of Joshua's miracle: the sun seems to stand still as on that occasion, only that now it stands in the wrong place, and gives light to the Antipodes. The very noises of the street come stifled and smothered through that suffocating medium; din is at a pause; the town is silenced; and the whole population, biped and quadruped, sympathize with the dead and chilling weight of the out-of-door world. Dogs and cats just look up from their slumbers, turn round, and go to sleep again; the little birds open their pretty eyes, stare about them, wonder that the night is so long, and settle themselves afresh on their perches. Silks lose their gloss, cravats their stiffness, hackney-coachmen their way; young ladies fall out of curl, and mammas out of temper; masters scold; servants grumble; and the whole city, from Hyde Park Corner to Wapping, looks sleepy and cross, like a fine gentleman roused before his time and forced to get up by candlelight. Of all detestable things, a London fog is the most detestable.

Mary Russell Mitford, OUR VILLAGE

AN ACCOUNT OF THE ARCHITECTURAL AMENITIES
OF THE SAVOY HOTEL

THIS IMPORTANT ADDITION to the hotels of the metropolis has many features quite novel to London. Its handsome river frontage, facing the gardens on the Thames Victoria Embankment, commands an extensive and highly interesting panoramic view – on the one hand St. Paul's Cathedral and the Tower of London; on the other, the Houses of Parliament at Westminster. Cleopatra's Needle stands in the foreground; on the opposite bank of the Thames lies the frontage of Lambeth; and in the far distance may be clearly seen the Crystal Palace and the Surrey hills.

The site of the Savoy Hotel, covering three quarters of an acre, is adjacent to the Savoy Theatre, whose manager and proprietor, Mr. R. D'Oyly Carte, is one of the directors of the Hotel Company; other directors are the Earl of Lathom, Mr. Hwfa Williams, and Sir Arthur Sullivan. The architect is Mr. W. Young, and Mr. G. H. Holloway was the builder.

A fine exterior view of the building is that of the south front, overlooking the Victoria Embankment, the gardens, and the Thames. To every floor there is a terraced balcony, supported either by granite columns or pillars of cream colour, having gilded capitals. Red and white striped blinds may be drawn at pleasure; and the combined effect of the colours, red, white, cream, and gold, in an edifice rising from the roadway eight floors high, is very attractive.

The carriage entrance, on Savoy Hill, from the Strand, brings visitors into a rectangular central courtyard, having an area of 6000 square feet, in the middle of which a fountain plays in a bower of flowers. Bright blossoms adorn the windows which pierce the lofty surrounding walls – walls that can never become smoke-begrimed, as they are built wholly of glazed white brick. At two corners, inclosed in towers which form portions of the square, have been provided American elevators, by means of which passengers may conveniently ascend to the top floors.

On the first floor is the restaurant, 70 ft. in length by 40 ft. in width, and capable of being temporarily subdivided. It is splendidly mounted in mahogany, carved and inlaid, and the chairs are covered with red leather. French windows open upon the broad balcony, where after dinner the grateful cup of coffee and cigarette may be enjoyed in the open air. Conveniently at hand are the kitchens, connected with the vast underground store-rooms, and the cellars, which are already stocked with carefully selected

LOUNGE ROOM

THE RESTAURANT

INTERIOR VIEWS OF THE SAVOY HOTEL

From the ILLUSTRATED LONDON NEWS 1889

champagnes, burgundies, and clarets, not to mention casks of ale and huge butts of spirits. The restaurant may in part be considered as distinct from the hotel, for it can be used by anyone who is attracted to it from the Strand, by which it is reached through Beaufort-buildings, a glazed corridor, leading therefrom to the dining-rooms, both public and private. Of course the Strand entrance is equally available to the regular visitor.

Another separate department is the banqueting-hall on the mezzanine floor, below the restaurant, having beneath it the ball-room; these three spacious rooms or halls corresponding in size and general characteristics, but differing, of necessity, in decoration. In the banqueting-room there is space sufficient to seat 360 people, and its acoustic properties are good, so that it will probably be hired for public meetings. The ballroom, treated in white and gold, has the advantage of a long alcove, and in the same wing there are reception- and cloak-rooms. A special entrance to this portion of the establishment is arranged in Savoy-place.

In the lower floors of the building are lounge-rooms, bureaus, cloak-rooms, smoke-rooms, and other conveniences which are the outgrowth of modern civilisation. In the depths of the cellars are four electric light engines – for no gas, except for cooking, is needed – water-heaters, pumps, and an artesian well, sunk over 420 ft. Here, too, a Turkish bath and swimming-bath will be constructed. The Savoy Hotel will make no charge for lights or for baths.

The majority of the four hundred and odd rooms which compose the hotel establishment derive light either from the river frontage windows or from those which open into the inclosed courtyard. A corridor, over 6 ft. wide, gives access to these apartments on every floor. It is possible to make a self-contained suite, consisting of one or more bed-rooms and private sitting-rooms, with a separate lavatory and bath-room, by the simple expedient of locking the double doors communicating with the next suite. With the doors thus closed the flat is complete, having nothing in common with its neighbour save the use of the main corridor or passage.

The bed-rooms, in their size and proportions, fittings, furniture, and decoration, are much alike; of course they vary in style, in tone, and in detail. All the suites of rooms are upholstered and arranged on a scale which can only be equalled in a grand mansion. Messrs. Maple have supplied pile carpets, brass 'twin' bedsteads, inlaid cabinets, and sets of mahogany, walnut, or enamelled ash, carved dados and mantlepieces, wall hangings of Japanese papers, or of tapestry designs, friezes of gold, and pottery of the choicest description. Nothing is wanting to please the educated eye or gratify the taste, as well to ensure comfort. It is expected that the rooms most in demand will be those which are at the greatest altitude, for the higher one goes the purer the air becomes, and the wider the prospect.

The provision of private bath-rooms, of which there are sixty-seven in all, is a new idea, and one that will no doubt be appreciated as an indispensable adjunct to the suite or flat system, which will be principally encouraged, as the basis of a fresh business. There is constant inquiry for such suites of rooms. On every floor there is a service-room, with lifts for luggage and speaking-tubes to the kitchen and offices. The hotel clerk, in his office, can, by looking at a dial, tell at a glance how long it is before any call has been answered by a servant.

It is intended that the Savoy shall cater for families of the highest class, and it can never be a cheap hotel, but it will not be unduly expensive. In all such details as plate, glass, china, and table-linen, great pains have been taken to procure the best. The manager of this new hotel is Mr. W. Hardwicke; the steward is M. François Rinjoux, formerly of the Grand Hotel at Monte Carlo, and M. Charpentier, late 'chef' at White's, is the ruler of the kitchen.

The building is entirely fireproof, as from basement to roof the materials employed are incombustible, the floors being of concrete and the joists of steel. Of wood there is none, except in the doors, window-frames, and furniture. One noticeable point is the completeness with which the electric lighting has been carried out, the current being cut off at will or utilised in prettily shaded lamps of the most convenient pattern.

ILLUSTRATED LONDON NEWS, 26 *October*, 1889

THE LONDON

CHRONICLER

DURING THE NINETEENTH CENTURY

SELECTED MAINLY FROM
CONTEMPORARY SOURCES
AND INCLUDING

SOME ACCOUNT OF THE FORMATION OF
THE LONDON FIRE-ENGINE ESTABLISHMENT IN 1833
FROM KNIGHT'S 'LONDON,' 1842

OBSERVATIONS UPON
THE POPULARITY OF THE GREAT EXHIBITION
EXHIBITION NOTABILIA
MACHINERY AT THE GREAT EXHIBITION
FROM 'THE UNIVERSAL EXHIBITOR,' 1851

AN ACCOUNT OF A BATTLE IN HYDE PARK
FOUGHT ON BEHALF OF GARIBALDI IN 1862
BY LOUIS BLANC

SOME ACCOUNT OF LONDON NEWSPAPERS
FROM KNIGHT'S 'LONDON,' 1877 EDITION

MEMORIES OF A VICTORIAN CHILDHOOD
BY MARY MACCARTHY, 1924

TOGETHER WITH
OTHER BRIEFER REFERENCES
AND NOTICES

The nation sits in the immense city they have builded, a London extended into every man's mind, though he live in Van Dieman's Land or Cape Town.

R. W. Emerson, ENGLISH TRAITS 1882

IN THE YEAR 1833, most of the insurance companies, seeing the benefit of mutual co-operation, and the effectual working of a system which had been put in force in Edinburgh, joined in the formation of the present 'London Fire-Engine Establishment.' The companies were ten in number, viz. the Alliance, Atlas, Globe, Imperial, London Assurance, Protector, Royal Exchange, Sun, Union, and Westminster. Subsequently, five others, the British, Guardian, Hand-in-Hand, Norwich Union, and Phœnix, joined the establishment; as did two or three recently-formed companies; and there are now only two fire-offices in London not belonging to it.

The affairs of the new Association were placed under the management of a committee, consisting of a Director from each of the associated insurance companies, which subscribe towards its support in certain agreed proportions. London was divided into five districts, which may be briefly indicated thus: – 1st, Eastward of Aldersgate Street and St. Paul's; 2nd, thence westward to Tottenham Court Road and St. Martin's Lane; 3rd, all westward of the 2nd; 4th, South of the river, and East of Southwark Bridge; 5th, South of the river, and west of Southwark Bridge. In these five districts were established engine-stations, averaging about three to each district; at each of which was one, two, or three engines, according to the importance of the station.

Such were the general arrangements as to distribution.

Since the year 1833 various minor changes have been made, according as experience pointed out the necessity for them; and at the present time the arrangements are nearly as follow: The establishment belongs to eighteen fire-insurance companies. There are fourteen stations, of which the most eastern is at Ratcliff, and the most western near Portman Square. At these stations are kept thirty-five engines, for whose management about ninety men are employed. The men are clothed in a uniform, and are selected with especial reference to their expertness and courage at fires; they are collectively known as the 'Fire Brigade,' and are all under the orders and direction of Mr. Braidwood, the superintendent of the establishment. A certain number of these men are ready at all hours of the day and night, and the engines are also always ready to depart at a minute's warning in case of fire. As a rule for general guidance, it is arranged that, when a fire occurs in any district, all the men and engines in that district shall repair to the spot, together with two-thirds of the men and engines from each of the two districts next adjoining to it, and one-third from each of those most removed from it; but this arrangement is liable to modification, according to the extent of a fire, or the number which may be burning at one time.

The general economy of the establishment, and the fearlessness of the brigade-men, have won a large measure of praise from nearly all classes in the metropolis. If self-interest were the chief motive which led the insurance companies to the establishment of a system likely to reduce their own losses, there is anything but selfishness in the risks which the men encounter in saving lives and property, the poor as well as the rich, the uninsured as well as the insured.

It has been often supposed that there are observatories on the roofs of the insurance offices or engine-houses, where watchmen are posted at all hours of the night to detect the appearance of fire, and to give notice to those below. This, if ever acted on, is not observed by the Fire-engine Establishment. There is an arrangement made by the Police commissioners, that a policeman, on observing a fire, communicates instantly to the nearest engine-station; and for so doing the Association gives him a gratuity of ten shillings. This, and a smaller gratuity to other persons who 'call an engine,' is found sufficient to command prompt information on the occurrence of a fire. It is true that the lovers of mischief so far show their silliness as to give 'false alarms,' to an average extent of some sixty or seventy per annum; and that the brigade-men are sometimes tantalized by atmospherical phenomena. It has often happened, in reference to the latter point, that an *aurora borealis* has so deceived the beholders as to lead to the impression that a great conflagration has broken out; in such case the engines are sent for precipitately, and all is in commotion. Two remarkable instances of this occurred about six years ago. On the first of these, twelve engines and seventy-four brigade-men were kept in constant motion from eleven in the evening till six the next morning, in endeavouring to search out what appeared to be a large conflagration; some of the engines reached Hampstead, and others Kilburn, before it was found that the glare was the effect of the 'northern lights.' On the other occasion, a crimson glare of light arose at the north-east part of the horizon, at about eight o'clock in the evening, seemingly caused by a fierce conflagration; and the resemblance was increased by what appeared to be clouds of smoke rising up after the glare, and breaking and rolling away beneath it. Thirteen engines and a large body of men went in search of the supposed fire, and did not detect their error till they had proceeded far to the north-east. Subsequent accounts showed that the military and fire-patroles at Dublin, Leyden, Utrecht, Strasbourg, Troyes, Rennes, and Nantes, had been similarly deceived by the atmospherical phenomena on the same night.

When, however, it is really a conflagration to which the attention of the brigade is called, there is an admirable coolness and system displayed in the whole proceedings. The water companies, by clauses in the Acts of Parliament regulating their foundation, are bound to furnish water freely in case of fire; and the hose or suction-pipe of every engine is speedily placed in connexion with the temporary pool of water derived from the street-plug. Then is observable a singular instance of the confidence which the firemen have that they shall obtain the aid of bystanders, for the firemen belonging to each engine are wholly insufficient to work it. The director or captain of each engine is empowered by the companies to pay – we believe at the rate of one shilling for the first hour, and sixpence per hour afterwards, together with a supply of 'creature-comforts' – for the services of as many strangers as he may need. It requires from twenty or thirty men to work each engine; and so extensive is the service thus rendered, that, at one of the large fires a few years ago, more than five hundred temporary servants were thus engaged.

While the supernumeraries are thus engaged with the engines, the brigade-men are directing the stream of water on the destructive element which they have to combat. Clothed in a neat and compact dress, with a stout leathern helmet to protect the head, they face the fiercest heat, alternately drenched with water from the pipes of the various engines, and half scorched by the flaming materials. Over and under, through and around the burning house, they direct their energies, braving alike the fire itself and the dangers attendant on falling ruins. It is lamentable to think that men, while thus engaged in a work of humanity, should lose their own lives; but such is the case, although, on account of the judicious arrangements of the corps, not very frequently.

Many of the most serious dangers attendant on a fire arise from the suffocating influence of the vast body of smoke which usually accompanies it. It has been thought, by those well qualified to form an opinion, that the calamity of being 'burnt to death' rarely, if ever, occurs, in the strict sense of the expression; that the real cause of death is suffocation from smoke, the burning and charring of the corpse being an after effect. To rescue individuals enveloped in smoke is thus a matter of anxious solicitude, and, to facilitate the exertions of the firemen to this end, they are provided with a very ingeniously-constructed smoke-proof dress. This dress is nearly analogous in principle to that of Mr. Deane, the diver. It consists of a leathern jacket and head-covering, fastened at the waist and wrists, whereby the interior is made tolerably smoke-proof. Two glass windows serve for the eyes to look through; and a pipe attached to the girdle allows fresh air to be pumped into the interior of the jacket, to support the respiration of the wearer. Thus equipped, the fireman may dare the densest smoke, although the dress is not so formed as to resist flame.

G. Dodd, KNIGHT'S LONDON, 1842

MUSIC IN LONDON IN THE EARLY NINETEENTH CENTURY

THE PHILHARMONIC WAS established in 1813, and from a somewhat similar motive to that which originated the Ancient Concerts. Grand instrumental compositions of the highest class, by modern musicians, had ceased to have a home, as the more important of the subscription concerts before mentioned lost their popularity and became gradually extinct. 'Never was a society formed in a better spirit and with a more commendable aim than the Philharmonic. It began where it ought; it was governed as it ought. There was no hunting after titled patrons or subscribers; no weak subserviency to mere rank. The most eminent members of the profession took the whole affair into their own hands, and entered upon their duties strong, and justly strong, in their own strength. They merged all claims of rank or precedence in one great object – the love of their art. Men of the highest musical rank were content to occupy subordinate stations in the orchestra. Every man put his shoulder to the wheel; and this very fact impressed the public with a conviction that they were in concert.'[1] Among the early members were John Cramer, Clementi, Crotch, Horsley, Bishop, Attwood, François Cramer, Spagnoletti, and Braham. It was fitting that the man who had before done so much in the cause in which they were engaged should preside at the opening meeting. Salomon, then an old man, led the concerts with 'a zeal and ability that age had in no degree impaired.' The progress of the Philharmonic was for some years equal to the preparation; and it is impossible to over-estimate the services rendered by it to the art during that period. Its band was, perhaps, the finest in the world.

KNIGHT'S LONDON, 1842

[1] *Spectator*, 1643.

THE REJOICINGS OF THE PEOPLE

UPON THE OCCASION OF

THE CHRISTENING OF THE PRINCE OF WALES, 1842

THE ILLUMINATIONS on Tuesday evening, although pretty numerous, were not so general as might have been anticipated upon so auspicious an occasion as the christening of the infant Prince of Wales, the future sovereign of these realms, which we believe may be attributed to the want of some official announcement that a general illumination would take place. None of the Government offices, the houses of Her Majesty's Ministers or of the Foreign Ambassadors (with a few exceptions) were lighted up; and the illuminations were, therefore, confined to the different club-houses, the houses of the royal tradespeople, and of a few private and patriotic individuals. The streets of the Metropolis, particularly at the West End, were from dusk densely thronged by respectably dressed persons of both sexes, who, regardless of the mud and slosh occasioned by the rain and the thaw in the morning wended their way from all directions towards the principal thoroughfares, which were crowded until long after midnight. Large bodies of the metropolitan and city police were stationed at the corners of the streets and at every available point, for the prevention of accidents and the preservation of property.

A notice was put up at the General Post Office Money Letter-office, stating that in consequence of the christening of the Prince of Wales that office was closed for the day. At Woolwich Dock-yard and Greenwich Hospital a good English dinner was given to the workmen and gallant veteran tars of Old England. The day was generally observed as a holiday at the West End; the shops and places of business were partially closed in the forenoon which became pretty general in the afternoon.

Among the many proofs of the prevalence of this well-timed philanthropy we mention the following: –

Royal Free Hospital. – The inmates of the Royal Free Hospital, to the number of fifty, as many as were convalescent, were feasted upon roast beef and plum pudding, with a pint of ale for each person.

Ward Schools. – In the city of London most of the children belonging to the various ward schools were regaled at their respective school rooms with the substantial fare of Old England. After dinner 'God Save the Queen' was sung.

Indigent Blind. – The 140 inmates of the School for the Indigent Blind had a holiday.   SUNDAY TIMES, 30 *January*, 1842

75

A DESCRIPTION OF
A MOST DARING ATTEMPT BY JOHN FRANCIS
TO ASSASSINATE THE QUEEN

THE ASSASSIN IS a young man not apparently more than twenty-two years of age; he is rather short and stout. He is deasently dressed, and his general appearance betokens respectability, his name is John Francis, the son of Mr. W. Francis, head machinist at the Theatre Royal, Covent Garden, for a number of years, and bears irreproachable character and much respected. It is stated that he exactly answers the description given of the miscreant who made an attempt to assassinate Her Majesty on Sunday evening. We were not inclined to credit this story of a previous attempt on Her Majesty's life on Sunday evening, but on enquiry, we learn from the highest authority that it is too true that such an attempt was made.

It appears that previous to Her Majesty's return to Buckingham Palace, yesterday evening, from her usual drive, the assassin attracted considerable attention in the Park, saying that the Queen lived upon the vitals of the people, at the same time making use of the most abusive epithets. Her Majesty was in the low pony phaeton, drawn by 8 greys and just as the phaeton reached the spot where the maniac Oxford made his attempt on Her Majesty's life, the individual now in custody, drew a pistol from his breast, and presenting it at Her Majesty discharged it, providentially without effect. The miscreant was arrested amidst the execration of the bystanders, who seemed almost inclined to execute summary vengeance on him; he was conveyed to one of the lodges of the Palace, and partially searched. The pistol which he thrust into his bosom was discovered to be loaded with ball, so that the difficulty of proving the intent will not occur in this case that occurred in the case of Oxford. He was subsequently conveyed to the Gardeners-lane Station house, where he was subjected to the most minute examination, but weather or not any other weapon has been found on him, we were unable to ascertain as the strictest orders were given to the authorities to observe the greatest secrecy on the subject. The prisoner does not present the slightest appearance of insanity, and seems perfectly calm and collected. We understand he refuses to state his place of abode or indeed any particulars about himself. At half-past seven he was conveyed from the Station house to the Home Office, where he went under a private examination before a privy council. Sir Robert Peel, Sir J. Graham, Lord Wharncliffe, and all the Cabinet Ministers, were assembled at the Home Office for the purpose of being at his examination.

The whole of Whitehall was crowded with persons anxiously waiting to catch a glimpse of the assassin on his return from the Home Office. St. James's Park also was thronged with people, pressing forward to make enquiries as to the well-being of the Queen.

Prince Albert was with Her Majesty in the phaeton at the time the attempt was made, but neither of them seemed aware of what had occurred until their return to the Palace.

About half-past six o'clock Sir James Graham was observed to enter the House of Commons, and walk towards the Speaker's end of the House, with a face evidently betraying anxiety.

A printer's broadsheet produced 30 *May*, 1842

OBSERVATIONS UPON THE POPULARITY
OF THE GREAT EXHIBITION

THE TIDE HAS fairly set in, and sixty thousand people pay daily visits to the Great Exhibition; and yet does London in no way differ in its appearance from that which it ordinarily presents at this time of year. 'Many persons,' says a lively French writer, 'who have not seen it, indulge in the idea that London is a town. Two millions of habitants, distributed in little more than two hundred thousand houses, seems an agglomeration sufficiently compact to justify that opinion. In reality, however, and despite appearances, London is but an immense hive. Its houses are but the cells of an honeycomb, and the diligent and industrious population is nothing more than a swarm of bees. I scarcely know anything that can give an idea of the prodigious activity which reigns in the twelve thousand streets, which are, as it were, the arteries and veins of its gigantic body. The only thing I may compare it to is an ant-hill, just at the moment when a child introduces a blade of grass into its subterranean passages. And yet this is but a weak comparison. The movements of its ebb and flow, can alone afford an idea of the continuous oscillations of the human multitude as there it onward flows, continually renewing itself without giving place to a single interval of time. This extraordinary activity is evidently a manifestation of universal toil. Meanwhile, however, some of those ingenious calculators whose province it is with impunity to group figures together, without being called on to prove them, do allege that in England there are not more than ten millions of individuals devoted to toil. This leads us to suppose the existence of a contemplative and parasitical population, amounting to about fifteen

THE 'DAY DREAMER' EASY CHAIR

*The easy chair thus appropriately named was designed by H. Fitz Cook, and
manufactured in papier mache by the exhibitors, Messrs. Jennens and Bettridge,
of Belgrave Square. The chair is decorated at the top with two winged thoughts –
the one with bird-like pinions, and crowned with roses, representing happy and
joyous dreams; the other with leathern bat-like wings – unpleasant and trouble-
some ones. Behind is displayed Hope, under the figure of the rising sun. The
twisted supports of the back are ornamented with the poppy, heartsease, convol-
vulus, and snowdrop, all emblematic of the subject. In front of the seat is a shell,
containing the head of a cherub, and on either side of it pleasant and troubled
dreams are represented by figures. At the side is seen a figure of Puck lying
asleep in a labyrinth of foliage, and holding a branch of poppies in his hand.*

THE UNIVERSAL EXHIBITOR, 1851

millions. Such a calculation astonishes me. If I have sometimes seen idlers, it was only in the large windows of the clubs. Though not very evident, still, after all, the statistical account may be correct. But even amongst these parasites, of every class and condition, what activity and quickness of motion is to be found! What, at first, surprises a stranger in London, is the spaciousness of the streets and the multiplicity of the squares, which form, as it were, oases in the inextricable ramification of the Babylonian routes which people naturally suppose to have a commencement somewhere, but the end of which is never seen. I cannot contemplate without affright the insupportable confusion that would exist if wise forethought had not opened such spacious paths for English activity. Were the "ant-like" toil of London transferred to our narrow streets, Paris would certainly burst asunder beneath the pressure of such a crowd, just like a boiler in which an excess of steam has accumulated. An idea of the relative manner in which Paris and London daily increase in size may be given by saying, that the former enlarges itself by rising upward, and the latter by spreading laterally. Were a person who lived in the reign of George III to be now restored to life, he would at the present day in vain seek for Primrose-Hill, Paddington, Islington, or Hampstead. All these charming retreats, with many others, have been incorporated with the Metropolis. As the population of London increases, a new village is made use of for accommodating the excess, and the town is thus led onwards. Babylon and Thebes, with its hundred gates, about which so much noise is made in ancient story, are assuredly but miniatures when contrasted with this monster Leviathan. Immensity in anything superinduces seriousness of thought. The ocean saddens me; a plain, bounded by the horizon, stupifies me; London, in its prodigious development, makes me weak and languid. I never met a traveller who, having visited London, did not bring away with him a depressingly unpleasant feeling. For this, however, the English are not to blame. There is not, certainly, a people in the world more anxious to please strangers than the English, and I am persuaded that they experience some regret in not having as yet been able to transfer the climate of India to the banks of the Thames, as they have done with respect to the incomparable "Mountain of Light." '

The mention of the Koh-i-noor naturally leads up to the transept of the Crystal Palace, and once there, we as naturally look around. We have visited it many times, but we are not yet familiar with anything more than the mere geography of the building. On the whole, the array of contributions present themselves to the mind in three groups: steam machinery, statues and models, and furniture. The machines are a type of Power; the art-models and the best statuary, Imaginative Beauty; and the furniture – at once so gay and grand, so elegant and substantial – the gleaming glass fountains, gorgeous carpets, handsome carved bedsteads with embroidered curtains, inlaid ormolu, gold, silver, and precious stones, textile manufactures, cloth, linens, laces, stuffs, silks, ribbons, satins, velvets, furs and leathers, mirrors and porcelain vessels, even the pictures exhibited – all, in fact, that may be comprehended under the term Furniture, convey that idea of Use to the mind for which Englishmen have a peculiar affection. And thus we have symbols of power, and beauty, and usefulness, the elements of civilization. In the display of Power, England reigns supreme. There in the might and symmetry of iron, and steel, and brass, stand the giant steam-engines which have won for us by their speed, and power, and immensity of production, the palms of commercial conquest in all the regions and over all the seas of the globe.

THE UNIVERSAL EXHIBITOR, 1851

EXHIBITION NOTABILIA

Purchases at the Great Exhibition. – We understand that at a meeting of Goldsmiths' Company, held a few days ago, a resolution was unanimously passed that the sum of £5,000 should be expended in the purchase of some of the magnificent plate, exhibited at the Crystal Palace, for the use of the splendid hall. At the next Court of Common Council, Alderman Copeland is to bring forward a motion 'that a sum not exceeding £5,000 be voted from the City cash to purchase some of the works of art in the Exhibition of the Industry of all Nations, adapted for the decoration of the City of London.'

The First Shilling Day. – Notwithstanding the general anticipation of a great crowd, the Duchess of Sutherland and Lady Blantyre were present with a party, among whom were the Earls of Jersey and Wilton, besides many others of the aristocracy.

The Exhibition Post-Office. – A 'post' has just been erected in the centre of the south half of the transept, after the fashion of such as are used in Belgium. It is a hollow cylinder (tastefully decorated, and in imitation of bronze), with a mouth similar to that of a common letter-box in this country; the post times being inscribed upon a ticket inserted in the top of the 'post.' It is, we understand, intended to adapt this to the uses of the Exhibition establishment, which, we may here mention, includes a post-office

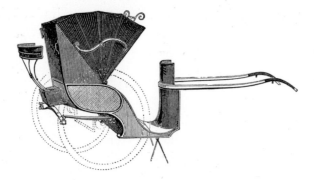

THE HANSOM SAFETY CAB

The body is required to be very low for the convenience of access, and therefore the shaft is not carried backward behind the dash-iron stays. The springs are three, one on each side, with a cross spring at the back attached to the footboard of the driver's seat.

MANUAL OF DOMESTIC INSTRUCTION, 1857

IMPROVED CONVERTIBLE CARRIAGE

An improved carriage, exhibited at the Great Exhibition, which may be used as A LIGHT OPEN BAROUCHE IN SUMMER AND FAIR WEATHER, *or* CONVERTED INTO A CLOSED CARRIAGE FOR WINTER. *It is constructed to seat four persons and the coachman. An examination of the illustration will show how, by removing the glass front and letting down the leather back, which is supported by springs in the usual way, the double Brougham becomes an open barouche. The dotted lines show the connection between the two vehicles.*

THE UNIVERSAL EXHIBITOR, 1851

department, the business of which is very extensive, and is conducted by Mr. Osmond Jones. In this office on an average about 500 letters are despatched daily, and about 300 arrive. Letters sent out are registered, and letters received are distributed to all the various parties engaged in the vast edifice. Posts arrive and leave thrice a day – 11, 3, and 5. The Postmaster-General sends direct for the letter bats, which do not pass through any branch office, and great accommodation is thus afforded to the public.

Educational Adaptation of the Exhibition. – The proposition to make the Exhibition a means of popular education by explanations and descriptive lectures, &c., has been most favourably received, and the University of Oxford not only countenances the scheme, but has given a series of lectures, in accordance with the idea in preparation for the general visit of the members of the University to the Exhibition. Professor Ansted has announced a series of eight lectures on successive Friday and Saturday mornings, between the hours of nine and twelve o'clock, in explanation of the mining processes, mineral products, and manufactures forwarded for exhibition from various parts of the world. The first of these lectures took place on Friday, 23rd of May, and was of an introductory character – treating of the general nature of the materials of which the earth is composed. He then discussed in their order mineral fuel, iron, other metals, stone, clay, various earthy minerals, and gems. The number of his class is limited, and a detailed list of the objects illustrated will be issued previous to each lecture. Lord Dufferin has suggested that a number of the pupils of the Belfast School of Design should be sent to London to have the benefit of seeing the Great Exhibition. His Lordship has headed a list of subscriptions for the purpose with a contribution of £30; and it is hoped that his excellent suggestion will not only be carried out in Belfast, but that the hint will be taken by other schools of design also.

The Official Catalogue is now understood to be quite useless to visitors; for notwithstanding the late improvements made in it, the impossibility of finding an object by reference to its pages, or having found it, of gleaning any intelligence beyond the name of the exhibitors, becomes daily more apparent.

New Arrivals. – A vessel just arrived in the docks from Charente, has brought some packages of chestnuts, almonds, figs, raisins, and grapes, which are officially stated to be for the purpose of exhibition in Hyde-park. The arrivals of the last two or three days from abroad have included, besides the above, some contributions from France and the Hanseatic States, and also some packages from Colombo, Ceylon, &c.

Lodgings. – A central registration office has been established in Exeter-change, Catherine-street, Strand, and a classified list of lodgings has been prepared. The accommodation at the disposal of the office ranges in price from twenty-five guineas per week to one shilling per night. The establishment has been extremely active in its endeavours to extend the lower priced list, and with all the obstacles in its way, has succeeded in obtaining the command of accommodation for about 2,000 persons, at prices which place it within the means of the artisan visitors; and it has, on the whole, the disposal of accommodation for some four or five thousand persons.

Her Majesty has, we understand, purchased at the Exposition a tiara of sapphires of great lustre and size, and a brooch, consisting of two enormous rubies, set round with diamonds, by Lemonnière, of Paris.

A Graceful Act of liberality on the part of his Royal Highness Prince Albert towards the young ladies, pupils at the Government School of Design, Somerset-house, has just become known. A few days before the opening of the Great Exhibition, the senior female students (several of whom are exhibitors) prepared a memorial to Prince Albert, praying that they might be present at the inauguration of the 'world's fair' by Her Majesty. The Prince immediately replied to Mrs. M'Ian, the principal of the female branch of the school, regretting his inability to grant the free admissions required, but requested that the young ladies would accept a dozen season tickets, and that she would be pleased to present them to twelve of her most deserving pupils. Shortly after this communication from the Prince, Mr. Redgrave, the principal of the male department, received from the Earl of Granville the following note: 'Bruton-street, April 29. Mr. Labouchère and I have much pleasure in offering twelve season tickets to the Government School of Design, if you will, with the other head masters, select those students who appear to you the most deserving. It will give us pleasure if these tickets give pleasure and instruction to those to whom you may allot them.' THE UNIVERSAL EXHIBITOR, 1851

MACHINERY IN THE CRYSTAL PALACE

THE LEVIATHAN *Lord of the Isles* is one of the ordinary class of engines constructed by the Great Western Company since 1847. It is capable of taking a passenger-train of 120 tons at an average speed of sixty miles an hour upon easy gradients. The evaporation of the boiler when in full work is equal to 1,000-horse power, of 33,000 lbs. per horse – the effective power, as measured by a dynamometer, is equal to 743-horse power. The weight of the engine in working order is 35 tons, which does not include the tender, which, under similar circumstances, weighs 17 tons 13 cwts. The diameter of cylinder, 18 inches; length of stroke, 24 inches; diameter of driving wheel, 8 feet; and the maximum pressure of steam, 120 lbs. The stately proportions of this engine are seen to great advantage in the Crystal Palace; and, contrasted with the light locomotives of Messrs. Adams and England, seems quite a giant of power and capability. To see this engine, however, in its full glory, the spectator should be at its side when it stops, after a heavy run at express speed – when the furnace is too white with heat for the naked eye to look upon without pain, and the steam, blowing off like thunder, shakes the very ground. One of these engines was nicknamed by the men the *Emperor of Russia*, on account of his extraordinary appetite for oil and tallow! In order to distribute the weight more equally over the rails, it will be observed that the engine alone has eight wheels. The cylinders are laid horizontally under the front end of the boiler, and can in this case be very conveniently inspected, together with the rest of the working parts, by going down into the pit provided for that purpose under the engine.

This system, as may be imagined, is best suited for main lines, where the traffic is very heavy. It had, however, been foreseen by some of our engineers that the rage for heavy engines would carry railway managers too far, and that when their eyes became open to the fact that more than half their power was exerted in moving *itself* merely, and knocking the rails and sleepers to pieces, they were as anxious to get back their light engines as they had formerly been to discard them. This led to the introduction of the light 'locomotive carriage' of Mr. Adams, and the light engine of Mr. England. The specimens which they have exhibited, whilst possessing all the advantages which experience and skill have worked out in the heavy engines, are not more than one-third of the weight and half the cost. Mr. Adams' plan consists in combining the engine and carriage in one, so that there is no superfluous weight; the stoker can act as guard and take the tickets. The boiler is a cylinder full of tubes placed vertically; but this plan, in subsequent engines, has been given up in favour of the ordinary horizontal construction, as shown in the locomotive carriage in the Exhibition.　　THE UNIVERSAL EXHIBITOR, 1851

THE LIGHT 'LOCOMOTIVE CARRIAGE' OF MR ADAMS

THE LEVIATHAN 'LORD OF THE ISLES'

RAILWAY ENGINES AT THE GREAT EXHIBITION

We may pause here a moment to notice the gradual rise in men's minds of our present ideas of speed. The directors of the London and Birmingham did not begin at a higher rate than eighteen miles an hour, then gradually advanced to twenty, twenty-two and a half, and ultimately to above twenty-six, including stoppages; whilst excluding stoppages from thirty-six to forty-two miles per hour is run upon the Northern and Eastern, the South Eastern and the Brighton, and not infrequently forty-five on the Great Western, which, on several occasions of importance, considerably exceeds even that enormous rate.

J. Saunders, KNIGHT'S LONDON, 1842

AN ACCOUNT OF A LONDON BATTLE
FOUGHT ON BEHALF OF GARIBALDI
IN OCTOBER, 1862

I RESIDE A FEW STEPS from Hyde Park, whence I have just returned. What a sad, what a disgusting spectacle! What an odious battle! In that immense park, – usually intended for peaceable promenaders, and which, even at the season when life is over-flowing in the capital, is animated only by brilliant cavalcades and the innocent rivalry of dashing equipages, – scenes have been enacted this day which make one shudder. Imagine well nigh 90,000 men gathered together and all terribly excited; furious encounters; hand to hand combats; heads broken by cudgels; terrified groups of runaways rushing against one another; women knocked down and trampled under foot; morning coats, soldiers' uniforms, working men's jackets, paupers' rags, all mingled together, all swept away in the same whirlwind; and by the side of individuals half murdered for having shouted, 'Garibaldi for ever!' other individuals half murdered for having shouted, 'The Pope for ever!' Such were the scenes presented to view in Hyde Park, barely an hour ago.

And why? Because, probably, our so much boasted civilization has not yet done with the demon of religious wars; because the number of idiots who deem it a holy work to cut their neighbours' throats for the glory of God, is still very considerable; because brutality is the child of ignorance, and because ignorance belongs to the brood of superstition; because the Papacy is represented in London by a mob of brutalised Irishmen, who even in the dens where the scum of the population boils over, form the scum of that scum; lastly – and this is at once the most important and the most melancholy reason – because it depends upon one solitary man in Europe to keep minds in suspense, to prolong indefinitely the uneasiness that arises from a situation where all is darkness, to change through impatience this feeling of uneasiness into fury, and to make the protracted occupation of Rome a source of agitation for the whole world.

Even on Sunday last the black speck that ushers the storm was seen in Hyde Park. An orderly meeting of English workmen, who had assembled to express aloud their sympathies for the hero of Aspromonte, was furiously assailed by a host of ragged Irishmen, armed with heavy bludgeons. Blows were exchanged, much passion was displayed, and many wounds inflicted. This was the prelude. Sinister reports had also been in circulation the whole week. A more serious engagement was announced. That efforts were made to prevent it is certain, but men's minds were greatly irritated by the rumour spread among the working classes, that the Irish had boasted in their own haunts, that they could prevent by force the manifestation of sympathies contrary to their own. Instead, therefore, of assembling to-day in Hyde Park to the number of five or six thousand only, as on Sunday last, the English workmen had gathered together to the number of forty or fifty thousand, without reckoning those who were drawn thither by curiosity. On their side, the Papists had counted up their forces, had provided themselves with weapons, and held themselves in readiness. Who was it who had marshalled this host? They certainly appear to have acted in conformity with some previous system of organization. In serried ranks, shoulder to shoulder, after the manner of a regiment on the march, they proceeded to the spot to which confusion and strife accompanied them. A mound formed of rubbish, which, on the previous Sunday, had served as a platform for the orators of the meeting, and afterwards as a field of battle, was the point towards which, this day also, the steps of the assailants were directed. It was thither chiefly that the 'defenders of religion' hastened to uphold their cause with sticks, stones, and fisticuffs; and there, more than elsewhere, bones were broken and faces covered with blood.

Never was a citadel attacked with greater impetuosity, or defended with greater obstinacy. Never was a strategic position more frequently taken and retaken. It seemed as if the fortune of pontifical Rome was attached to the possession of that heap of rubbish, to which, doubtless with a view to render it historical, has been given the name of Redan! Military honour happening thus to be interested in the affair, soldiers of the Guards regiments joined in the *melee*, and took part in the assault amid the enthusiastic acclamations of the people. Needless to add, that numerous detachments of the police were dispatched to the scene of disorder, where they exhibited great intrepidity and self-possession. But their interference availed not to prevent bloodshed. It is said that some lives were lost. A large number of persons were conveyed to the hospitals in a condition that causes serious apprehensions as to their ultimate recovery. At least, so I heard while returning to my home, after having witnessed the riot from a spot sufficiently distant to avoid any chance of being mixed up in it. If it be true that Cardinal Wiseman's carriage was seen driving through the Park, his Eminence, as well as every intelligent Catholic, must have deplored the mode in which the Church was being upheld.

The English workmen, Garibaldi's partisans, would no doubt have acted wisely if they had abstained from this open-air meeting, especially since it was almost certain that a savage conflict would be the consequence; but, after all, they were in the right. Not only are open-air meetings authorised in England, but it may even be said that they form an essential part of public life. There is not a park here, not a public garden, no large open space, where you do not, on Sundays, find groups gathered around some well-meaning preacher, who, mounted on a chair, explains the Bible to the passers-by, and preaches to them religion after his own views. It is a relic of the practices engendered by the spirit of the Reformation. 'Every man is a priest,' said Luther. Room, therefore, for whosoever deems himself capable of preaching, and room for whosoever feels any curiosity to hear him preach! If the Irish had desired to oppose manifestation to manifestation, nothing prevented them from doing for the Pope what the English workmen had resolved to do for Garibaldi. There would have been no want of room in Hyde Park. They could there have erected, to their own satisfaction, altar against altar. No one, assuredly, in this free country, would have quarrelled with them had they voted the martyr's palm to the Pope, or to Napoleon the title of Saviour of Religion – of religion placed by him, as all know, under the edifying protection of his bayonets. They could even have asserted, without any one thinking for a moment of stopping their mouths, that the States of the Church are the best governed on the face of the earth. But no: to these wretched slaves of a gross fanaticism it seemed far more simple to refute with their bludgeons the arguments of those who differ in opinion from themselves. Is it their fault? I deny it. The real culprits are those who, exercising over this ignorant mob an unbounded influence, inflame their passions instead of enlightening their minds.

Louis Blanc, LETTERS ON ENGLAND, 5 *October*, 1862

THE GAROTTERS IN LONDON

A GOOD WAY for the inhabitants of London to get the better of the garotters would be by learning the art of self-defence. If a man carries a stick, or any other weapon, it is of consequence that he should know how to make use of it; and if he is not armed, it is of consequence that he should know how to make use of his fists.

From London Sportsman, SATURDAY REVIEW, 1862

LITTLE DID HONEST Nathaniel Butter, when in 1622 he began to publish 'Certain Newes of the present Week,' contemplate the extent to which the trade which he was inventing was destined to grow. In little more than two centuries the small weekly newspaper has expanded into 1,585 daily, weekly, &c., newspapers in the three kingdoms. The activity set in motion to keep up these papers may be partly inferred from what has been stated above: so many news-collectors incessantly perambulating the streets, peeping into the senate and courts of justice, into the theatres and other places of public amusement, or posting night and day to and from public dinners, agricultural and political meetings in all the provinces of the empire – so many honest spies residing in the capitals both of Christendom and Islam, gathering and transmitting to the London newspapers every rumour of court intrigue – so many theatrical and artistical critics, and writers of essays, all for the edification of the patrons of the London newspaper press – so many editors devising means of rendering their paper more attractive, collecting matter from all ends of the earth – so many telegraph wires to convey information to the newspapers, or the newspapers to their readers – so many reporters listening (what a penance!) to the lengthy speeches of modern orators, and translating them into grammar and English idiom, in order that they may not discredit the columns of the newspaper – so many newsvenders, with their bags, fetching, and folding, and despatching, by foot-messengers, by post, and by railway-trains. It is a brave bustling life, and one in which there is no stint or stay. No sooner do the night-owls, whose business it is to 'compose' the morning papers, quit work, than their brother typos, who work by day, are setting to work upon the evening papers. The last copy of the Sunday paper is scarcely 'worked off' when the compositors on the Monday morning journals are beginning to bestir themselves. Sunday and Saturday are alike days of sale with the newsvender. The half-opened shop-window, the wall beplastered with placards announcing the contents of the Sunday newspapers, show that the newsman is at his receipt of customs: and at the omnibus-stands and the steamboat piers the volunteer venders of the newspapers attend to supply the country-going parties with something to read should the time hang heavy on their hands. These last are the lingering remnants (sadly tamed down) of the vociferous itinerants, the Horn Boys with their cries of 'Glorious News.'

The printers of newspapers are much like other printers, but both the authors of newspapers (editors, writers of 'leaders' and reviews, reporters, penny-a-liners, &c.) and the newsvenders are classes with marked distinctive characters. The latter have been described above, but their light-foot Mercuries (their errand-boys) must not be passed unnoticed. We have an affection for the little creature, who, be it storm or sunshine, rain or snow, duly brings our newspaper at breakfast-time. It would be a hard heart indeed that could grudge him his Christmas-box annually petitioned for in verse from the Catnach mint. Charles Lamb has celebrated an annual dinner given in days of old to the chimney-sweeps. Had he lived till this time he might have recorded – as he only could – the annual dinner of the newsvenders' boys. But as such blazon may not be, let us take the account of their last festival, evidently from the pen of some precocious imp of the tribe. We sorely suspect our own juvenile, whom we have more than once caught, on returning from an early walk through the green-lanes in our neighbourhood, taking a furtive glance at the columns of our newspaper, totally regardless of the plight we should have been in had the tea and toast been ready before it arrived.

'The newsvenders' servants' anniversary dinner, which is given by the proprietors of the London papers to the newsvenders and their servants, took place yesterday at Highbury Barn Tavern, and was very numerously attended by the class for whom it was more particularly intended, and their wives. The dinner, or rather series of dinners – for there were two, not to mention a tolerably solid supper at eight o'clock, for those whose engagements prevented their earlier attendance – was plain and substantial, and was duly honoured by the guests, whose style of dealing with the viands set before them would seem to prove that the calling of a newsman is by no means a hindrance to the possession of a remarkably sound and vigorous appetite. Indeed we have seldom seen more able performers than the lads who partook of the first dinner at one o'clock; meat-pies, pudding, and drink vanished with inconceivable celerity, and the cry was still for more. At last the young folks were satisfied, and their elder brethren and their families then partook of the second dinner at three o'clock, which being finished, the chairman rose and proposed successively the "Queen," "Prince Albert," and the "Proprietors of the London Newspapers," all of which toasts were drunk with the most vociferous applause. After rising from the table the company proceeded to amuse themselves in the grounds till nine o'clock, when the ball, which usually succeeds these festivities, being opened under the able direction of that *skilful but eccentric master of the ceremonies*, dancing-master Wilson, the ladies and gentlemen present commenced dancing, which they kept up with great spirit long after we were *compelled to depart*. The festivities of the day were well conducted by Mr. Wylde, the chairman, assisted by the stewards, and seemed to give general satisfaction; and the company, though abundantly uproarious, appeared to enjoy themselves greatly after their own way. To the credit of the party it should be observed, that *out* of nearly five hundred individuals, young and old, who were present, we did not see one tipsy man or woman.'

It is a more delicate matter dealing with the character and position of the literary labourers in the newspaper vineyard. They wield goose-quills too, and are noways slow to betake themselves to their tools, either in attack or defence. A great deal of melancholy cant has of late been vented about the social estimation of journalists as below their deserts. The intellectual character of British journalists, too, it has been said by those who ought to know better, is inferior to the French. Neither assertion is true. The cry about the degraded *status* of journalists has been got up by a knot of kid-glove democrats, who wish to be pets of the saloons, as some French journalists are. The *prestige* which attaches to the literary character in France, and to writers in journals along with the rest, cannot be expected here. In England a man takes his place in public esteem, not on the strength of his profession, but of his personal character – and may this long be the case. No one need expect to find here a company awed into respect by the announcement that he is Mr. ———, editor of the ———; but neither need he fear, if his conduct is what it ought to be, that the announcement will make him less regarded. Journalists may command, and do, and have commanded, as much respect in this country as members of any other profession. As to the alleged superiority of the French newspaper press, it is, in respect of news, both as concerns quantity and quality, decidedly inferior to the English; and, without any wish to undervalue the high talents dedicated to journalism in France, there have been, and are, talents quite as high embarked in the profession in London. That the character of mercantile speculation preponderates in our newspapers is, in so far as politics are concerned, rather an advantage than the contrary. The fears of proprietors put a check upon such crude and rash speculations as distinguished the French 'Globe' in the days of its St. Simonianism. There may be less of the parade of scientific

inquiry in English journals, but there is more of practical states-
manship. The men who are trained to political controversy in
association with the party-leaders of their day, and the most active
members of the great mercantile interests, are trained in a better
school than sentimental and imaginative belle-lettrists, like
Lamartine and De Tocqueville.

Within our limits, it would indeed be impossible to sketch the
characters of the three hundred and odd newspapers published in
London alone. All that can be done is to group them in classes,
indicating the peculiarities of each class by a few of the more
prominent individuals belonging to it. The daily papers are a class
by themselves. They are in the news department less narrators of
events than mirrors of the transactions themselves. The full,
almost *verbatim*, reports of speechifying meetings, the long collections of protocols and other official documents, are given with a
conscientious fidelity that renders these papers sometimes almost
as tiresome as the facts they chronicle. There was a time when the
newspapers were not allowed to report the proceedings of Parliament, and then they must have been deficient in a very interesting
feature. But the fidelity with which the debates in Parliament are
now reported has become wearisome. The public has been sur-
feited with Parliamentary eloquence. To wade through these inter-
minable columns, a man would require to have no other avocation.
So strongly is this felt, that all the daily papers are now in the
habit of giving, along with their full Parliamentary report (which is
intended probably as a matter of record or a *piece justificatif*), an
abstract of it in the editorial column – and few readers, we suspect,
venture upon any more. Each of the leading daily papers has a
strongly-marked spirit of individuality, impressed upon it in some
instances by the first projector, and retained through many
changes of proprietorship and editorship. *The Times* is right John
Bull; always vigorous and vehement, sometimes to a degree ludi-
crously disproportioned to the subject of discussion. Shrewd and
energetic, it is *borné* in the last degree when any question comes to
be discussed in which the insular prejudices of England come into
play. The *Standard* is marked by clear logic, strong prepossessions,
and a high gentlemanly tone. It is the paper of a ripe scholar, and
withal somewhat of a recluse. The *Globe* is characterized by a
diplomatic *retenue* and the natural easy tone of a man of the world.
This it inherits from a former editor: the present writers have
caught up his mantle, but a flippancy at times breaks out which
contrasts disagreeably with the usual tone of the paper. The *Post* is
apt to be looked upon as a mere fashionable paper: this is a mis-

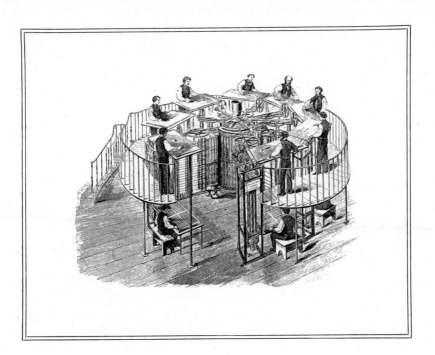

APPLEGATH EIGHT-FEEDER

VERTICAL CYLINDER PRESS

AS SUPPLIED TO 'THE TIMES', 1848

In 1848, a remarkable invention was introduced at 'The Times' office, the credit of which was due to Mr. Applegath. The types, instead of being laid on a table, traversing a sort of railroad – a correct description of the old process – were built up as it were on the face of a drum of cast iron. Eight printing cylinders were arranged round this drum, and instead of the four impressions taken by the old machine in its double journey, eight sheets were printed in every revolution of the cylinder. Eight men, on a raised gallery, were employed to feed the machine, by carefully pushing successive sheets into its eight mouths, each man doing this at the rate of one sheet in four seconds. Directly under these eight men were a similar number on the ground, employed in taking off and piling the printed sheets thrown out by the machine. So astonishing is the velocity of this press, that the eye vainly attempts to follow the numerous sheets of paper in their rapid motion. Ten thousand copies an hour can be thrown off by means of it, and if necessary twelve thousand. Indeed, it is said that a sufficiently large cylinder, with corresponding apparatus, could as easily produce one hundred thousand as ten thousand copies an hour.

CAXTON AND THE ART OF PRINTING

93

take – there is much vigorous writing and unconventional thought, both in the literary and political departments.

The London weekly papers are literary, or political, or sporting, or fashionable, or agricultural, or commercial, or blackguard. To these may be added class papers.

There are some exclusively literary papers; such, for instance, as the *Athenæum* and the *Academy*. The leading political weekly papers are the *Saturday Review*, the *Spectator, Examiner, John Bull, World, Guardian, Weekly Dispatch*, and *Weekly Times*. The *Weekly Times* and the *Examiner* represent the opinions of two sections of the middle-class liberals; the *Dispatch* is affected by the hard-headed artisans; the *John Bull* is still nominally the representative of the class which yet glories in the designation of Tory, though it also, like the *Guardian*, aims at representing the Established Church. *Bell's Life in London* is the oldest exclusively sporting paper. It is a goodly mass of small type, recording all feats of racing, hunting, boating, coursing, cricketing, and, in short, every *ing* that flourishes in the fields of merry England. The *Sunday Times*, however, supplies its readers with a fair proportion of sporting intelligence. The *Era*, though chiefly theatrical, is looked up to by some sporting characters as a fair record of the events of the turf. The so-called fashionable papers are the *Court Journal* and *Court Circular*; they are patronised by the same class that patronised the fashionable novels in their day. Foremost among the agricultural papers stands one of the oldest London papers, *Bell's Weekly Messenger*. This journal has for nearly a century been considered, *par excellence*, the farmers' journal. The *Mark Lane Express* is rather the journal of the corn-factors than of the agriculturists, and is circulated weekly among the frequenters of corn-markets. The commercial journals are the *Commercial Gazette*, the *Commercial Weekly Statement of Stocks*, the *Journal of Commerce*, and the *Mercantile Shipping Register*, with a whole host of *Stock and Share Lists, Trade Lists, Circulars*, &c., &c. Almost every class and profession have now their special journals: soldiers and sailors have their *Naval and Military Gazette, The Navy*, and *United Service Gazette*; the gardeners have a *Gazette* and a *Chronicle*; the lawyers have their *Law Times* and *Solicitors' Journal*; speculators in steam and railways have the *Railway Times*; the colonial interest has its *Colonial Gazette*; and some colonies and dependencies (as, for example, New Zealand and India), have journals of their own published in London. Every sect in religion almost has its newspaper: – the evangelical churchmen have their *Record*; the high-churchmen their *Guardian* and *Church Times;* the ruling body of the Dissenters their *Patriot;* and their opposition the *Noncon-formist:* one section of the Wesleyans patronise the *Watchman;* another the *Wesleyan Chronicle;* and our Roman Catholic brethren have their *Tablet, Weekly Register,* and *Universe.* Perhaps the blackguard papers above alluded to may be named as class papers, and the best way to put a stop to them may be to mark down as blackguards all their supporters. The 'illustrated' journals are a comparatively recent invention. Of these the *Illustrated London News* stands first on the roll, having been established as far back as 1841, by the late Mr. Herbert Ingram, a native of Boston. The *Graphic* may be classed as next in importance. Besides these, there are the *Pictorial World,* the *Illustrated Sporting and Dramatic News,* and two or three others of very questionable taste.

Charles Knight, LONDON, 1842
with Walford's additions, 1877

ADVERTISEMENTS IN THE PRESS

THERE is a dramatic interest about the advertisements which belongs to no other department of a newspaper. They tell us what men are busy about, how they feel, what they think, what they want. As we con them over in the pages of *The Times* or *Telegraph,* we have the whole busy ant-hill of London life exposed to our view.

Many of them have such a suggestive mystery about them, that they almost deserve a place in the 'Romance of Real Life.' In corroboration of this we take up a file of *The Times,* and open at random, turning to the top of the second column of the first page, the locality most affected by this class. There is an imploring pathos about the very first that meets our eyes, that might suggest matter for at least three chapters of a modern novel: – 'F. T. W. is *most urgently intreated* to communicate his address to his friend J. C., before *finally determining upon so rash a course of conduct* as that mentioned in his letter of yesterday. *All may and will be arranged.* The address, if communicated, will be considered confidential.' Still more heart-rending are the images conjured up by the address upon which we stumble next: – 'To A.M. Your brother *implores* that you will immediately return home, and every arrangement will be made for your comfort; or write me, and relieve the dreadful distress in which our parents are at your absence.' The next strikes the note of generous enthusiasm: – 'Grant. Received 5*l.* 6*s.,* with thanks and admiration for the rare probity exhibited.'

Charles Knight, LONDON, 1842

FOR SOME YEARS NOW, after Adela and I had left the school-room, it had been our custom to spend the end of the season in London. This came about every year because the wife of a Colonel in the Guards persuaded my mother to let her occupy our house at Eton, while she lent us her house in London.

'So good for sweet Adela and Mary to have a little fling? So good for darling Evelina's lessons?' reads my mother from the persuasive Mrs. Darcy's letter.

'And so good for Mrs. Darcy to have the river, the garden, and the library,' adds the Warden a little tartly over the rim of *The Times*.

Once more the four-wheeler piled with luggage has brought us away from Paddington and turned into the eighteenth-century square, as into a hushed cove, out of the roaring sea of Oxford Street. We alight at Mrs. Darcy's house. My mother is at once perfectly happy in the drawing-room with its long mirrors and Buhl furniture, where at a great escritoire she seats herself and writes imaginative letters telling her friends where to come and find her.

But Mr. Kestell sits in the over-furnished boudoir with Adela, Mary, and Evelina, and they all grumble together in the drowsy afternoon heat, surrounded on all sides with Adonises of the Guards in silver frames, which presently they will put away.

'The Colonel, you may be sure, doesn't like my study, and I don't like his,' says Mr. Kestell. He has thrown one knee over the other and is shaking his foot impatiently. 'It's a mere tank with his racing calendar and spurs and a stale smell of cat rising up from the pavement.'

'Mother is probably writing a letter upstairs saying that the Warden is as happy as a king in the Colonel's study,' says Adela drowsily.

'And Mrs. Darcy is probably writing a letter saying that the Colonel is as happy as a king in Mr. Kestell's dear, delightful, dowdy study,' Mary suggests.

'No: – dear, delightful, dowdy Mr. Kestell's study,' suggests Evelina, throwing her arms round the Warden's neck.

'You see, father, it was exceedingly tiresome of you to submit to the exchange again this year,' she adds.

'Oh, well, your mother does so much enjoy London, and it is really useful to me to be at the British Museum every day just now, I must remember. You will enjoy your season.'

'Oh, no, father, we shall not for a single moment. We have no clothes – we are dowdy. Nothing could satisfy me but to be simply tremendously smart and dash round the Park, driving a barouche and pair with a tiger on the back seat,' says Mary fiercely, a swift vision of a totally unattainable elegance darting into her head.

Adela then grumbles too. 'Yes, and just look at our engagements. The Archbishop's Garden Party and the Bishop's Garden Party. Old Sir Theodore's jaunt, and then there's that hop at Lady A's. She only knows about twelve young men – all under life-size or with squints.'

'This is absurd,' says Mr. Kestell. 'You want me to exclaim over and over again like Mrs. Allen, when she took Catharine Morland to Bath: "If only we had some acquaintance here!" As a matter of fact you know perfectly well that lots of fun will crop up, and before you know where you are, you are in a whirl of most delightful parties, my dear children,' says Mr. Kestell, thinking that the grumbling must really cease.

But Mary goes on querulously. 'Then the awful shopping. Everything lovely too expensive – dying of heat in shops, and coming out with nothing but a nervous breakdown!'

'My dear, my dear! Your father ought to have had ten thousand a year at least. You must be *good*!' says Mr. Kestell.

'Mary, you adore shopping,' says Adela severely.

We have all been rather like babies waking up from sleep and wailing at absolutely nothing. But it is a thundery, stifling afternoon. After some fragrant tea out of Mrs. Darcy's Crown Derby, we feel refreshed, and soon our mood completely changes. We see Mr. Kestell off affectionately, at the front door, in his scholarly, black morning-coat and Ruskinian-blue tie drawn through a ring. Though he will only be out until the evening, we all embrace him as if he were going on a far journey; and though we have all just spent some hours together he wishes to know exactly when he is to see us all again.

'Remember we shall spend a great deal of money on clothes when we go out,' says Adela.

'Yes, you will be punished for bringing us here by our extravagance,' Mary says with a Goneril-like thrust at the last.

'No, no, no. Poor, but clean. Poor, but clean,' and he runs down the steps and disappears down the street. He may be going to the London Library to look up some point for the book on Mediæval Chivalry that he is writing, or to look in at Sotheby's to see some Elzevirs that he feels with pain will certainly be bought for

America; then he will probably call on an old lady at St. James's Palace; or visit the Athenæum where he will hide behind pillars from other old gentlemen; or hear an anthem at the Abbey before he has finished his day.

Adela and I in the late afternoon stroll through Hanover Square and Bond Street, tantalized as we flatten our noses abstemiously in the 'street of elegant shops.' We both adore shoes, hats, and gowns. Then we jingle down to Knightsbridge in a hansom, and here we flatten again, and then make a self-indulgent plunge inside. We buy green shoes, to wear with white muslin Sir Joshua dresses.

'Cleanliness *can't* be combined with poverty,' says Adela, remembering Mr. Kestell's injunctions, among billows of flowered chiffon.

'No, I know, it's impossible,' says Mary, and she pounces upon white silk stockings to wear with green shoes. In the end we spend a great deal, and everything is put down to Mrs. Kestell's account. It is 'feast' not 'fast' just now. 'Le grand livre' will lie in its drawer for many a day after the exchange of houses with Mrs. Darcy, for no one will have the courage to bring it out.

That evening, Mrs. Kestell at her writing-table is writing to one of her friends:

'Adela and Mary are off, radiant, to their dance, looking like flowers in their calyxes, with their sweet young faces in their white and green.'

'Why *do* they say these things to each other?' says Adela in the hansom trotting across the Park to the dance at Mrs. Tallboys' on Campden Hill. She has just repeated the words that she read over her mother's shoulder to Mary and Mr. Fitzgerald, who is accompanying them to the dance, and peals of laughter have floated out of the hansom into the summer dusk.

'Yes, and all the time mother knows quite well what a devil's heart lies under Mary's Burne-Jonesy sweetness,' says Adela.

'And that M. Anatole France isn't in it for Adela's cynicism, though she drifts about being thought a very sweet creature!' says Mary.

'Which part of you is the calyx, do you suppose?' says Fitzgerald, leaning out over the hansom doors, enjoying the girls' conversation and his cigarette.

The latter is our greatest friend. We cannot do without him. He seems to have unlimited time, and though he strolls through life as if it were a vast exhibition, at any booth of which he can tarry as long as it pleases his fancy, he never appears in the least demoralized by leisure; though there are grave head-shakings over his 'career.' Everyone may be concerned about him, but he quietly goes his own way.

He seems to set our minds free from the pressure of social primness of the outer circle at Eton. We are natural and happy with him as he takes us round with him, making a diverting Lord George Sanger-like show for us out of social London, by his subtle observation, his humane humour, and his detachment.

And now we are trip-clip-clopping, trip-clip-clopping up through the leafy bowers of Campden Hill, and stop at a tall Norman-Shaw architected house – alight, and pass through marble, up marble, through a close conglomeration of Italian shrines, caskets, cabinets, marqueterie; against the tangled background of William Morris's pomegranates; past the pictures by Rossetti, Sir Frederick Leighton, Burne-Jones, Holman Hunt, and Mr. Watts, of which the host is the renowned possessor. On and across the parquet floor to the fascinating, artistic, gracious hostess, and to the massive, comfortable chaperons in their rich waisted velvets and long trains, seated in formidable yet customary array.

We have dance programmes given us, on which is printed only one word, 'Valse,' all the way down, interspersed twice with the word 'Lancers.' Soon, in our shimmering white or pink satins, with our long white kid gloves, elegant waists and sprays of flowers on the left side of our bodices, our hair coiled on the nape of our necks or on the top of our heads, our trains first swirling about our feet, then gracefully caught up and managed, we fall with our partners into the swinging rhythm of that old 'Blue Danube' Valse.

Duennas and chaperons were fast going out even at that date; but at this house many lorgnons still bristled, and elderly heads nodded together over the young things whirling round the centre of the room; for Mrs. Tallboys had a passion for young people, and invited her eminent contemporaries to come and watch them as though they were a lot of young sea-lions plunging about, at whom it was a great pleasure to look. Thus many of her friends would come and look on, diverted by the antics of the young creatures and secretly prognosticating mating. We were used to this. Had the phalanx been a dull one it would have been depressing, but as a matter of fact the fine vitality of the elderly and eminent, both male and female, of Mrs. Tallboys' acquaintance, gave a certain spice to the dances in her house. She had a particular atmosphere and 'tenue' of her own.

Over one's partner's shoulder one would see, for instance, that Mr. Henry James had come in. A few more whirls round, and one has a glimpse at his face, which betrays that nervous suffering which a sense of the shortcomings of words was apt to throw him into at any moment. It was an artist's agitation carried to an extreme over possible failure in expressing his fine and complicated idea; a hesitation that postponed the moment when he must eventually let the inadequate little phrase pass from between his lips at a run, since his listener waited.

At the amusing phrase at last chosen the hostess would throw back her head a moment, laughing, and then perhaps she carried him off to look at a Corot or Whistler in the next room.

Another round of the long Valse and one perceives that old Herr Joachim and his quartette have come in after a concert, and Mrs. Tallboys takes him down to the dining-room to sup with the *elite* of his English musical circle of adorers.

One steps with a little more freedom for the absence of the elderly and eminent. Many members of the younger generation of this circle, 'faithless and perverse' just like any other generation, wanted to get out of the atmosphere in which they were brought up. This seems to be a general rule and not confined to any particular generation; and it is no conclusive criticism of the receding period. Our elders, after all, had won all their refined and graceful art and sounded the high, noble note of poetry and symbolism, through rebellion against Philistine ugliness and the narrow terrors of an outworn evangelical creed. And now here were many contrary young creatures already feeling they were simmering in a syrup. They were just beginning to seek for fresh values, telling each other that they were stifled by emphatic and misty gush and 'couleur de rose' rapture. But at present there was only a dissatisfied groping for fresh expression.

The arrogance which perhaps became a necessity of self-assertion for a while, and has been a decided characteristic of the first twenty years of the twentieth century, had not yet come into fashion – piquant in a very few, vile in the pretentious. Some bold and definite spirits of this set had already declared they wouldn't have their roots growing in drawing-room flower-pots any longer; they were all for 'Beachcombing,' whatever that might mean; just a few disappeared. Count Tolstoi was beginning to make a profound disturbance with his exposition of Christianity. Since the Great War many people have found it easy enough to turn a fork in a potato patch, from choice or necessity; but even Count Tolstoi himself, as a pioneer, in the nineteenth century, found himself baulked by his wife's gardeners – so the difficulties of these young rebels can be imagined. Tolstoi's youthful followers were many, but they were all baffled by the ease, comfort, and established order of the nineteenth century. Many young women, intending to become artists and writers, were beginning to feel the need of opportunities and independence. In contrast, however, to such tentative seekers, there were also a number of young Philistines among the dancers, who thought all the future artists, poets, men of letters of this circle, outsiders. They were intending themselves to find a more conventional set as soon as possible, having a great respect for will-power, but a horror of the Imagination.

But I am not thinking, of course, of these things in the whirl of the Valse. The Joachim quartette have by this time demolished several cold fowls and boot-shaped tongues, and it is time for the dancers to swarm down to the dining-room.

And now, at this distance of time, I hear a faint popping of corks, and laughter at the 'flash' of talk that passes across the little supper-tables in the tapestried room; I remember rapid exchanges of confidences with intimate cousins; a light tap with a fan on my shoulders draws my attention. I feel the absorption of happy lovers, or the hidden tragedies of men loving and not loved, or of young girls loving and not loved; sentimental Valse music tearing at their hearts.

The bright trivial animation of the ball-room I cannot reproduce. I feel it is muffled now, faded, and ghostly.

Once when I passed with my children by the door of Mrs. Tallboys' high house, I suddenly remembered a spring afternoon when a famous singer at the piano carolled, as though one with the nightingales and thrushes, in the romantic manner so abandonedly enjoyed by her nineteenth-century audience, who as they listened then were gazing vaguely out among the leaves and spreading branches of the great chestnut tree in the Square garden.

'Wait one minute! The house we are passing is full of ghosts to me,' I said to the children. They attended for a second with their ball lifted – then thought better of hearing me out – threw their ball before them and ran off.

So I never speak of my memories as I pass the house now, with whomever I may be; I know I shall not be able adequately to reanimate the shades, and shall only be a bore. But in silence, and just for myself, I like to pass again in mind through the door and up the marble stairs, and find Mrs. Tallboys among her cabinets and damask, with Mr. Henry James, and all her idealistic, romantic, highly sophisticated, delicate-minded contemporaries.

When her dance is over, 'Who were the blots?' Mrs. Tallboys asks an intimate friend as she comes back into her emptied room, having said good-night to most of her guests. Though gracious and romantic, Mrs. Tallboys is also satirical

Adela and I, animated and dishevelled, still a little out of breath after the last extra, get into our hansom and wave good-night to Fitzgerald.

As the horse trots gently through the London dawn, we begin to yawn and feel a great fatigue; then we lie back in our corner silent; two puppets limp on their strings after the drama is ended.

Mary MacCarthy, A NINETEENTH CENTURY CHILDHOOD, 1924

THE LONDON

SPORTSMAN

DURING THE NINETEENTH CENTURY

SELECTED FROM
VARIOUS CONTEMPORARY SOURCES
AND INCLUDING

DESCRIPTION OF
VARIOUS SPORTING CONTESTS
AND ESTABLISHMENTS
INCLUDING
AN ITALIAN TURN-UP AT WESTMINSTER
AND A VISIT TO TATTERSALL'S REPOSITORY
FROM PIERCE EGAN'S 'LIFE IN LONDON,' 1821

AN ACCOUNT OF
AN ASCENT OF A NEW SMOKE BALLOON
FROM THE SURREY ZOOLOGICAL GARDENS
FROM 'THE MIRROR OF LITERATURE, ETC.,' 1838

AN ACCOUNT OF THE 'DEAD HEAT'
IN THE UNIVERSITY BOAT RACE, 1877
FROM 'THE TIMES'

AN ACCOUNT OF THE SECOND TEST MATCH
PLAYED AT LORD'S, 1899
FROM WISDEN'S 'CRICKETER'S ALMANACK,' 1900

AND OTHER
BRIEFER NOTICES
AND REFERENCES

London Town's a dashing place
 For ev'ry thing that's going,
There's fun and gig in ev'ry face,
 So natty and so knowing.
Where Novelty is all the rage,
 From high to low degree,
Such pretty lounges to engage,
 Only come and see!
  What charming sights,
  On gala nights;
  Masquerades,
  Grand parades,
  Fam'd gas lights,
  Knowing fights,
  Randall and Cribb
  Know how to fib!
  Tothill-fields
  Pleasure yields;
  The Norwich bull
  With antics full.
  Plenty of news,
  All to amuse;
  The Monkey 'Jacco'
  All the crack O!
  Ambroghetti's squall,
  Match girls' bawl!
  Put on the gloves,
  Playful as doves,
  Then show your forte
  At the Fives Court;
  Conjurors rare
  At Bartlemy fair;
  Polito's beasts,
  See city feasts,
  Lord Mayor's day—
  Then the play.

                    Pierce Egan, LIFE IN LONDON, 1821

AN ADVERTISEMENT

AND BRIEF DESCRIPTION OF

A SURPRISING NOVELTY

AT THE WESTMINSTER PIT

AN ITALIAN TURN-UP

Surprising Novelty in the Sporting Circle.

On Tuesday next, September 5, at Seven o'Clock in the Evening,

A special grand Combat will be decided at the WESTMINSTER PIT,

FOR ONE HUNDRED GUINEAS,

Between that extraordinary and celebrated creature, the famed Italian Monkey,

JACCO MACCACCO

of Hoxton, third cousin to the renowned Theodore Magocco, of unrivalled fame, and a Dog of 20 lbs. weight, the property of a Nobleman, well known in the circle.

N.B. The owner of the Monkey having purchased him at a great expense, on account of his wonderful talents, begs to notice to his friends of the FANCY that another person has started a match, with a common Monkey, on the day preceding this match, with an intent to injure him and deceive the public.

After which, a DOG-FIGHT, for Ten Pounds, between the CAMBERWELL BLACK AND TANNED DOG and the well-known STRATFORD DOG; and a match between two Bitches, the property of two Gentlemen well known in the Fancy. To conclude with BEAR-FIGHTING.

‡‡‡ Regular Nights, Mondays and Wednesdays.

THE DOG-PIT WAS FILLED in a few minutes, and numerous persons went away *grumbling*, as if they had lost the finest sight in the world, at the disappointment they had met with in not being able to procure places. Some little delay having occurred before the performances commenced, a costard-monger, from the upper storey, roared out, 'I say, governor, how long are *ve* to be kept in this here *rookery* before you give us a sight of this *Phenomony?*' JACCO MACCACCO was at length produced in a handsome little wooden house, amidst the shouts, and loud whistling of the audience. But he was not *polite* enough to bow in return for this mark of approbation paid to him. JACCO had a small chain of about two yards in length placed round his loins, which was fastened to a strong iron stake, drove a considerable depth into the ground. He

105

was then let out of his house. The dog was immediately brought and let fly at him; but the monkey previous to this attack, gathered himself up with as much *cunning* as a prize-fighter would do, in order to repel the shock. The dog immediately got him down, and turned him up; but the monkey, in an instant, with his teeth, which met together like a saw, made a large wound in the throat of the dog, as if done with a knife; and from the great loss of blood the dogs in general sustained, who were pitted against JACCO MACCACCO, several of them died soon afterwards. The monkey seldom met with an injury in any of these contests; but he is of so ferocious a nature that his master deems it prudent to have a plate of iron before him, in case he might make a mistake and bite his legs. '*What a deep covey,*' said a greasy butcher, with his mouth open, a red night-cap on his nob, and pointing towards JACCO MACCACCO. 'I'll bet a thigh of mutton and *smash*, that the monkey wins. Blow me tight, if ever I saw such a thing in my life before. It really is wonderful. And what a *punisher* too! Why he seems to *mill* the dogs with as much ease and sagacity as if he had been fighting matches with them for years.' A small volume might be filled with the singular remarks and gestures made by this noisy motley group on the *finishing* qualities possessed by JACCO MACCACCO. Some laughed; others shouted vehemently; and numbers of them were continually jumping up and down in a sort of ecstasy, knocking their sticks against the ground, not unlike the inmates of a lunatic asylum when free from their *strait*-waistcoats. The matches being over, some clean water was thrown over the monkey, in order to refresh him, when he appeared little the worse from the effects of his battles; and was immediately put into his wooden house.

Pierce Egan, LIFE IN LONDON, 1821

A BRIEF DESCRIPTION OF

CORINTHIAN JACK JACKSON

AND HIS ROOMS

THE ROOM MIGHT be deemed a CORINTHIAN *set-out* altogether; and no man is more deserving of the appellation of CORINTHIAN JACK than Mr. JACKSON. Indeed, he is acknowledged to be such by the very first classes of society, from that self-knowledge of propriety, gentlemanly deportment, and anxiety to please, which plays round his character at all times. Servility is not known to him. Flattery he detests. Integrity, impartiality, good-nature, and manliness, are the corner-stones of his understanding. From the highest to the lowest person in the Sporting World, his *decision* is law. He never makes a *bet;* therefore, he has no undue influence on his mind. There is nothing *'creeping'* or *'throwing the hatchet'* about this description. It is the plain and naked truth. His room is not common to the public eye; but, nevertheless, the taste of it is not *caviare* to the million. No person can be admitted without an introduction. As a teacher of the Art of *Self-Defence*, Mr. JACKSON has no competitor.

In one corner of the room a picture is to be seen, framed and glazed, with the following inscriptions painted upon it, and which is a present. 'FROM THE RIGHT HON. W. WINDHAM, M.P., to Mr. JACKSON.

'The fatal effects of a Roman quarrel, in the Piazza del Popoli la Coltellata, in the Roman costume.' The subject in question represents a person lying dead, killed by an assassin, who is seen making his escape, with the dagger in his hand. Women and children are shrieking with agony over the body. Several men, in cloaks, looking at the deed, terrified, as it were, yet all afraid to stop the flight of the assassin.

'Humbly recommended to the consideration of those who are labouring to abolish what is called the brutal and ferocious practice of boxing.'

The above Plate speaks volumes in favour of the manly and generous mode resorted to by Englishmen to resent an insult or to decide a quarrel.

Pierce Egan, LIFE IN LONDON, 1821

ANNOUNCEMENT FOR A MAIN OF COCKS

A MAIN OF COCKS will be fought, on Monday, the 3d of June, at the Cockpit Royal, Tufton-street, Westminster, a double days' play, between the Gentlemen of Middlesex and Shropshire, for 5 guineas a battle, and 50 the odd battle. To begin fighting the first ingo at 2 o'clock, and the second at 5 o'clock. Briggs, for Middlesex, Davis, for Shropshire, Feeders.

TIMES, 1 *June*, 1822

ANNOUNCEMENT FOR A CHICKEN MATCH

COCKING. A Chicken Match to be fought, between Nash and Mr. Crawley, on the 15th and 16th of December for £5 a battle, and £20 the odd, at the Cock-pit, Little Grosvenor-street, Milbank. Feeders, Nash and Hall.

TIMES, 13 *December*, 1828

TATTERSALL'S WILL ALWAYS PROVE an agreeable lounge, if no direct purpose call a person thither. If nothing more than INFORMATION be acquired, that *alone* to a man of the world is valuable at all times. Besides, TATTERSALL'S gives a *tone* to the *sporting* world, in the same way that the transactions on the ROYAL EXCHANGE influence the mercantile part of society. It has likewise its '*settling days*' after the great races at *Newmarket, Doncaster, Epsom, Ascot*, &c. I do not know about the *bulls* and *bears;* but if it has no *lame ducks* to *waddle* out, it has sometimes *Levanters* that will not *show* for a time, and others that will *brush off* altogether. But this does not happen very often: and TATTERSALL'S has its '*good* MEN' as well as the '*Change;* and whose '*word*' will be taken for any amount. It has also its 'subscription room,' which is extremely convenient for gentlemen and other persons, who feel any inclination to become acquainted with the events of the sporting world, at the moderate charge of *one guinea* a year. Indeed there is an air of sporting about this place altogether; elegance, cleanliness, and style, being its prominent features. The company, I admit, is a *mixture* of persons of nearly all ranks in life; but, nevertheless, it is that sort of *mixture* which is pleasingly interesting: there is no *intimacy* or *association* about it. A man may be well known here; he may also in his turn *know* almost every body that visits TATTERSALL'S; and yet be quite a *stranger* to their habits and connexions with society. It is no matter who *sells* or who purchases at this repository. A *bet* stands as good with a LEG, and is thought as much of, as with a *Peer,* – MONEY, being the *touchstone* of the circumstance. The 'best judge' respecting sporting events is acknowledged the 'best man' here; every person being on the 'look-out,' to see how he *lays* his *blunt*. The DUKE and the *Parliamentary Orator*, if they do not know the properties of a horse, are little more than cyphers; it is true, they may be *stared* at, if pointed out as great characters, but nothing more. The *nod* from a *stable-keeper* is quite as important, if not more so, to the Auctioneer, as the *wink* of a RIGHT HONOURABLE. Numbers of persons, who visit TATTERSALL'S, are or wish to appear *knowing;* from which '*self*'-importance they are often most egregiously duped. In short, if you are not as familiar with the *odds* upon all events as CHITTY in quoting precedents – show as intimate an acquaintance with the *pedigree* and *speed* of race horses as a GULLEY

TATTERSALL'S

Tattersall's, it has been remarked more than once, has given a tone to the sporting world, and in this respect it has, probably, had a more beneficial effect than the Jockey Club itself. That representative of the power of the organised turf can only deal with overt acts of an ungentlemanly or dishonest character. But Tattersall's – 'the glass of fashion and the mould of form' – has set the whole sporting-world to 'assume a virtue,' even when they have it not. Its influence in this way has been materially promoted by the institution of the subscription-room, which took place at a very early date subsequent to the opening of the mart. For a while, at first, the court was the only place of meeting for all parties; but as soon as it became a place of resort for the news of the sporting world, it was soon found advisable to fall upon some means to keep at a distance the crowd of questionables. With this view, the subscription-room was opened for the accommodation of gentlemen, as the Tap had been opened for the accommodation of their servants. The regulations of the room have not undergone any material alteration since. Its frequenters are, in a manner, the natural aristocracy of Tattersall's, and the lower orders frame their manners 'ad exemplar regis,' as like those of the subscribers as possible. This has contributed in no small degree to diffuse a recognition of the point of honour (in theory, at least) through all ranks of sporting characters.

W. *Weir*, KNIGHT'S LONDON, 1842

109

– and also display as correct a knowledge of the various capabilities of the prize pugilists as a JACKSON – if GAIN is your immediate object, you are 'of no *use*' at TATTERSALL'S.

It is an excellent mart for the disposal of carriages, horses, dogs, &c., and many a fine fellow's *stud* has been *floored* by the hammer of TATTERSALL. There is a capacious TAP attached to the premises, for the convenience of the servants of gentlemen in attendance upon their masters, or for any person who stands in need of refreshment. TATTERSALL'S, for the purposes intended, is the most complete place in the Metropolis; and if you have any desire to witness 'real life' – to observe *character* – and to view the favourite *hobbies* of mankind, it is the resort of the *pinks* of the SWELLS, – the *tulips* of the GOES, – the *dashing* heroes of the military, – the fox-hunting clericals, – springs of nobility, – stylish coachmen, – smart guards, – saucy butchers, – natty grooms, – tidy helpers, – knowing horse-dealers, – *betting* publicans, – neat jockeys, – sporting men of all descriptions, – and the picture is finished by numbers of real gentlemen. It is the tip-top sporting feature in London.

Pierce Egan, LIFE IN LONDON, 1821

AN ACCOUNT OF AN ASCENT OF

A NEW SMOKE BALLOON FROM THE

SURREY ZOOLOGICAL GARDENS

WE HAVE OFTEN had occasion to notice novelties in nature, science, or art, as first introduced to the public at the Surrey Zoological Gardens; but never one more extraordinary than the immense aerostatic machine bearing the above cognomen, which made its first ascent from these excellently adapted grounds on Thursday last. Since the first discovery of balloons by Stephen and Joseph Montgolfier in 1782, there has not been an ascent of so extraordinary a nature, or which has excited so intense and general an interest. It is the first that has ever taken place in England with an aerostat on this beautifully simple, but seldom used plan. The balloon has been constructed by a party of gentlemen, interested in the art of aerostation; and its fabrication has occupied many months of uninterrupted labour, during some period of which upwards of 100 women have been engaged in sewing the seams of the vast machine together.

The New Montgolfier is the largest and most powerful aerial machine ever built in this country, being 130 feet from the bottom of the car to the upper rim of the balloon, and 200 feet at its greatest circumference. It is, therefore, the height of the York

ASCENT OF THE NEW MONTGOLFIER SMOKE BALLOON

FROM THE

SURREY ZOOLOGICAL GARDENS, 24 MAY, 1838

Column; and its circumference is nearly half that of the dome of St. Paul's Cathedral. It contains, when fully inflated, 170,000 cubic feet of air. The car is 15 feet by 8, gorgeously ornamented, and made of cane: it has an aperture in the bottom, through which part of the furnace drops. The furnace is of very ingenious and peculiar construction. The chimney from it is placed in the lower aperture of the balloon, while the aeronauts are able, with the most perfect convenience, to regulate the quality of fuel. The degree of heat can be raised to 200 of Fahrenheit in three minutes, and depressed to that of the surrounding atmosphere almost as quickly; and the balloon can be fully inflated by the great power of this furnace in eight minutes. When in that state it presents the peculiar egg shape represented in our Engraving, being cut off quite abruptly at the bottom, and there leaving an aperture of 46 feet in circumference. This is formed of rope bound with basil, and lies as flat as any other part of the machine, until the inflation takes place. To this another very strong hoop, formed of ash, bound with cane, is suspended, and on it depends the weight of the car and its appurtenances. There is no net-work, as in the gas balloons; but its absence is supplied by a line being sewn down each of the 58 gores with the material, and terminating in the neck-rope before described.

The grapnel is the invention of the constructor of the balloon, and is very powerful: it weighs 85 lbs., and is so made, that in case of any single fluke, of which there are six, being broken off, it can be easily replaced by means of a nut and screw. Having a swivel head there is also less danger of breaking the cable attached to it. The fuel consists of small bundles of wood prepared in a particular manner, chopped straw, and willow rinds, &c.; many hundred pounds of which materials will be taken up. The machine has an ascending power equal to the weight of fifteen or twenty persons. The fabric is lawn, covered with a peculiar varnish, and thus made impermeable. It is extremely light. The apparatus for inflating it is very extensive; a large platform being raised about twelve feet above the Lake in the Gardens, with an aperture from which the heated air ascends into the balloon. It is necessary to elevate the crown of the balloon to about half its height before the inflation is commenced; and for this purpose two large, stout spars, of about ninety feet in height, are raised; and by means of a rope passing through blocks, the machine is hauled up, until it gains sufficient ascensive power to sustain its own weight.

THE MIRROR OF LITERATURE, AMUSEMENT, AND INSTRUCTION,
26 *May*, 1838

AMONGST THE many inventions and improvements with which the nineteenth century is pregnant, the original from which our sketch is taken is not the least worthy of notice. The respect in earlier ages for the hero was incomplete, did not his skill as a charioteer rank equally high with his valour. In fact, the many instances around us of the benefit the horse is to man leads us to rejoice at every object or idea that can render the life of toil more endurable to the noble animal. And the contrast between the former savage mode of making beasts of burden draw from the tail with the more Christian harness before us, gives as unqualified a feel of pleasure as the contrast between a clown seated upon a Pegasus, hauling like a coal porter, with the steady hand and unshaken seat of an individual who has learned the difference between the reins of a bridle and the ropes of a swing-swang, which often is illustrated in the riding school in the Harrow Road.

THE PICTORIAL TIMES, 1843

THE NEW GAME OF POLO AT HURLINGHAM

THE PRINCE AND Princess of Wales, with their two elder boys, Prince Albert Victor and Prince George, were among the spectators of the polo-match, on Saturday afternoon, in the grounds of the Hurlingham Park Club. The Duke of Cambridge, Prince Edward of Saxe-Weimar, and many of the nobility were present. The whole assemblage numbered several thousand; and the weather being fine, it was a very bright and lively scene. Their Royal Highnesses were accommodated in the pavilion or marquee prepared for their reception, and shelter was provided for some of the general company. Numerous 'drags' and other carriages were on the ground. The band of the 2nd Life Guards performed at intervals during the afternoon. The polo-match was between five officers of the Royal Horse Guards and five of the 17th Lancers – the former being distinguished by white and blue, the latter by red and white. They contended for a silver cup, the gift of the Prince of Wales, to be handed by the Princess to the captain of the winning team. The game was kept up with great spirit and skill during an hour and a quarter. The only 'goal' was obtained by Mr. J. F. Brocklehurst, one of the Royal Horse Guards. His side thereby won the prize, which was received by the Hon. Charles Fitzwilliam on their behalf. The Princess, in giving him the cup, expressed her pleasure in seeing such a fine display of dexterity and good horsemanship and such an example of the new game. Another match is to be played this afternoon.   ILLUSTRATED LONDON NEWS, 1875

IT CAME TO PASS then that off the Bull's Head, at the lower end of the village of Barnes, Cambridge once more put on a brilliant spurt, so that Oxford, though again irregular in their rowing, led by a third of a length. From the Bull's Head to the Bridge, as the Cambridge spurt died out, Oxford slowly increased their advantage and passed under the centre railway arch nearly a length ahead, but not yet quite clear. In the next two hundred yards the Oxford crew drew clear for the first time in the race, and opposite the White Hart led by a length and three feet, a yard of daylight intervening between the rudder of one boat and the nose of the other. At this point the Oxford boat was sheered to the left, in order to avoid a barge which projected into the course, having apparently shifted from its moorings, and thus got close in front of Cambridge; but as the crew of the latter made another effort and gained upon the leading boat which was somewhat out of its course, the Oxford crew suddenly went all abroad, and a perfect scramble ensued amongst the bowside oars, even if there was not crab catching in the rough water which was here running as the wind became foul. During this momentary disorder the bow oar of Oxford became irretrievably damaged, and the bowman was thereafter unable to do more than keep time with his crew, without feathering his oar. The Cambridge crew meanwhile were not only overlapping Oxford, but fast reducing their lead off the Limes, getting up within half a length off Godfrey's, and still further gaining at Mortlake Brewery. The inside of the turn in the river to some extent aided the Oxford crew in their difficulties so that they continued to hold the lead as far as the Ship, where their boat's nose was just two feet in front. The efforts of the rival crews at this period of the contest needs to have been seen to be fully appreciated, for it is impossible to do justice to them on paper. Oxford, partially disabled, were making effort after effort to regain their winning lead, while Cambridge, who, curiously enough, had settled together again, and were rowing almost as one man, were putting on a magnificent spurt at 40 strokes to the minute, with a view of catching their opponents before reaching the winning post. Thus struggling over the remaining portion of the course, the two eights raced past the flag alongside one another, and the gun fired amid a scene of excitement rarely equalled and never exceeded. Cheers for one crew were succeeded by counter cheers for the other, and it was impossible to tell what the result was until the

HAMMERSMITH BRIDGE

THE FINISH

THE BOAT RACE 'DEAD HEAT'

I was so excited, as both boats flashed past the Judge's chair in front of the Ship, that if you had flung a handful of gold into my lap, I couldn't have told you which had won. PUNCH, 24 *March,* 1877

Press boat backed down to the Judge and inquired the issue. John Phelps, the waterman, who officiated, replied that the noses of the two boats passed the post strictly level and that the result was a dead-heat. This decision he unfortunately failed to communicate to the Umpire, and when the latter returned to his steamer to seek him, his boat could nowhere be found in the crowd and confusion which reigned afloat; but at a later period of the day Phelps was taken up to Lincoln's-Inn, and there officially made known to Mr. Chitty his decision.

THE TIMES, *Monday*, 26 *March*, 1877

THE SECOND TEST MATCH, 1899

PLAYED AT LORD'S

THURSDAY, FRIDAY, SATURDAY, 15, 16, 17 JUNE

THE SECOND OF THE Test matches was the only one of the five brought to a definite conclusion, and its result was a heavy blow to English cricket, the Australians gaining a brilliant victory on the third afternoon by ten wickets. They played a winning game all the way through, fairly beating the Englishmen at every point. The match, indeed, furnished one of the most complete triumphs gained by Australian cricketers in England since Gregory's team came over and astonished us in 1878.

Without in any way attempting to make excuses for an over-whelming defeat, it must be said that the committee in picking the England eleven laid themselves open to obvious criticism. They made no fewer than five changes from the side that had done duty at Trent Bridge a fortnight before, A. C. MacLaren, Townsend, G. L. Jessop, Lilley and Mead taking the places of W. G. Grace, William Gunn, Hirst, Storer and J. T. Hearne. As regards batting, they were probably right to leave out Grace and Gunn, but having done that they ought assuredly to have invited Shrewsbury to play. The Nottingham batsman had given conclusive evidence that he was in form, and with Grace standing down there would have been no difficulty about his fielding at point. A still more serious blunder, however, was committed in connection with the bowling. It was tempting providence to go into the field on a fine day at Lord's with no other fast bowler than Jessop, and it was a dangerous experiment—by no means justified by results—to give Walter Mead the preference over J. T. Hearne on the latter's favourite ground. There was, too, some risk in playing MacLaren, who had not so far taken part in any first-class cricket during the season.

THE NEW, OR OVER-HAND SYSTEM,

DEMONSTRATED AT LORD'S GROUNDS, 1842

On Monday an interesting match took place at Lord's Grounds, wherein the relative merits of the fast and slow systems of bowling were tried by eight gentlemen and players, with three bowlers on the new system and the same number with three slow bowlers. The same event has been contested on four previous occasions and the match excited considerable interest. The fast bowlers were Alfred Mynn, Esq., Redgate, and Dean, with E. Bayley, William Felix, R. W. Keate and F. Thackeray, Esqrs., Box, Butler, Dorrington, and Guy, against Lillywhite, Hillier, and Nixon, with the Hon. R. Grimston, R. Kynaston, and Anson, Esqrs., with G. Lee, Hammond, Pilch, and Wenman, on the old systems. The first innings only was completed on each side, when the wickets were struck – the result being in favour of the fast bowlers by 115 runs to 89. Of the players of the swift bowling side, Box secured 35 runs, and W. Felix, Esq., 23; while the Hon. R. Grimston scored 41 runs, and carried his bat out, at the conclusion of the opposing party. The match was concluded on Tuesday, the fast bowlers coming off victorious by a majority of 47 runs on the two innings. The numbers scored by the players on the new, or over-hand system, was 194, while their opponents scored only 147. PICTORIAL TIMES, 1842

In this case, however, the committee had reason to congratulate themselves, MacLaren playing a magnificent second innings and making a great, though fruitless, effort to save the game.

The Englishmen really lost the match during the first hour or so on the opening day. They won the toss and when they went in to bat on a carefully-prepared wicket it was confidently expected they would stay for the whole of the afternoon. To the dismay of the crowd, however, six wickets went down for 66 runs—a deplorable start from which the team were never able to recover. Jackson and Jessop by putting on 95 runs together saved their side from complete collapse, but Jackson, who played a superb innings, might have been run out by several yards when England's score stood at 70. It was felt when the innings ended for 206—Jones's terrific bowling being the chief cause of the breakdown—that the Australians had an immense advantage, and so it proved. For a little time there seemed some chance of an even game, Worrall, Darling and Gregory being got rid of for 59 runs, but thenceforward the Australians were always winning. The turning point of the game was the partnership of Clement Hill and Noble. The two batsmen had carried the score from 59 to 156 at the drawing of stumps, and on the following morning they took the total to 189 before Noble left. Then came another good partnership, Hill and Trumper putting Australia well in front with six wickets in hand, and increasing the score to 271. At this point Hill was brilliantly caught by Fry in the deep field. Later on Trumper found a valuable partner in Trumble, and it was not until after four o'clock, that the Australian innings ended, the total reaching 421, or 215 runs ahead. In their different styles Hill and Trumper, who curiously enough made exactly the same score, played magnificent cricket. Trumper's innings was by far the more brilliant of the two, but inasmuch as Hill went in while there was still a chance of an even game, and had to play the English bowling at its best, it is only right to say that the left-handed batsman had the greater share in the ultimate success of his side. Hill, who was missed at slip by Ranjitsinhji when he had made 119, was batting just over four hours, and hit seventeen 4's, seven 3's and eighteen 2's. Trumper, who so far as could be seen gave no chance whatever, hit twenty 4's, four 3's and six 2's, and was at the wickets for three hours and a quarter.

Going in for the second time against a balance of 215, the Englishmen had a very gloomy outlook, and their position was desperate when at 23 their third wicket went down, the batsmen out being Fry, Ranjitsinhji and Townsend. Hayward and Jackson made things look a little better, but just before the time for drawing stumps Jackson was easily caught and bowled in playing forward at Trumble, the total at the close being 94. Hayward batted well, but when he had made a single he was palpably missed by the wicket-keeper, standing back to Jones. On the third morning MacLaren joined Hayward, and so long as these two batsmen stayed together there was still a chance of England making something like a fight. Indeed, things were looking comparatively cheerful when 150 went up without further loss. However, on Laver being tried Hayward, Tyldesley and Jessop were caught in quick succession, and with seven wickets down for 170 the match was as good as over. MacLaren, who so long as Hayward stayed in had been steadiness itself, hit in wonderful form from the time that Lilley joined him, but despite his efforts England were all out for 240. Never has MacLaren played a greater innings. The Australians only required 26 runs – a trifling number, which after lunch Darling and Worrall obtained without being separated.

ENGLAND

Mr. C. B. Fry c Trumble b Jones	13	b Jones	4
Mr. A. C. MacLaren b Jones	4	not out	88
K. S. Ranjitsinhji c and b Jones	8	c Noble b Howell	0
Mr. C. L. Townsend st Kelly b Howell	5	b Jones	8
Mr. F. S. Jackson b Jones	73	c and b Trumble	37
T. Hayward b Noble	1	c Trumble b Laver	77
J. T. Tyldesley c Darling b Jones	14	c Gregory b Laver	4
Mr. G. L. Jessop c Trumper b Trumble	51	c Trumble b Laver	4
A. A. Lilley not out	19	b Jones	12
W. Mead b Jones	7	lbw b Noble	0
W. Rhodes b Jones	2	c and b Noble	2
B 2, l-b 6, w 1	9	B 2, l-b 2..........	4
	206		240

AUSTRALIA

J. Worrall c Hayward b Rhodes	18	not out	11
J. Darling c Ranjitsinhji	9	not out	17
C. Hill c Fry b Townsend...........	135		
S. E. Gregory c Lilley b Jessop	15		
M. A. Noble c Lilley b Rhodes	54		
V. Trumper not out	135		
J. J. Kelly c Lilley b Mead	9		
H. Trumble c Lilley b Jessop	24		
F. Laver b Townsend	0		
E. Jones c Mead b Townsend	17		
W. P. Howell b Jessop	0		
L-b 4, n-b 1	5		
	421		28

THE LONDON

RAMBLER

DURING THE NINETEENTH CENTURY

SELECTED FROM
VARIOUS CONTEMPORARY SOURCES
AND INCLUDING

AN EXPLORATORY PERAMBULATION
FROM THE WEST TO THE EAST OF LONDON
FROM 'BENTLEY'S MISCELLANY,' 1838

A NOTE ON
THE FIRST OMNIBUS
IN THE LONDON STREETS IN 1829
FROM THE 'MORNING CHRONICLE,' 1850

DESCRIPTION OF VARIOUS
SHOPS AND BAZAARS
PRESENTED TO VIEW IN THE STREETS OF LONDON
FROM KNIGHT'S 'LONDON,' 1842

SOME ACCOUNT OF THE
POSTERS, EXTERNAL PAPER-HANGERS,
PERIPATETIC AND VEHICULAR PLACARDS
IN THE STREETS OF LONDON
FROM KNIGHT'S 'LONDON,' 1842

The park of saintly James invites
This errant gaze to calm delights;
There cows lactiferously mild
Give solace to the thirsty child.
There Phyllis and her Strephon stray,
And spoon the fleeting hours away.

AN EXPLORATORY PERAMBULATION
FROM THE WEST TO THE EAST
OF LONDON

THE OCEAN-STREAM of life flows adown the Strand, whose courts, lanes, and blind alleys, are so many creeks and inlets; the Mississippi of existence rolls along Holborn Hill in a tremendous tide, while its eddies are reflected into the mouths of a thousand tributaries, ever absorbing and pouring out their atoms of human life. These comparisons may appear somewhat turgid and magniloquent, but we should be glad to know what less grand and majestic images are worthy to typify the rolling masses that flood a living tide along London streets.

These courts, lanes, and alleys, have a character peculiarly their own, bearing no analogy to the by-places of great provincial towns: the courts of London, those at least interlacing with the leading thoroughfares, are no more nor less than narrow streets, sacred to the pedestrian, where, undisturbed by noises vehicular, and the chaotic intermixture of waggon, 'bus, and cab, he can saunter at his ease, pausing to look about him, without obstructing the thoroughfare, or wending his desultory way, without being himself obstructed.

SIDNEY ALLEY, the first of these, our favourite *viæ sacræ*, has its origin hard by the place where Hamlet – not Hamlet the Dane, but Hamlet the Jeweller, – whilom rejoiced to inhabit, where Coventry Street, that supplemental Piccadilly, wonders to find itself cut off in mid career by the rectangular interposition of Princes' Street. The direct communication with Leicester Square, which Coventry Street, by means of its 'most lame and impotent conclusion,' is unable to carry out, is facilitated for pedestrians only by Sidney Alley, a very favourable specimen of our metropolitan by-ways, and one to which we first introduce the reader, in order that we may be able to carry him the more pleasantly from one to another. In this short anastomosing artery of pedestrian life, the shopkeepers devote themselves almost exclusively to the fair sex, and to those decorative essentials that make even the fair sex still more fair. Here are bargains of lace and veils, infinite choice of stays, from six-and-sixpence, *upwards;* variety inexhaustible of baby-frocks, boys' caps and tunics, and, in short, every modification of frippery, ticketed so low, indeed, that it is a wonder how anybody can venture into places where, the shopkeepers assure you, every article is *alarmingly* low. When once, in, however, your alarm of the most timid is speedily dissipated, as they will find,

123

perhaps to their cost, that whatever they may happen to want has in itself the elements of an *alarmingly* upward character.

Emerging from Sidney Alley into Leicester Square, we pause to look about us, meditating as we contemplate this, by no means one of our most select localities, upon the migratory tendencies of the world of fashion, since first we had the happiness to rejoice in the possession of a fashionable world. The houses now introducing themselves to our notice, presenting us their addresses in great gilt wooden letters, as WATERLOO HOUSE, DIMITY HOUSE, LEICESTER HOUSE, and devoted to the sale of haberdashery, boasted, some three quarters of a century since, a very different style of occupants. Mansions now occupied by gunmakers, cheap booksellers, cigar-dealers, porter and ale merchants, *restaurants*, and the like, were tenanted by such men as Hogarth and Sir Joshua Reynolds. Where Miss Linwood has now her curious exhibition of needle-work, and where a mob is daily and nightly congregated to witness the transit of pasteboard cavalieros across a pane of glass, – indication sufficient of the attraction of the sixpenny show within, – stood the mansion of the Sidneys – Philip and Algernon –

> 'Ah! how unlike to Gerard Street,
> Where beaux and belles together meet,
> Where gilded chairs and coaches throng,
> And jostle as they troll along'

and in later times the royal residence of Frederick Prince of Wales, the friend and patron of the poet Thomson. Not far from this spot, in Gerard Street, Soho, Dryden lived and died; and nearer still, in St. Martin's Street, was the residence of Newton; Hogarth, Wool-lett, and Sir Joshua Reynolds inhabited houses in the square.

With the progression of London westwards, it is curious to observe how, while the commercial world stood still, clinging with mercantile tenacity to its original shop, *the City*, where it flourishes supreme to this day; the fashionable world, on the contrary, had an instinctive tendency to escape from place to place, as the world of business, and bustle, and every-day toil pressed upon its outskirts. We find, at an early period, the great mansions of our people of fashion, in Ely Place, for example, in Southampton Buildings, in Gray's Inn. Some time later, when the class became less warlike, and more gregarious, we have them erecting noble mansions along the *then* suburban line of the Strand. As this class increased in numbers, jostled by plebeian wealth, detached mansions were out of the question, and we find the fashionable world condescending to sit down round the circumference of Lincoln's-inn Fields;

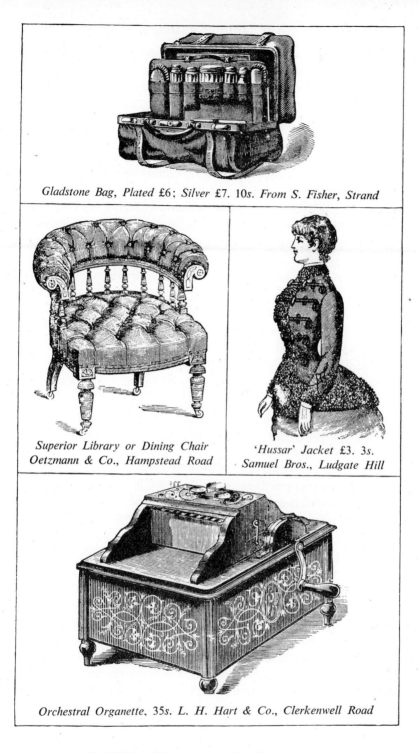

Gladstone Bag, Plated £6; Silver £7. 10s. From S. Fisher, Strand

Superior Library or Dining Chair
Oetzmann & Co., Hampstead Road

'Hussar' Jacket £3. 3s.
Samuel Bros., Ludgate Hill

Orchestral Organette, 35s. L. H. Hart & Co., Clerkenwell Road

BARGAINS IN THE LONDON SHOPS IN THE EIGHTIES
FROM THE ILLUSTRATED LONDON NEWS

thence they migrated to Leicester Square, and the streets immediately adjacent. Here the world of fashion contentedly remained, until Marylebone began to provide, in Portman and Cavendish Squares, new hives for the migrating swarm. Here, in a parallelogram, contained within Oxford Street, Piccadilly, Bond Street, and Park Lane,

'The twice two thousand for whom earth was made,'
together with their dignity, pride, airs, assumption, ambition, jealousy, pug-dogs, footmen, and the rest of their equipage remained, till the original genius of a Cubitt struck out the grand idea of Belgrave Square. Then, and not till then, was it discovered that a new migration was necessary; a city of palaces arose, as it were by magic, in the swamp that formerly desecrated the future site of Belgrave Square, and the streets and squares adjacent. Yet, who shall cease to admire the fickleness of fashion, and the 'vain, transitory splendour' of palaces wherein it dwells; Hyde Park Gardens, with another, and a yet more magnificent city at its back, sprung up in a twinkling on the northern side of the Park, and behold! the world of fashion, ere the rooms are well dry, migrate in myriads to this delectable location. How long they may remain, or where next the tide of change and the accumulation of conveniences may waft them, yet remains for future historians to record; but, we confess, we expect nothing less than that the third next following generation of the fashionable world, should the migratory tendency still set in a western direction, having progressed by easy stages from parish to parish, will find itself pleasantly seated in the flowery meads, somewhere about Windsor and Eton.

Now we leave the square for Cranbourne Alley, grand repository of bonnet and stay-makers. At every door stands, half in and half out of the shop, like a spider in its web, a pale-faced, sickly-looking young woman, in a cloth cloak and faded silk bonnet: these are canvassers for customers, or, as they are technically called, 'touters,' and are unrivalled by the other sex in pertinacity of solicitation.

Indeed, it is by no means an uncommon occurrence in Cranbourne Alley for a lady, with whom you have been walking along very pleasantly, interchanging the compliments of the season, or any other compliments, suddenly to disappear, as it were by the magic wand of an enchanter. Lost in amazement, you look round, wondering by what accident your companion has been spirited from your side; in ten or fifteen minutes you discover her in the dusky recesses of one of the bonnet-shops, when she very naturally inquires if you happen to have five-and-thirty shillings, to pay for a small purchase she was tempted to make, – such a love of a bonnet, – *so* cheap, &c., &c. You find, while disbursing the 'needful,' that your fair friend had been only 'touted,' not *spirited* into the bonnet-shop. Having paid for the love of a bonnet, to the tune of five-and-thirty shillings, like another Orpheus, you once more conduct your Eurydice to the realms of day.

Sometimes worse consequences attend the fatal curiosity to which ladies wandering in Cranbourne Alley are prone, of speculating upon the 'loves of bonnets' in the windows. Two rival 'touters' may happen to seize the unsuspecting damsel at the same moment, and, as this predatory animal was never known to let go its hold, the lady is attempted to be dragged into two bonnet-shops at the same time, with the almost inevitable result of the deposit of the skirt of her gown in the one, and her head-dress in the other.

Cranbourne Alley, like all the other alleys that form the subject of our present contemplation, has its tributary alleys. Old print, and older book-shops, picture-dealers' dusky galleries, and public houses, retired into private life, abound. One wonders, wandering up and down, how people who have money to spend discover these unobtrusive retreats.

Crossing St. Martin's Lane, which may serve as our meridian of Greenwich, we keep a southerly course for a short distance, until the inlet of May's Buildings, bristling on either side, like the mouth of a dragon, with rows of artificial teeth, arrests our devious course. This is the paradise of dentists and cuppers; every variety of artificial tooth, molar, incisor, canine, is displayed in every variety of artificial gum, waxen, composition, golden; a profusion of ruined grinders, 'elegant extracts,' as we may say, are displayed, by way of contrast, oftentimes set out in the form of a star – we presume a *Tuscan* ensign of nobility – and tempting announcements of the low prices of dental apparatus, invite the preference of those whose mouths are to let *unfurnished*. The small boys, with large livery buttons, running hither and thither, are the dentists' and cuppers' boys; a small boy, in large livery-buttons, being an indispensable appendage to dentists and cuppers, as well as to all other medical and surgical establishments.

We pass under a low archway into Little May's Buildings, and pause before the window of a surgical instrument maker's, to contemplate the awful machinery by which the accidents and ills that flesh is heir to are relieved. What frightful apparatus is this of saws, and double-edged knives, and probes, scalpels, forceps, and

127

PATENT ROAD AND STREET CLEANSING MACHINE

This machine has lately been set to work in Regent Street and the neighbourhood, under agreement with the Commissioners of Woods and Forests, and has accordingly excited some attention in the metropolis. The principle of the invention consists in employing the rotary motion of locomotive wheels, moved by horse or other power, to raise the loose soil from the surface of the ground, and deposit it in a vehicle attached. The apparatus for this purpose consists of a series of brooms suspended from a light, wrought-iron frame, hung behind a common cart, the body of which is placed near the ground for greater facility in loading. As the cart-wheels revolve, the brooms successively sweep the surface of the ground, and carry the soil up an inclined or carrier-plate, at the top of which it falls into the body of the cart. The draught is easy for two horses, and, whilst filling, scarcely a larger amount of force is required than would be necessary to draw the full cart an equal distance. Proceeding at a moderate rate through the streets, the cart leaves behind it a well-swept track, and it has repeatedly filled itself in the space of six minutes; and it sweeps, loads, and carries, as it were, in one operation. When going at the rate of only two miles an hour, with brooms three feet wide, the patent machine will clear nearly sixty superficial yards per minute, which is about the average rate of work done by thirty-six men. The water collected in the cart can be let off by means of a pipe, having its interior orifice some inches above the level of the mud after settlement; the cart, when full, is drawn to the side of the street, at some distance from a sewer grid, and the pipe-plug being withdrawn, the water flows into the channel. The pressure of the brooms on the ground is regulated by a series of weights, and the whole apparatus may be raised from the ground by means of a handle turned by the driver, when ever necessary. Wood pavement, when swept with this machine, is stated to be no longer slippery. An indicator attached to the sweeping apparatus shows the extent of surface swept during the day, and acts as a useful check on the driver. By use of the machine, it is estimated that the streets may be swept at one fifth of the present cost.   ILLUSTRATED LONDON NEWS, 1843 the horrible machinery of the surgeon's art! What powerful rhetoric in the hands of a popular preacher would be this infinite variety of instruments of torture!

Stop – let us peruse this embossed card: –

'BLACKWELL'S ROSTRAKIZION;
OR,
INIMITABLE CURLING COMB.
Insert the comb in hot water, press the spring at A, the comb disappears; withdraw, and the curl is complete.'

Nothing is more characteristic of London ingenuity and enterprise than the perpetual fertility of invention that distinguishes the professors of every art and trade. Here, in Blackwell's Rostrakizion, or inimitable curling-comb (a pair of curling-tongs, with a concealed comb, elevated or depressed by a spring), we have a good example of the apparently trivial things to which invention can descend; the list of patents weekly published, illustrate the fact at greater length. When we recollect that the fees for taking out a patent for the United kingdoms of Great Britain and Ireland, amount to nearly three hundred pounds, we can scarcely find words to express our astonishment and admiration at the enterprise of men who are content to risk such a sum, upon the remote possibility of their invention being sufficiently appreciated by the public, as to secure them a return.

London furnishes everyday illustrations of the theory of human perfectibility. To-day, you walk forth, and see, for example, scavengers at work, with their huge shovels projecting the mud of our streets, having first swept them, into their frightful carts; to-morrow, you see a gaudily-painted machine, drawn by a great horse, and attended by one man, performing simultaneous operations of sweeping, shovelling, and carting the *alluvium* of our streets, without difficulty or delay, as if merely working for its own amusement.

Perhaps, while you are sauntering about, your attention is arrested by the laying down of the new wooden pavement; you consider it a wonderful invention, and go away, satisfied in your own mind that we have at length gained perfection in the desirable matter of street-paving; returning in six weeks, you find the blocks being taken up, and some of improved construction being laid in their stead, and this goes on, ripping up, and repairing our wooden streets, until you begin to imagine the heads of those who authorise these perpetual revolutions must be of a material somewhat ligneous.

Where will this perpetuity of improvement have an end, or to what shall the children of men at last attain? we often ask ourselves, and nowhere so often as in progressive London; yet the inquiry is vain; the only limit to the social progressiveness of mankind would appear to be the point of cessation, by–natural laws, of the tractability of the natural agents subjected to man's will, and disciplined for his service by the power of his intellect.

Let us proceed; infinite, and infinitely various, to be sure, are the methods of getting a living in London. Here is one:–

'W. DAVIS,
Handles put to tea-cups, mugs, jugs, &c.; stoppers taken out of decanters.'

We are now in Covent Garden; we pass on to the principal entrance of Drury Lane, where we plunge once again into the loved obscurity of VINEGAR YARD, RED LION COURT, RUSSEL COURT, and their sub-denominations.

This is strictly a theatrical and bacchanalian neighbourhood; here commercial enterprise appears to be divided between spirituous liquors and theatrical properties; Hamlet's dresses, and heavy-wet; rabbit-skin robes, and rum-shrub; peppermint cordial, and point lace; brandy and buskins. Russel Court, however, is an exception; literature here is worthily represented in a profusion of second-hand bookshops; of these, some are ticket-shops, others are not; at the former, as might be expected, you pay a high price for what is little better than waste paper, at the latter, you may have works of sterling literary value, at their exact commercial value; our experience telling us that a really good book is not, save by the merest accident, to be obtained, save at a really good price; and this is just as it should be.

Here – at the sign of THE SHERIDAN KNOWLES we pause, for rest and refreshment; we choose this sign, because the landlord pays respect to literature by placing over his door the head of our greatest living dramatist, and deserves to be encouraged for his sign's sake.

'Boy, a pint of old ale, the paper, and a screw of tobacco.'

Leaving The Sheridan Knowles, we stalk, like a giant refreshed, across Drury Lane, and are lost in the intricacies of WHITE HORSE YARD. Here, although only across the street, the alleys have a totally different character from those tributary to Vinegar Yard. The habitations are poor and dilapidated, as are also the inhabitants; ruined faces and places stare you out of countenance on every side; chandler's shops, rag and bottle warehouses, penny-a-bottle ginger-beer establishments, marine stores, old-iron ware-houses, give abundant evidences of a population struggling against imminent want, and the small necessities of life perpetually recurring.

Holding our course right onward, noticing by the way a street full of stunted old women, each with a short pipe in her mouth, seated by a basket of carrots, turnips, lettuces, the stock-in-trade of each establishment averaging, perhaps, eighteen-pence. With this amount of capital, an old basket, and their time, do these poor creatures contrive to keep off absolute starvation, for, to say that they gain a livelihood were to insult their misery; in all weathers, poorly clad, badly shod, with no solace but their pipe, and no luxury save an occasional 'drop o' gin,' which by hook or crook they contrive to procure, they manage to exist, until a hard winter, or long-continued wet weather, dismisses them to their fate, in the workhouse or the hospital.

We now enter Clare Market, the former abiding-place of the famous Orator Henley, with his congregation of butchers, whom he used to edify with ebullitions of atheism; Henley has been long since dead, or, as he would say himself, *annihilated*, but the town never wants a babbling infidel. Here is always one or more loud-talking Antichrists holding forth to vagabonds of both sexes, and only persecution, which, unluckily for themselves, they do not suffer, can bring them into notoriety, or elevate them from obscure infamy to the bad eminence of apostles of infidelity.

Talking of hospitals, here is an hospital appropriately located in a grave-yard, in Portugal Street, which, although not exactly a court, or alley, is yet so directly in our way that we feel an irre-sistible desire to explore it. Here, indeed, we have the Valley of the Shadow of Death; almost in juxtaposition, the College of Surgeons, King's College Hospital, and the burying-ground of St. Clement's Danes.

Portugal Street is not merely a medical, but a medico-legal neighbourhood; were we to make a *catalogue raisonné* of the public buildings, we might enumerate the College, the Hospital, and the Insolvent Court, which, in truth, is only an hospital for incurables in, or rather out of pocket.

What a melancholy place! spectators seem as if they had already passed the ordeal of the court, and despite the dingy hue of their faces and habiliments, we may safely infer that the majority have been lately *white-washed;* the rest seem to await their turn, paying minute attention to the interrogatories of the judge and counsel, addressed to a party now before the court.

Entering a narrow postern, we found ourselves in the spacious area called New Square, of Lincoln's Inn. Happy they who, like ourselves, have no other business here than that of indifferent spectators! Yet is there something melancholy in the dingy, desolate appearance of those dark staircases leading from doors inscribed with the densely-packed names of legal inhabitants to their respective chambers. Here would appear to have been obtained a perpetual injunction against sunshine, and we breathe as if our pulmonary organs were in Chancery.

We enter the spacious hall, emblazoned with gilded names of great lawyers inscribed in the oaken panels, the windows 'richly dight' with shields, escutcheons, quarterings, supporters, and all the blazonry of the herald's art, casting a 'dim *forensic* light'; the court has just risen; solicitors are busied forming into bundles their voluminous depositions, interrogatories, pleadings; barristers, especially the briefless, gossiping with professional fluency in groups throughout the hall.

The carriage of the Chancellor draws up before a private door; a crowd, lawyers' clerks, writing clerks, laundresses, nursery-maids, assemble to see the great man; the great man appears, languid and exhausted, as well he may be, who not only keeps the consciences of kings, but is guardian of all wards, custodian of all lunatics, and in a great degree administrator of not only the supreme law, but the general government of the country, – an aggregation of labour, responsibility, and power, in the person of one man, to which the universal world, we presume, can in a free country afford no parallel. And yet – what an example and a lesson for all men! – this great personage, taking, by virtue of his high office, precedence of every man in England not of the royal blood, has elevated himself to this giddy altitude from the condition of the son of a professional man, by naked talent and sheer industry. Wonderful country, that can include such tremendous prizes in the lottery of life; and not less wonderful men, who daringly put forth the powerful hand, and claim them as their own!

We are in Chancery Lane, or rather we steal across this ominously-sounding locality, and dive, like a rabbit, head foremost into a Thermopylæ of a place, where no more than one adventurer can go abreast, called Church Passage.

This is the most impoverished, most wretched of its class that we have yet visited. Frightful, one-eyed, pock-pitted creatures hang about the doors, or peer distrustfully through the patched and papered windows; ricketty children paddle in congenial dirt; here are shops where victuals are offered for sale much less eatable in

CHRISTMAS DAY ON THE PAVEMENT

A marked feature of the day in the streets is, that there is scarcely one of the people we meet who is not the bearer of some substantial evidence of the genial influences of the season; – they are all carrying gifts, like the Kings of Saboea. THE ILLUSTRATED LONDON ALMANACK, 1855 appearance, and probably in reality, than the cat's-meat of a respectable tripe-shop; here are rag-shops, with the customary black doll dangling by the neck above the door.

From this miserable abode of unfortunate humanity we proceed to the Liberty of the Rolls, as a chaotic aggregation of tumble-down tenements has the honour to be denominated. Certainly this Liberty is a most extraordinary place; every house is dressed in the unquestionable livery of a Chancery suit; we see here a lively illustration of the condition of tenements and tenants, where the law is the landlord.

From Little White Alley we get into Great White Alley; turning Poll's Corner, we leave Lee's Buildings, and Birch's Buildings on the left. Our next appearance is in Acorn Court; then turning and doubling with intricate sinuosity, worming our way, now to this side, now to that, like a corkscrew, we emerge from the more than Cretan labyrinth at Roll's Buildings, and rejoice to behold again the familiar face of Fetter Lane.

At the Horse Shoe and Magpie, in the lane, we turn down West Harding Street, and find ourselves in a mechanical or engineering literary neighbourhood. Here is the Glasgow and other type-founderies; here a trade, of whose existence we were as yet in ignorance, that of *printer's* smith; here, in New Street, an orna-mented iron gateway, surmounted with the royal arms, richly gilt, introduces us to the printing-house of Spottiswoode and Co., an establishment of itself, for its magnitude, management, excellence of workmanship, and minute division of labour, well worthy of a separate article.

Descending Harp Lane, half a century ago famous for its lower-class ordinaries, where the obsolete practice of diving for a dinner might once have been studied in perfection, and which then, as now, was a fifth-hand furniture mart, we find ourselves, at length, in Farringdon Street, the equatorial line of our devious and intri-cate voyage.

Here, we are compelled to emerge from the by-ways into the highways, as far as Basinghall Street – name abhorred by ship-wrecked merchants. The court is sitting, and in the presiding judge we recognise the caustic editor of the *Examiner*, examining a ruined horse-chaunter.

Here, nearly opposite the Court of Bankruptcy, begins that curious labyrinth, to whose entrance we have given the reader a clue, which he must needs unravel for himself. Who shall describe the intricacies of Leathersellers' Buildings, Blue Hart Court, White Rose Court, Swan Alley, Blue Anchor Court, Green Court, courts of every colour, every shape, running up and down in the heart of the blocks of city-warehouses, like children at play? Who shall delineate the various haunts of the thirsty votaries of Bacchus nestled within their precincts, or describe the statesmen, theologians, gossips of The Dr. Butler's Head, The Blue Last, or The Shepherd and his Flock?

John Fisher Murray, BENTLEY'S MISCELLANY, 1838

RAMBLER BY BUS OR A JOURNEY BY

MR SHILLIBEER'S NEW OMNIBUS, 1829

THERE WERE, for many days, until the novelty wore off, crowds assembled to see the omnibuses start; and many ladies and gentlemen took their places in them to the Yorkshire Stingo, in order that they might have the pleasure of riding back again. The fare was 1s. for the whole, and 6d. for half the distance, and each omnibus made 12 journeys to and fro every day. Thus Mr. Shillibeer established a diversity of fares, regulated by distance; a regulation which was afterwards in a great measure abandoned by omnibus proprietors, and then re-established on our present 3d. and 6d. payments, the 'long-uns' and the 'short-uns.' Mr. Shillibeer's receipts were 100l. a-week. At first, he provided a few books, chiefly magazines, for the perusal of his customers; but this peripatetic library was discontinued, for the customers (I give the words of my informant) 'boned the books.' When the young-gent conductors retired from their posts they were succeeded by persons hired by Mr. Shillibeer, and liberally paid, who were attired in a sort of velvet livery. . . . The short-stage proprietors were loud in their railings against what they were pleased to describe as a French innovation. In the course of from six to nine months, Mr. Shillibeer had twelve omnibuses at work. He feels convinced that had he started fifty omnibuses instead of two in the first instance, a fortune might have been realized. In 1831–2, his omnibuses became general in the great street thoroughfares; and as the short stages were run off the road, the proprietors started omnibuses in opposition to Mr. S.

MORNING CHRONICLE, 26 *September*, 1850

ALMOST ENDLESS WOULD BE the task of enumerating the fine and elegant shops presented to view in the streets of London, and the dazzling array of commodities displayed in the windows. The furnishing ironmonger sets off his polished grates, fenders, candle-sticks, &c., to the best advantage; the cabinetmaker, with his french-polished mahogany and his chintz furniture, does his best to tempt the passer-by; the tobacconist, abandoning the twisted clay-pipes and the pigtail tobacco of former days, displays his elegant snuff-boxes, cigar-cases, meerschaums, and hookahs; the perfumer decks his windows with waxen ladies looking ineffably sweet, and gentlemen whose luxuriant moustaches are only equalled by the rosy hue of their cheeks, and oils, creams, and cos-metics from Circassia, Macassar, &c. – nominally, at least; and so on throughout the list of those who supply the wants, real and imaginary, of purchasers. But there are, besides these shops, two or three classes of establishments which occupy distinct and separate positions in respect to the mode in which sales and purchases are made; such as bazaars and general dealers, which merit our notice.

A modern English bazaar is, after all, not a genuine representa-tive of the class. It is a mingled assemblage of sundry wares rather than wares of one kind. The markets of London might more fittingly claim the designation of bazaars, in respect to the class of commodities sold in each. Gay, writing above a century ago, says –

'Shall the large mutton smoke upon your boards?
Such Newgate's copious market best affords;
Wouldst thou with mighty beef augment thy meal?
Seek Leadenhall; St. James's sends thee veal!
Thames Street gives cheeses; Covent Garden fruits;
Moorfields old books; and Monmouth Street old suits.'

This, which in some of the items is applicable to our own day, represents the true bazaar principle of the East. However, as our bazaars are retail shops, we will take a rapid glance at them.

The Soho Bazaar stands at the head of its class. It was founded many years ago by a gentleman of some notoriety, and has been uniformly a well-managed concern. It occupies several houses on the north-west corner of Soho Square, and consists of stalls or open counters ranged on both sides of aisles or passages, on two separate floors of the building. These stalls are rented by females,

136

who pay, we believe, something between two and three shillings per day for each. The articles sold at these stalls are almost exclusively pertaining to the dress and personal decoration of ladies and children; such as millinery, lace, gloves, jewellery, &c., and, in the height of 'the season,' the long array of carriages drawn up near the building testifies to the extent of the visits paid by the high-born and the wealthy to this place. Some of the rules of the establishment are very stringent. A plain and modest style of dress, on the part of the young females who serve at the stalls, is invariably insisted on, a matron being at hand to superintend the whole; every stall must have its wares displayed by a particular hour in the morning, under penalty of a fine from the renter; the rent is paid day by day, and if the renter be ill, she has to pay for the services of a substitute, the substitute being such an one as is approved by the principals of the establishment. Nothing can be plainer or more simple than the exterior of this bazaar, but it has all the features of a well-ordered institution.

The Pantheon Bazaar is a place of more show and pretensions. It was originally a theatre, one of the most fashionable in London; but having met with the discomfitures which have befallen so many of our theatres, it remained untenanted for many years, and was at length entirely remodelled and converted into a bazaar. When we have passed through the entrance porch in Oxford Street, we find ourselves in a vestibule, containing a few sculptures, and from thence a flight of steps lead up to a range of rooms occupied as a picture gallery. These pictures, which are in most cases of rather moderate merit, are placed here for sale, the proprietors of the bazaar receiving a commission or percentage on any picture which may find a purchaser. From these rooms an entrance is obtained to the gallery, or upper-floor of the toy-bazaar, one of the most tasteful places of the kind in London. We look down upon the ground story, from this open gallery, and find it arranged with counters in a very systematical order, loaded with uncountable trinkets. On one counter are articles of millinery; on another lace; on a third gloves and hosiery; on others cutlery, jewellery, toys, children's dresses, children's books, sheets of music, albums and pocket-books, porcelain ornaments, cut-glass ornaments, alabaster figures, artificial flowers, feathers, and a host of other things, principally of a light and ornamental character. Each counter is attended by a young female, as at the Soho Bazaar. On one side of the toy-bazaar is an aviary, supplied with birds for sale in cages; and adjacent to it is a conservatory where plants are displayed in neat array.

The Pantechnicon is a bazaar for the sale of larger commodities. It is situated in the immediate vicinity of Belgrave Square, and occupies two masses of building on the opposite sides of a narrow street. Carriages constitute one of the principal classes of articles sold at this bazaar: they are ranged in a very long building, and comprise all the usual varieties, from the dress carriage to the light gig, each carriage having its selling price marked on a ticket attached to it. Another department is for the sale of furniture, and consists of several long rooms or galleries filled with pianofortes, tables, chairs, sideboards, chests of drawers, bedsteads, carpets, and all the varied range of household furniture, each article, as in the former case, being ticketed with its selling price. There is a 'wine department' also, consisting of a range of dry vaults for the reception and display of wines. The bazaar contains likewise a 'toy-department'; but this is not so extensive as those noticed in the preceding paragraphs.

The Baker Street Bazaar bears some resemblance to the Pantechnicon, inasmuch as it contains a large array of carriages for sale. But it has somewhat fallen off from its original character; for it was opened as a 'horse bazaar' for the sale, among other things, of horses. Horses are, we believe, no longer exposed here for sale; and the chief commodities displayed are carriages, harness, horse-furniture and accoutrements, furniture, stoves, and 'furnishing ironmongery.' The 'wax-work' and the 'artificial ice' are exhibitions no way connected with the bazaar other than occupying a portion of the too-extensive premises.

There is, in the upper part of the Gray's Inn Road, a building called the North London Repository, which gained some kind of celebrity a few years ago as a locality where the principle of 'labour-exchange' was put to the test. Every article sold had a price fixed upon it, such as would afford sixpence per hour for the time and labour of the artificer who made it, and this was to be bartered for some other article priced in a similar way. The scheme was an utter failure; and the building appropriated to it has been since converted into a kind of furniture and carriage depot, or bazaar.

If the Burlington or Lowther Arcades contained shops of one kind only, they would bear a closer resemblance to the Oriental bazaars than any other places in London; for they are arranged in the long vaulted manner which pictures represent those of the East to be; but they contain paper-hangers, bootmakers, book and print sellers, music-sellers, besides toy-sellers and others. The Lowther Bazaar, opposite to the Lowther Arcade, is simply a large shop, carried on by one owner, but decked out with a variety of fanciful wares. The Opera Colonnade was once somewhat of a bazaar; but it has been shorn of many of its attractions, and is a spiritless affair.

Next let us glance at the shops where commodities having already rendered service to one set of purchasers are exposed to the view of a second, or perhaps a third. The pawnbroker, the dealer in marine stores, the common broker, the 'old-iron shop.' – these are terms which point to our meaning. As to the multifarious articles displayed in the window of a pawnbroker, they have had a probation of a year and a day, and have been brought from the hidden recesses of the pawnbroker's store-rooms again to see the light. Each article – whether it be a telescope, a gown, a pair of pistols, a coat, a watch, a Bible – has its own tale of sorrow and poverty, and is suggestive of reflection on the ruinous rate of interest and loss at which the poor borrow money.

But a more remarkable class of such shops includes those which are commonly known as 'broker's shops' and which contain almost every imaginable kind of commodity. Let a pedestrian walk through Monmouth Street and St. Andrew's Street, the New Cut, or any other part of London in a dense and poor neighbourhood, and observe the motley assemblage of articles, some good enough, but not in general requisition, some useful, but shabby, some to all appearance useless, yet all for sale, and he will acquire a general notion of the miscellaneous nature of the lower class of shop trading. Old furniture shops, or curiosity shops, such as we find in Wardour Street, are a new species – and amongst the most interesting. Humbler collections of curiosities are to be found in Monmouth Street, St. Andrew's Street, and the New Cut. We cannot, however, mention Monmouth Street without thinking of its array of second-hand clothing. Gay spoke of it more than a century ago, and it remains the same in principle to the present day. As fashions change, so does the cut of the garments in Monmouth Street change; but the dealers never change: they are the same people, actuated by the same motives, trafficking on the same system, as in by-gone days. In no other part of London is the use of cellar-shops so conspicuous as in Monmouth Street. Every house has its cellar, to which access is gained by a flight of steps from the open street; and every cellar is a shop, mostly for the sale of second-hand boots and shoes, which are ranged round the margin of the entrance; while countless children – noisy, dirty, but happy brats – are loitering within and without.

Holywell Street, in the Strand, and Field Lane, near Saffron Hill, are two other places where second-hand garments are exposed for sale. The former still maintains a character given to it long ago, that a passenger needs all his resolution to prevent being dragged into the shops whether he will or no; so importunate are the entreaties by which he is invited to buy a brand-new coat, or a splendid waistcoat. Field Lane has a reputation somewhat more equivocal. Its open unsashed windows are loaded with silk handkerchiefs, displayed in dazzling array; and if it be asked how they all came there, we may perhaps arrive at an answer by solving the following police-problem: given, the number of handkerchiefs picked from pockets in the course of a year, to find the number exposed for sale in Field Lane in an equal period. In the immediate vicinity of Drury Lane is another curious assemblage of shops for the sale of old commodities: a small street is occupied almost entirely by open shops or stalls belonging to 'piece-brokers,' who purchase old garments, and cut out from them such pieces as may be sound enough to patch up other garments; whereby a market is furnished which supplies many a 'jobbing' tailor.

A word or two respecting the daily economy of London shops. It is curious to mark the symptoms of the waking of huge London from its nightly sleep. Stage-coach travellers, unless where driven to a new system by railroads, have often means of observing this waking when entering or leaving London at a very early hour. There is an hour – after the fashionables have left their balls and parties, the rakes have reached their houses, and the houseless wanderers have found somewhere to lay their heads, but before the sober tradesmen begin the day's labour – when London is particularly still and silent. Had we written this a year ago, we might have had to allude to the poor sooty boy's shrill cry of 'Sweep!' but we may now only speak of the early breakfast-stalls, the early milkmen, and a few others, whose employment takes them into the street at an early hour. Very few shops indeed, even in the height of summer, are opened before six o'clock; but at that hour the apprentices and shopmen may be seen taking down the shutters from the windows. Time has been when these shutters slid in grooves at the top and bottom of the window, but they now rest on a well-polished brass sill at the bottom, and are fastened with much neatness. The splendour of modern shops has in some cases reached to the shutters themselves, which are highly polished, and not unfrequently figured and decorated with gold; while in the recently-constructed windows of large dimensions sliding shutters of sheet-iron are occasionally used. When the shutters, whatever be their kind, are taken down, we soon see busy indications of cleansing operations going on: how sedulously the glass is wiped, the floor swept, the counters dusted, let the busy apprentice tell. Then comes the shopman or the master, who lays out in the window the goods intended to be displayed that day. Some trades, it is true, allow the goods to remain in the window all night; but in many the shop-window is cleared every evening, again to be filled the next morning. There is singular art and dexterity displayed in this part of the day's proceedings, in laying out the commodities in the most attractive form, especially in the mercers' and drapers' shops. Then, hour after hour, as the streets become gradually filled with walkers and riders, the shopkeeper prepares to receive his customers, whose hours of purchasing depend greatly on the nature of the commodities purchased; the baker has most trade in the morning and afternoon, the butcher and the greengrocer in the forenoon, the publican at noon and in the evening, and so on. In occupations relating to the sale of provisions, a small number of persons can transact a tolerably large trade; but in the drapery line the number of hands is remarkably large, there being some of these establishments in which the shopmen, clerks, cashiers, &c., amount to from fifty to a hundred. One of these, called the 'shop-walker,' has a singular office to fill: his duty being to 'walk the shop,' with a view to see who enters it, and point out to them at what counter, or at what part of the counter, they may be served with the particular commodity required.

As the evening comes on, the dazzling jets of gas become kindled in one shop after another, till our principal streets have a brilliancy rivalling that of day. The evening-walkers are often a different class from the mid-day walkers, and make purchases of a different kind: some, too, seem to expect that shops shall be kept open for their accommodation till nine, ten, or eleven o'clock, while others uniformly close at seven or eight o'clock. This question of shop-shutting has been a subject of much discussion lately; the shopmen to drapers, druggists, and many other retail traders, having urged the justice of terminating the daily business at such a time as will leave them an hour or two for relaxation or reading. This does not seem to be unreasonable; but, at the same time, a little caution seems to be needful in carrying the plan into practice, since the convenience of the purchasers, in respect to the hours at which they make their purchases, must always be an element to be considered.

That some streets should be exclusively private, while others are as exclusively occupied by shopkeepers, is a system for which there is good and sufficient reason. It is, in fact, one mode of exemplifying the bazaar-system, in which, when purchases are to be made, a saving of time is effected by congregating the sellers near polis. The rapid progress of the work of metropolitan improvement, as it assails now one and now another quarter of the city, is perpetually forcing the exhibitors of these monster advertisements to be changing their locality.

The attractive character of the objects exhibited sufficiently accounts for the crowds of lounging amateurs which may at almost every hour of the day be found congregated around them. There are colossal specimens of typography, in juxtaposition with which the puny letters of our pages would look like a snug citizen's box placed beside the pyramids of Egypt. There are rainbow-hued placards, vying in gorgeous extravagance of colour with Turner's later pictures. There are tables of contents of all the weekly newspapers, often more piquant and alluring than the actual newspapers themselves. Then there are pictures of pens, gigantic as the plumes in the casque of the Castle of Otranto, held in hands as huge as that which was seen on the banisters of the said castle; spectacles of enormous size, fit to grace the eyes of an ogre; Irishmen dancing under the influence of Guinness's Dublin Stout or Beamish's Cork Particular; ladies in riding habits and gentlemen in walking dresses of incredible cheapness; prize oxen, whose very appearance is enough to satiate the appetite for ever. Then we have highly-coloured views of famous watering-places, whither cheap excursion trains run at frequent intervals during the summer months, offering strong inducements to the weary and toil-worn Londoner to be off and spend 'nine hours by the seaside.'

The announcements of the grand fêtes and gatherings at the Crystal Palace, and other public places of resort, also add considerably at times to the pictorial adornment of our vacant spaces, and make our 'dead walls' live again in all the beauties of nature. Lastly, there are 'bills o' the play,' lettered and hieroglyphical, and it is hard to say which is the most enticing in the eyes of the multitude – possibly it is the one which is most sensational. These pictorial bills o' the play-houses, especially of the lesser houses, perhaps, bring before our startled eyes a 'Domestic Tale,' illustrating a touching scene in such romantic dramas as 'The Prayer in the Storm,' 'Led Astray,' 'The Peep o' Day Boys,' and many others of a similar character.

The external paper-hangers themselves are a peculiar race; well known by sight from their fustian jackets with immense pockets, their tin paste-boxes suspended by a strap, their placard-pouches, their thin rods of office, with cross-staff at the extremity, formed to join into each other and extend to a length capable of reaching the loftiest elevations at which their posting-bills are legible. A cor-

THE VEHICULAR PLACARD

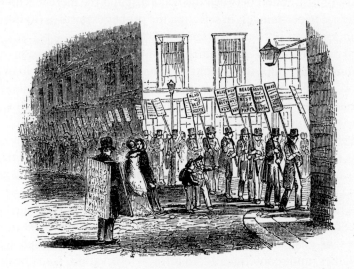

PROCESSION OF PLACARDS

The art and science of advertising even in London did not reach the state of perfection in which we find it all at once. But our fathers, though not quite equal to us, were, after all, pretty fellows in their way; they understood something about advertising, too. The art of advertising is perhaps in our days more universally known and practised – there are no such crude unlicked lumps of advertisements as there were.   W. Weir, KNIGHT'S LONDON, 1842 porate body they are, with consuetudinary bye-laws of their own, which have given rise to frequent litigations in the police courts. The sage judges of these tribunals have found ere now the title of an external paper-hanger to his station as puzzling as that of a sweeper to his crossing. Then there seems to be a kind of apprenticeship known amongst them, though, from cases which have been made public, there is room to doubt whether the rights and duties of master and 'prentice have hitherto been defined with sufficient precision. The period for which a placard must be exposed to public view before it is lawful to cover it over with a new one is a nice question, but seems settled with tolerable certainty. And, to the honour of London external paper-hangers be it said, that there is rarely found (even at the exciting period of an election) among them that disregard of professional etiquette, or rather honour, which leads the mere bill-sticker of the provinces to cover over the posting-bills of a rival before the latter have well dried on the wall. Great judgment is required, and its possession probably is the best mark of distinction between the real artist and the mere mechanical external paper-hanger, in selecting the proper exposures (to borrow a phrase from horticulture) for bills.

'Any man,' said an eminent member of the profession with whom we had once the honour to argue the question, 'any man can stick a bill upon a wall, but to insinuate one gracefully and irresistibly into the hands of a lady or gentleman, is only for one who, to natural genius, adds long experience.'

Peripatetic placards are comparatively a recent invention. The first form they assumed was that of a standard-bearer, with his placard extended like the Roman vexillum at the top of a long pole. Next came a heraldic anomaly, with placards hanging down before and behind like a herald's tabard: Boz has somewhere likened this phenomenon to a sandwich – a piece of human flesh between two slices of pasteboard. When these innovations had ceased to be novelties, and, consequently, to attract observation, some brilliant genius conceived the idea of reviving their declining powers by the simple process of multiplication. This was no more than applying to the streets a principle which had already succeeded on the stage. Of late the practice has, in a great measure, been restricted to a weekly newspaper of enormous size and enormous circulation, which seems to have discovered that the public could only be made aware of the great number of copies it purchased by this mode of chronicling the intelligence.

To peripatetic placards succeeded the vehicular. The first of these were simple enough – almost as rude as the cart of Thespis

THE LONDON

GOURMET

DURING THE NINETEENTH CENTURY

SELECTED FROM

CONTEMPORARY SOURCES

AND INCLUDING

AN ACCOUNT OF THE CULINARY ARRANGEMENTS

OF THE REFORM CLUB

WITH PARTICULAR REFERENCE TO M. SOYER

SOME ACCOUNT OF EATING-HOUSES

OF VARIOUS KINDS

IN THE METROPOLIS

REPORT OF AN ENQUIRY INTO

THE OPERATION OF THE IMPORT DUTIES

WITH PARTICULAR REFERENCE TO COFFEE-HOUSES

THE DRINKING OF BEER IN LONDON

WITH NOTES AND STATISTICS UPON

THE PRODUCTION OF THE PRINCIPAL BREWERS

FROM KNIGHT'S LONDON, 1842

They use a plentiful and nutritious diet. The operative cannot subsist on water-cresses. Beef, mutton, wheatbread, and malt-liquors, are universal among the first-class labourers. Good feeding is a chief point of national pride among the vulgar, and, in their caricatures, they represent the Frenchman as a poor, starved body.

R. W. Emerson, ENGLISH TRAITS, 1882

THE REFORM CLUB very closely resembles the other distinguished clubs at the West End: but it is by the possession of its
famous *kitchen* that this club has gained a peculiar notoriety; a
kitchen which baffles the conception of those who are accustomed
only to ordinary culinary arrangements. The 'genius loci' is M.
Alexis Soyer, whose occupation is that of chief cook to the club,
and whose invention the general arrangement of the kitchen seems
to have been. The gastronomic art, certainly, never before had so
many scientific appliances at its disposal. We have seen many
large factories, where furnaces and boilers are largely employed;
but, with one single exception, we know of none which can rival
this kitchen in the arrangements for *economizing heat*. The
arrangement is somewhat as follows : –

The kitchen, properly so called, is an apartment of moderate
size, surrounded on all four sides by smaller rooms, which form
the pastry, the poultry, the butchery, the scullery, and other subordinate offices. There are doorways, but no doors, between the
different rooms; all of which are formed in such a manner that
the chief cook, from one particular spot, can command a view of
the whole. In the centre of the kitchen is a table and a hot closet,
where various knick-knacks are prepared and kept to a desired
heat, the closet being brought to any required temperature by
admitting steam beneath it. Around the hot closet is a bench or
table, fitted with drawers and other conveniences for culinary
operations. A passage, going round the four sides of this central
table, separates it from the various specimens of cooking apparatus, which involve all that modern ingenuity has brought to bear
on this matter. In the first place there are two enormous fire-places
for roasting, each of which would, in sober truth, roast a sheep
whole. The screens placed before these fires are so arranged as to
reflect back almost the entire of the heat which falls upon them,
and effectually shield the kitchen from the intense heat which
would be otherwise thrown out. Then, again, these screens are so
provided with shelves and recesses as to bring into profitable use
the radiant heat which would be otherwise wasted. Along two
sides of the room are ranges of charcoal-fires for broiling and
stewing, and other apparatus for other varieties of cooking, which
will easily be conjectured by those who are learned in such matters. These are at a height of about three feet, or three and a half

149

feet, from the ground. The broiling fires are a kind of open pot or pan, throwing upwards a fierce but blazeless heat; behind them is a frame-work by which gridirons may be fixed at any height above the fire, according to the intensity of the heat. Other fires, open only at the top, are adapted for various kinds of pans and vessels; and in some cases a polished tin reflector is so placed as to reflect back to the viands the heat which would otherwise be an inconvenience. Under and behind and over and around are pipes, tanks, and cisterns in abundance, either for containing water to be heated by the heat which would otherwise be wasted, or to be used more directly in the multitudinous processes of cooking. A boiler, adjacent to the kitchen, is expressly appropriated to the supply of steam for cooking various dishes by the method of 'steaming,' for heating the hot closets, the hot iron plates, and similar apparatus which everywhere abound.

If we go to the adjacent rooms from the central kitchen, we find that – so effectually is heat economized – all are cool, and fitted to the object for which they are intended. In one small room the butchers' meat is kept, chopped, cut, and otherwise prepared for the kitchen. In the pastry all the appliances for making the good things which its name indicates are conveniently arranged around. In another room there are drawers, in the bottoms of which a stratum of ice is laid; above this a light covering; and above this such small articles of undressed food as require to be kept perfectly cool.

To tell how bright the pots and the pans and the cups are, and how scrupulously clean is every part of the range of rooms, and how quietly and systematically everything is conducted, and how neat are all the persons employed therein – is more than we can attempt; but the system of operations between the cooks and the consumers pertains so closely to our present object, that it must be noticed. In one corner of the kitchen is a little compartment or counting-house, at a desk in which sits the 'clerk of the kitchen.' Every day the chief cook provides, besides ordinary provisions which are pretty certain to be required, a selected list, which he inserts in his 'bill of fare' – a list which is left wholly to his own judgment and skill. Say three or four gentlemen, members of the club, determine to dine there at a given hour; they select from the 'bill of fare,' or order separately if preferred, or leave altogether to the choice of M. Soyer, the requisite provisions. A little slip of paper, on which is written the names of the dishes and the hour of dining, is hung on a hook in the kitchen on a blank board, where there are a number of hooks devoted to different hours of the day

KITCHEN RANGES

The kitchens are underground, which is universally the custom in London.

MANUAL OF DOMESTIC ECONOMY, 1857

Light in the kitchen, both by day and night, is one very important item that should always be attended to and also a proper ventilation.

MANUAL OF DOMESTIC ECONOMY, 1857

or evening. The cooks proceed with their avocations, and by the time the dinner is ready the clerk of the kitchen has calculated and entered the exact value of every article composing it, which entry is made out in the form of a bill – the cost price being that by which the charge is regulated. Immediately at the elbow of the clerk are bells and speaking-tubes, by which he can communicate with the servants in the other parts of the buildings. Meanwhile a steam-engine is 'serving-up.' In one corner of the kitchen is a recess, on opening a door in which we see a small square platform, calculated to hold an ordinary-sized tray. This platform or board is connected with the shaft of a steam-engine, by bands and wheels, so as to be elevated through a kind of vertical trunk leading to the upper floors of the building; and here servants are in waiting to take out whatever may have been placed on the platform. What will the steam-engine be made to do next?

KNIGHT'S LONDON, 1842

SOME ACCOUNT OF
EATING-HOUSES OF VARIOUS KINDS
IN THE METROPOLIS

THERE ARE, it appears, about two hundred places in London which can fittingly come under the denomination of eating-houses, occupying a place between the hotels on the one hand and the coffee-rooms on the other. At all of these places joints of meat are dressed every day, depending for variety on the extent of business done, but generally including boiled beef and roast beef, as well as the necessary appendages for the formation of a dinner. In some of these houses the quantity of meat dressed in a week is quite enormous; and it seems pretty evident that the greater the sale the better the quality of the articles sold – or perhaps we may take it in an inverse order, that the excellence of the provisions has led to the extent of the custom.

Some of these dining-rooms are the scenes of bustle during only a few hours of the day; while others, either from the extent of their trade, or the different classes of their visitors, present a never-ceasing picture of eating and drinking. Some, such as a celebrated house in Bishopsgate Street, are frequented almost entirely by commercial men and City clerks, who, during a few hours in the day, flock in by hundreds. Then again others, such as Williams's boiled-beef shop in the Old Bailey, and a few in the neighbourhood of Lincoln's Inn Fields, are frequented almost entirely by lawyers' clerks, witnesses, and others engaged in the law or criminal courts. In all such cases there is a 'best' room for those whose purses are tolerably supplied; and a more humble room, generally nearer to the street, for such as can afford only a 'sixpenny plate.' Again, on going farther westward, we find, in the neighbourhood of Covent Garden and the Haymarket, dining-rooms in great plenty, the visitants at which are altogether of a different class. Here we may see actors, artists, paragraph-makers, and foreigners, most of whom seem in much less haste than the City diners. In this quarter of the town there are many French restaurateurs, whose rooms present the agreeable variety of ladies dining without any restraint from the observation of the male visitors.

It is observable that in some houses the waiter gives the diner a long detail of the good things which are 'just ready,' while in others there is a printed bill-of-fare placed before him. The latter is certainly the most systematic method; for, by the time the nimble waiter has got through his speech, we almost forget the first items to which he directed attention. In the 'bill of fare' all the dishes customarily prepared at the house are printed in certain groups, and the prices are *written* opposite those which are to be had hot on any particular day, so that a customer can at once see what provisions are ready, and how much he shall have to pay for them. In the opposite case, where the visitor knows nothing of the matter but what the waiter tells him, the routine of proceedings may be thus sketched: – The guest, perhaps a man of business who has but little time to spare for his dinner, enters the room, takes the first seat he can find (the one nearest the fire in cold weather), takes off his hat, and asks for *The Times* or the *Chronicle*. While he is glancing his eye rapidly over the daily news, the active, tidy waiter, with a clean napkin on his left arm, comes to his side, and pours into his ear, in a rapid but monotonous tone, some such narrative, as the following: – 'Roast beef, boiled beef, roast haunch of mutton, boiled pork, roast veal and ham, salmon and shrimp-sauce, pigeon-pie, rump-steak pudding.' The visitor is perhaps deep in the perusal of 'Spanish Scrip' or 'Columbian Bonds,' or some other newspaper intelligence, and the waiter is obliged to repeat his catalogue; but, generally speaking, the order is quickly given, and quickly attended to. A plate of roast beef, which may be taken as a standard of comparison, is charged for at these places at prices varying from 4d. to 10d., generally from 6d. to 8d.; and other articles are in a corresponding ratio. When the meat and vegetables have disappeared, the nimble waiter is at your elbow, to ask whether pastry or cheese is wanted; and when the visitor is about to depart, the waiter adds up, with character-istic rapidity, the various items constituting the bill. 'Meat 8*d*., potatoes 1*d*., bread 1*d*., cheese 1*d*., &c.,' are soon summed up; the money is paid, and the diner departs.

At the alamode-beef houses the routine is still more rapid. Here a visitor takes his seat, and the waiter places before him a knife, a fork, and a spoon; and gives him the choice among sundry lumps of bread kept in an open basket. Meanwhile the visitor asks for a 'sixpenny plate'; and it may happen that two other customers ask at the same time, the one for a sixpenny, and the other for a four-penny plate. Out goes the waiter, calling, in a quick tone, for 'two sixes and a four'; a brevity which is perfectly well understood by those who are to lade out the soup from the cauldron wherein it is prepared. Presently he returns with a pile of pewter plates, containing the 'two sixes and a four,' and places them before the diners. There is a house near the theatres where this scene of operation continues almost uninterruptedly from twelve o'clock at noon till an hour or two after the theatres are over in the even-ing; some taking soup as a luncheon, some as an early dinner, some as a late dinner, some as a substitute for tea, and the remainder as a supper.

There is a lower class of soup-houses, where persons to whom sixpence is even too much for a dinner may obtain wherewithal to dine. Whoever has had to walk through Broad Street, St. Giles's, or down the northern side of Holborn Hill, may have seen shops, in the windows of which a goodly array of blue and white basins is displayed, and from which emanate abundant clouds of odour-giving steam. Around the windows, too, a crowd of hungry mortals assemble on a cold day, and partake (in imagination) of the enticing things within. A poor fellow, all in tatters, with a countenance which speaks strongly of privation, gazes eagerly through the window at what is going on within, and thinks how rich a man must be who can afford to pay twopence or threepence for 'a basin of prime soup, potatoes, and a slice of bread'; – for it is at some such charge as this that the viands are sold. As for the quality of the soup, we should, perhaps, only be just in supposing that it is good enough for the price. One thing is certain, that the quantity sold every day at these houses is extremely large.

The 'chop-houses' in the City form a class by themselves. They are neither eating-houses nor taverns, nor do they belong to classes hereafter to be noticed. The solid food here to be procured is chiefly in the form of a steak or a chop, with such small appen-dages as are necessary to form a meal. There is no hot joint from

THE LONDON GOURMET

'*Waiter, what have you got to-day?*'
'*Haunch of Venison, Sir, Boiled Turkey, Roast Veal and Ham, Roast Pork,
Boiled Fowls, Roast and Boiled Beef.*'
'*What vegetables?*'
'*Asparagus, Sea Kale, Broccoli, French Beans, Greens and Potatoes.*'
'*Oh, then, I'll take a small plate of boiled beef and a potato!*'

Robert Seymour, SCENES IN LONDON, 1834

155

which a guest may have a 'sixpenny' or a 'ninepenny' plate; nor are there the various dishes which fill up the bill-of-fare at a dining-room. Every guest knows perfectly well what he can procure there. If a chop or a steak will suffice, he can obtain it; if not, he goes to some house where greater variety is provided. With his chop he can have such liquor as his taste may prefer. There are some of these houses which have been attended by one generation after another of guests, comprising merchants, bankers, and commercial men of every grade. The portrait of the founder, or a favourite waiter, may perhaps be seen over the fireplace in the best room; and the well-rubbed tables, chairs, and benches tell of industry oft repeated. Sometimes the older houses exhibit a waiter who has gone through his daily routine for half a century. There is a dingy house in a court in Fleet Street where the chops and steaks are unrivalled. Who that has tasted there that impossible thing of private cookery – a *hot* mutton chop, a second brought when the first is despatched – has not pleasant recollections of the never-ending call to the cook of 'Two muttons to follow'?

At most of the respectable eating and chop houses it is a pretty general custom to give a penny or twopence to the waiter when the 'reckoning' is paid. This is a bad system. It would be much better to pay an extra penny for the price of the dinner, and let the waiter be paid by the master; instead of, as is at present the case, the waiter giving the master a *douceur* for permission to hold the situation. But whether such a change would change the characteristics of a waiter, we cannot say; certain it is that a London waiter is quite a character. Here is Mr. Leigh Hunt's picture of one: – 'He has no feeling of noise, but as the sound of dining, or of silence, but as a thing before dinner. Even a loaf with him is hardly a loaf: it is so many "breads." His longest speech is the making out of a bill *viva voce* – "Two beefs – one potatoes – three ales – two wines – six and twopence," – which he does with an indifferent celerity, amusing to new comers who have been relishing their fare, and not considering it as a mere set of items.'

Many houses have what is termed in France a *table-d'hôte*, or in England an *ordinary;* that is, a dinner ready for all comers at a fixed hour in the day, and at a fixed charge. The host determines on the choice of good things to constitute the bill of fare; and the diner partakes of such as may best accord with his palate. Some of these places are attended day after day by nearly the same persons, while others see a constant succession of new faces. There is one such house near or in Billingsgate, celebrated for the excellence of the *fish*, which forms a component part of the cheer; and which is, on this account, much frequented by the connoisseurs in fish. Nay, we have heard that so far does the demand for table-room exceed the supply, that the 'knowing ones' have their seat at the table half an hour before the prescribed dinner-time, as the only way to be prepared for the fish by the time the fish is prepared for them. A public-house (really one) in a street near Covent Garden has an ordinary of three courses, which the lovers of economical good cooking, who cannot dine without fish and pastry, delight to haunt. But there are few of these. The *ordinaries* of the days of Elizabeth have left few successors.

Besides the dining-rooms and chop-houses, properly so called, there are many places where a man can get a dinner by a sort of indirect arrangement. Not to mention oyster-rooms, which are frequented rather for suppers than dinners, or pastry-cooks' shops, which are rather for lady-like delicacies than for stout, hearty food which will enable a man to buffet through the world, or Garraway's, and one or two similar houses, where a sandwich and a glass of wine or ale may be rapidly swallowed, there are public-houses where a *gridiron* is kept always at hand for cooking a steak or a chop belonging to a customer. If we draw a circle of a few hundred yards radius round the Royal Exchange, we shall find more than one place of which the following is a sketch. A butcher's shop within a door or two of a public-house supplies a purchaser with a steak or a chop at a reasonable price. He carries it into the public-house (or tavern, if the name be preferred) and places it in the hands of a waiter or servant, who speedily dresses it on an enormous gridiron, the bars of which are so constructed as to save a great portion of the fat from the meat. For this service the small sum of *one penny* only is charged, in addition to an equally moderate charge for bread, potatoes, and whatever drink may be called for.

Some of these houses are celebrated for the 'fine old cheese,' or the 'baked potatoes,' or the 'mutton pies,' which they provide for their customers; each place having a reputation for some one or other welcome dish. In humble neighbourhoods, again, all such dainties as 'sheeps' trotters,' 'sheeps' heads,' 'pigs' faces,' 'faggots,' &c., are to be had hot at certain hours of the day; but these are not supplied by the owners of public-houses; they are procured at shops adjacent, and very often demolished in the tap-rooms of the public-houses.   KNIGHT'S LONDON, 1842

AN AMERICAN IN LONDON

THEY DOUBT a man's sound judgment, if he does not eat with appetite, and shake their heads if he is particularly chaste.

R. W. Emerson, ENGLISH TRAITS

REPORT OF AN ENQUIRY INTO
THE OPERATION OF THE IMPORT DUTIES
WITH PARTICULAR REFERENCE TO COFFEE-HOUSES

ON THE 5th of May, 1840, the House of Commons directed a Committee to inquire into the operation of the Import Duties; and in the Report which the Committee made to the House on the 6th of August in the same year many curious details occur respecting coffee-houses, coffee-house keepers, and the class of persons who frequent coffee-houses. The evidence arose out of the consideration of the duty upon coffee; but it involves statistical details of a highly curious character, and closely connected with the subject of our paper.

On one of the days of meeting, five coffee-house keepers, residing in as many different parts of London, gave evidence before the Committee. It was there stated, by Mr. Humphreys, that the gradual increase of coffee-houses in London may be estimated at nearly a hundred per annum; that twenty-five years ago there were not above ten or twelve coffee-houses (of the kind now under consideration) in the metropolis; but that they had since increased to sixteen or eighteen hundred. The following are two of the questions put to Mr. Humphreys, and the answers given to them: –

'Has the charge for coffee, to the consumer, been reduced, in consequence of this competition (between rival coffee-house keepers)?' – 'Very materially. About twenty-five years ago there was scarcely a house in London where you could get any coffee under sixpence a cup, or threepence a cup; there are now coffee-houses open at from one penny up to threepence. There are many houses where the charge is one penny, where they have seven or eight hundred persons in a day. There is Mr. Pamphilon, who charges three halfpence per cup; and he has from fifteen to sixteen hundred persons a day.'

'It is the particular beverage that you sell which is the great attraction to the persons that come to your house?' – 'Yes; I have, on the average, four to five hundred persons that frequent my house daily; they are mostly lawyers' clerks and commercial men; some of them are managing clerks, and there are many solicitors likewise, highly respectable gentlemen, who take coffee in the middle of the day, in preference to a more stimulating drink. I have often asked myself the question, where all that number of persons could possibly have got their refreshment prior to opening my house. There are taverns in the neighbourhood, but no coffee-house, nor anything that afforded any accommodation of the nature I now give them; and I found that a place of business like mine was so sought for by the public, that shortly after I opened it I was obliged to increase my premises in every way I could; and at the present moment, besides a great number of newspapers every day, I am compelled to take in the highest class of periodicals. For instance, we have eight or nine quarterly publications, averaging from four shillings to six shillings each; and we are constantly asked for every new work that has come out. I find there is an increasing taste for a better class of reading. When I first went into business, many of my customers were content with the lower-priced periodicals, but I find, as time progresses, that the taste is improving, and they look out now for a better class of literature.'

There are other places, more generally designated 'coffee-shops,' where working men mostly congregate; and it is interesting to know that among this class also the growth of a taste for refreshing beverage and sober decency has been by no means slow. Mr. Letchford, one of the witnesses examined before the Committee, keeps a coffee-shop in a densely populated and humble part of the metropolis. When this shop had been established seven years, there were from seven to nine hundred persons visited it per day, most of them hard-working men. He has three rooms, in which the charges for a cup of coffee are respectively 1d., 1½d., and 3d., according to the kind of customers for which they are intended. The cheapest room is that which is most frequented, and which has a constant influx of customers from four in the morning till ten at night. To the question, 'Does a man come there and get his breakfast?' Mr. Letchford replied, 'Yes; he comes in the morning at four o'clock and has a cup of coffee, and a thin slice of bread and butter, and for that he pays 1½d.; and then again at eight, for his breakfast, he has a cup of coffee, a penny loaf, and a pennyworth of butter, which is 3d.; and at dinner time, instead of going to a public-house, at one o'clock he comes in again, and has his coffee and his bread, and brings his own meat. I do not cook for any one.' It was stated that nine newspapers were provided for these numerous but humble customers.

Another feature strikes the observer, in glancing over the evidence given before this Committee, viz., that the coffee-rooms have in many cases become also *dining*-rooms, and not merely places where breakfast or tea is taken. Mr. Humphreys stated that latterly the coffee-house keepers have been compelled to sell meat ready cooked. Persons became so desirous of having their meals in houses of this description, that they have gradually got into the

159

habit of dining there, as well as of purchasing the beverage for which the houses were originally established. 'I now sell,' said Mr. Humphreys, 'about three cwt. of cold ham and meat every week. I was first compelled to sell it by persons going to a cook's shop, and buying their meat, and bringing it in and asking me for a plate; and I found it a matter of some little trouble without any profit. It occurred to me that I might as well cook; and I have myself now, in consequence of that, a business during the whole of the day. A number of gentlemen come in and have a plate of beef for 4d., a cup of coffee for 2d., and a loaf of bread; and for 6d. or 7d. they have what is for them a good breakfast. In fact, a gentleman may come to my house and have as good a breakfast for 8d. as he can have in any hotel for 1s. 6d.' To the same effect was the statement of Mr. Pamphilon. He said that a large middle-day trade had sprung up among coffee-room keepers, in consequence of the pursuance of this system; and that he had often had a hundred people dining in his rooms in the middle of one day, off cold ham, and beef, and coffee. Mr. Hare, also, who keeps a first-class coffee-room in the City, gave evidence corroborative of the same view. He said that bankers' clerks, and mercantile men of a similar description, were constantly in the habit of having steaks and chops at his house, coffee being the beverage: he explained this latter point by saying that men of this class find that they can transact their afternoon's business better after coffee than after malt liquor. The same witness stated that when he commenced business, nine or ten years previously, he did not cook anything; the custom had its origin in the request, as a matter of favour, on the part of some of the gentlemen who took coffee at his house, that he would furnish them with the means of partaking of a chop or a steak without going to a tavern. He did so; and thus arose a custom which has now become very prevalent in the majority of the coffee-houses of London. As an item in the economy of London refreshment, confessedly brought into existence within the last dozen years, this is not unworthy of notice.

The cigar-divans and chess-rooms are modifications of the coffee-rooms. They are for those who require something more than coffee and reading, and yet at the same time wish to have those luxuries. The owners of these rooms are not so much accustomed to supply meals as evening refreshment. Your true chess-player can sit many hours without eating or drinking largely: his 'checking,' and 'castling,' and 'mating,' absorb nearly all his attention; and he has only time to whiff his cigar and sip his coffee once now and then. At some of the places here indicated the guest pays a shilling on entrance, for which he receives a 'fine Havannah' and cup of coffee; while at others he pays for what he may purchase, without paying for admission.

In closing this paper we must not forget the old woman who serves hot coffee to the coachmen and labourers at four in the morning; or the 'Baked tato' man, whose steaming apparatus glistens before us; or the 'Ham-sandwich' man, who encounters us on leaving a theatre. Respecting the first, it may suffice to say, that there are many labouring men abroad in the morning at an hour too early to find coffee-shops open; and for the supply of such customers with an early breakfast, a table is laid out *al fresco*, with sundry huge slices of bread and butter, an array of cups and saucers, and a vessel full of hot coffee – all served, we have no doubt, at a very small charge. The baked-potato dealer is a merchant of modern growth; he sprang up somewhere in the neighbourhood of St. George's Fields, and has since spread his trading operations to every part of London. His apparatus is really a very ingenious and smart-looking affair, and when lighted up at night constitutes a locomotive cook-shop, of which the last generation could have had no idea. How the man takes out a steaming potato, cuts it open, seasons it with butter, pepper, and salt, and exchanges it for a half-penny – every apprentice boy in London knows; and it must be owned that this is a ha'p'orth which would comfort many a hungry stomach. As for the ham-sandwich man, he is a nocturnal dealer: he puts on his white apron, lays his sandwiches in a small handbasket, which he holds before him, and takes his post opposite the gallery-doors of the theatres, where, at or near midnight, he attracts the notice of his customers by the cry of 'Ham-sandwiches, only a penny!'

KNIGHT'S LONDON, 1842

BEER IN LONDON

WHEN THE HEAD of the foremost of its colossal horses is seen emerging from one of those steep, narrow lanes ascending from the river side to the Strand (sometimes is it there seen, though the coal-waggon has pre-eminence in that locality of dark arches looking like the entrance to the Pit of Acheron), there is a general pause in the full tide of human life that flows along the thoroughfare. Heavily, as though they would plant themselves into the earth, the huge hoofs, with the redundant locks dependent from the fetlocks circumfused, are set down, clattering and scraping as they slip on the steep ascent; the huge bodies of the steeds,

thrown forward, drag upward the load attached to them by their
weight alone; in a long chain they form a curve quite across the
street, till at last the dray, high-piled with barrels, emerges from
the narrow way like a reel issuing from a bottle, and, the strain
over, the long line of steeds and the massive structure, beside
which the car of Juggernaut might dwindle into insignificance, pass
smoothly onwards.

It is no unimportant element of London life that is launched
with all this pomp and circumstance into its great thoroughfares.
There is a system organised, by which the contents of these huge
emissaries from the reservoirs of the breweries are diverted into a
multiplicity of minor pipes and strainers which penetrate and
moisten the clay of the whole population. From 'morn till dewy
eve' the huge, high-piled dray may be seen issuing from the
brewery gates to convey barrels to the tap-houses, and nine-gallon
casks, the weekly or fortnightly allowance of private families. At
noon and night the pot-boys of the innumerable beer-shops may
be seen carrying out the quarts and pints duly received at those
hours by families who do not choose to lay in a stock of their own;
or the mothers and children of families, to whom the saving of a
halfpenny is a matter of some consequence, may be seen repairing
with their own jugs to these beer-conduits. You may know when it
is noon in any street in London by the circulation of beer-jugs, as
surely as you may know when it is 11 A.M. by seeing housekeepers
with their everlasting straw reticules and umbrellas. And in addition to these periodical flowings of the fountains must be taken
into the account the 'bye-drinkings' of carmen, coal-whippers,
paviours, &c. at all hours of the day – of artisans at their 'dry
skittle-grounds,' and of medical students and other 'swells' at
taverns.

It is not easy to form an estimate of the quantity of beer annually strained through these alembics, but we may venture upon
what Sir Thomas Browne would have called 'a wide guess.' In
1836 the twelve principal brewers in London brewed no less than
2,119,447 barrels of beer. The quantity of malt wetted by all the
brewers in London in that year was 754,313 quarters; the quantity
wetted by the illustrious twelve, 526,092 quarters. According to
this proportion, the number of barrels of beer brewed in London,
in 1836, could not fall far short of 3,000,000. The beer manufactured for exportation and country consumption may be assumed,
in the mean time, to have been balanced by the importation of Edinburgh and country ales, and Guinness's stout. In 1836 the population of the metropolis was estimated at 1,500,000. This would give,

hand over head, an allowance of two barrels (or 76 gallons) of beer per annum for every inhabitant of the metropolis – man, woman, and child. This is of course beyond the mark, but perhaps not so much so as one would at first imagine. At all events, these numbers show that beer is an important article of London consumption: thus corroborating the inference naturally drawn from the high state of perfection to which we find the arrangements for injecting it into all the veins and arteries of the body corporate have been brought.

Beer is to the London citizen what the water in the reservoirs of the plain of Lombardy, or the kahvreez of Persia (which is permitted to flow into the runnels of the landowners so many hours per diem), is to the village peasantry of those countries. It is one of those commonplaces of life – those daily-expected and daily-enjoyed simple pleasures which give man's life its local colouring. The penning of the sheep in a pastoral country – 'the ewe-bughts, Marion' of Scottish song – is poetical, because the bare mention of it calls up all the old accustomed faces, and sayings and doings, that make home delightful. In London it is our beer that stands foremost in the ranks of these suggestions of pleasant thoughts. Therefore it is that a halo dwells around the silver-bright pewter pots of the potboy, and plays, like the lightning of St. John, about the curved and tapering rod of office of the brewer's drayman. Therefore is it that the cry of 'Beer!' falls like music on the ear; and therefore it is that in the song of the jolly companion, in the gibe of the theatrical droll, in the slang of him who lives 'on the step' (of the 'bus), in the scratching of the caricaturist, the bare mention of beer is at any time a sufficient substitute for wit. It needs but to name it, and we are all on the broad grin.

The genuine London beer (although we learn from the 'Brewers' Annual' that there are only three brewers in London – Reid, Meux, and Courage – who do not brew pale ale, and that there are a few who brew nothing else) is the brown stout. It is the perfection – the ideal of the 'berry-brown ale' and the 'but-brown ale' of the old songs. It is what the poet of those antediluvian days fancied, or a lucky accident enabled their brewers at times to approach. No disparagement to the pale and amber ales, infinite in name as in variety; to the delicious Winchester; to the Burton, which, like Sancho's sleep, 'wraps one all round like a blanket'; to Hodgson's pale India ale, so grateful at tiffin when the thermometer is upwards of 100, and the monotonousness-creating punkah pours only a stream of heated air on the guests; 'London particular' is the perfection of malt liquor. As Horace says of Jupiter, there is nothing 'similar or second to it' – not even among liquors of its own complexion. Guinness is a respectable enough drink, but we must say that the ascendancy it has gained in many coffee-houses and taverns of London is anything but creditable to the taste of their frequenters. Its sub-acidity and soda-water briskness, when compared with the balmy character of London bottled stout from a crack brewery, are like the strained and shallow efforts of a professed joker compared with the unctuous, full-bodied wit of Shakespeare. As for the mum of Brunswick, which enjoys a traditional reputation on this side of the water, because it has had the good luck to be shut out by high duties, and has thus escaped detection, it is a villainous compound, somewhat of the colour and consistence of tar – a thing to be eaten with a knife and fork. We will be judged by any man who knows what good liquor is – by a jury selected from the musical amateurs of the 'Coal-hole,' the penny-a-liners who frequent the 'Cock' near Temple Bar, and the more sedate but not less judicious tasters who dine or lunch daily at 'Campbell's' in Pope's Head Alley. Should it be objected that such a tribunal, composed exclusively of Londoners, might be suspected of partiality, let it be a jury half composed of foreigners – Lübeck, Goslar in Saxony, and any town in Bavaria can furnish competent persons to decide such a question.

But the favour in which London beer stands in so many and various regions of the earth may be received as the verdict of a grand jury of nations in its favour. Byron sings –

'Sublime tobacco, that from East to West
Cheers the tar's labours and the Turkman's rest';

and he might have added that wherever tobacco is known and appreciated, there too have the merits of London porter been acknowledged. The learned Meibomius,[1] who, in a Latin quarto, has dilated upon the subject of 'beer, tipple, antall other intoxicating liquors except wine,' with the completeness and minuteness of a true German naturalist, and with that placid seriousness which might make what he says pass for a joke if there were only wit in it, or for learning if it contained anything worth knowing, has judiciously remarked that smoke-drinking and beer-drinking are natural and necessary complements of each other. The mucilaginous properties of the beer are required to neutralise the narcotic adustness of the Nicotian weed; and London beer, being the perfection of its kind, naturally takes the lead of all other kinds of beer.   KNIGHT'S LONDON, 1842

[1] Joan. Henrici Meibomii de Cervisiis Potibusque et Ebriaminibus extra Vinum aliis Commentarius: Helmestadii, 1688, 4to.

THE LONDON

REFORMER

DURING THE NINETEENTH CENTURY

SELECTED FROM
VARIOUS CONTEMPORARY SOURCES
AND INCLUDING

DESCRIPTIONS OF
CERTAIN SOCIETIES, REFORMATORIES AND PRISONS
FROM PHILLIPS' 'MIRROR OF LONDON,' 1804

AN ACCOUNT OF THE PROGRESS AND PROCEEDINGS
OF THE LADIES' ASSOCIATION FOR IMPROVING
THE CONDITION OF FEMALE PRISONERS IN NEWGATE
FROM 'THE BRITISH MAGAZINE,' 1819

INCIDENTAL NOTICES
UPON EDUCATION IN LONDON
FROM 'KNIGHT'S LONDON,' 1842

THE REPORT OF THE FIRST RAGGED SCHOOL
AS PRINTED BY ORDER OF
THE HOUSE OF COMMONS, 1850

A PROPOSAL BY GENERAL WILLIAM BOOTH FOR
A HOUSEHOLD SALVAGE BRIGADE
FROM 'IN DARKEST ENGLAND AND THE WAY OUT,' 1890

TOGETHER WITH
OTHER BRIEFER REFERENCES
AND NOTICES

*I could fill volumes with stories of the war against vermin, which is part of th[e]
campaign in the slums, but the subject is too revolting to those who are ofte[n]
indifferent to the agonies their fellow creatures suffer, so long as their sensiti[ve]
ears are not shocked by the mention of so painful a subject.*

General William Booth, IN DARKEST ENGLAND AND THE WAY OUT, 189[?]

Society for Bettering the Condition of the Poor, Parliament-Street

THIS SOCIETY was instituted in 1796. Its object is, every thing that concerns the happiness of the poor, To remove the difficulties attending parochial relief, and the discouragement of industry and economy, by the present mode of distributing it; to correct the abuses of workhouses; and to assist the poor in placing out their children in the world; in the improvement of their habitations, gardens, the use of fuel, &c.

The following are the subjects of information upon which the society is desirous of obtaining and circulating information. 1. Parish relief; 2. Friendly societies; 3. Parish workhouses; 4. Cottages; 5. Cottage gardens; 6. Parish mills; 7. Village shops; 8. Village kitchens; 9. Fuel and fire-places; 10. Apprentices; 11. County gaols; 12. Beggars, &c.

Upon all the topics, and others connected with them, the reports of this society (published in numbers) speak amply, and present a body of knowledge at once practical, interesting, and important, highly to the credit of the promoters of this institution; it commenced when the distresses of the poor were most urgent, and when the dearness of all articles of subsistence required every possible plan of economy to be studied and earnestly enforced through each class of the community. Subscriptions are received at Messrs. Ranson and Co.'s, Bankers, Pall Mall; and a donation of ten guineas at once, or one guinea annually, intitles the subscriber to two copies of each publication of the society, and so in proportion upon a larger sum.

Philanthropic Society, St. George's Fields

THE GREAT object of this society, instituted thirteen years since, is to unite the purposes of *charity* with those of *industry and police;* to rescue from destruction the offspring of the vicious and dishonest.

They have at present 167 children, male and female; among these, there are several who have been taken from prisons, others who have been rescued from the retreats of villainy, and the haunts of prostitution. For their employment, buildings are erected, in which, under the direction of master workmen, various trades are carried on; and the girls are bred up to work at their needle, and to do those household offices, which render them serviceable to the

167

community, and enable them to obtain an honest living. The whole number of children, of both sexes, that have been received by the society, amount to 489; among whom were many, though *young in years yet old in iniquity*.

The committee feel themselves indebted to any well disposed and judicious persons, whether subscribers or not of the society, who favor the institution with a visit, and a book is kept to insert any remarks which may occur on such an inspection.

Newgate Prison

IS THE GAOL for the county of Middlesex, and of course is a place of confinement both for criminals and for debtors; but, though the building is large, the accommodations are by no means sufficient for the reception of those unfortunate persons, whose pecuniary embarrassments rob them of their liberty, and who are here crowded together, in a manner which is disgraceful to the metropolis, and dangerous to the public health. The number of debtors is generally upwards of 300, and these are, almost without exception, of the poorest class, as all who can procure the means, get themselves removed either to the Fleet or King's Bench. That side of Newgate which is for felons, is sufficiently capacious, and the criminals are better accommodated than those who are confined for debt, except such as are under sentence of death, who are kept in irons and in cells. Part of the felon's side, distinguished by the name of the state side, contains large and comfortable rooms.

The keeper of Newgate, Mr. Kirby, is a man of great humanity, and softens the rigours of a prison as much as possible; a conduct which has an excellent effect on all who are under his care, as they know that if they behave well, they will receive the good offices and good report of their judicious keeper.

This prison may be visited by strangers on paying two or three shillings to the turnkeys, and on submitting to the performance of a few acts of real charity among the distressed prisoners in the several yards.

The Fleet

IS A PRISON belonging to the Courts of Common Pleas and Chancery, to which debtors may remove themselves from any other prison, for the expence of six or seven pounds. It contains 125 rooms, besides a common kitchen, coffee and tap-tooms, but the number of prisoners is generally so great, that two, or even three persons, are obliged to submit to the shocking inconvenience of living in one small room!! – Those who can afford it, pay their companion or chum off, and thus have a room to themselves. Each person so paid off, receives four shillings a week. The prisoner pays one shilling and three-pence a week for his room without furniture, and an additional seven-pence for furniture. Matters are sometimes so managed, that a room costs the needy and distressed prisoner from ten to thirteen shillings a week.

Those who have trades that can be carried on in a room, generally work, and some gain more than they would out of doors, after they become acquainted with the ways of the place. During the quarterly terms, when the court sits, prisoners, on paying five shillings a day, and on giving security, are allowed to go out when they please, and there is a certain space round the prison, called *the Rules*, in which prisoners may live, on furnishing two good securities to the warden for their debt, and on paying about three *per cent.* on the amount of their debts to the warden. The Rules extend only from Fleet-market to the London coffee-house, and from Ludgate hill to Fleet-lane, so that lodgings are bad, and very dear. Within the walls of the prison, there is a yard for walking in, and a good racquet-ground.

Charitably disposed persons ought liberally to contribute to the poor's-box, placed on the pavement on the eastern side of Fleet-market, as all the money so collected is fairly and judiciously distributed among objects of real charity.

The King's Bench

IS IN MOST respect like the Fleet prison, but it is larger, more airy, and more conveniently laid out. The Rules, though more extensive, cost more to be obtained, and a prisoner in the inside, can only go out one day each term, or four days in a year, instead of the eighty or ninety days obtained in the Fleet. Being out of the town, the Bench, though more wholesome, is less in the way of friends who might call, which to the chief part of prisoners, is a considerable disadvantage. There are nearly 300 rooms in this prison, but the number of people confined is proportionally great, and decent accommodations are even more expensive than in the Fleet.

Other Prisons

THE MAGISTRATES of London commit those who are supposed to be guilty of crimes, provisionally to the Poultry Compter, a dark, small, ill-aired, dungeon, situated near the Mansion-house, in the street from which it takes its name; and the magistrates of Westminster commit, in like cases, to a prison called Tothill-fields Bridewell, which is a house of correction also.

There are other prisons, such as that in Giltspur-street, for debtors who are citizens of London; Clerkenwell Bridewell, the New Gaol in the Borough of Southwark, for the county of Surrey, on the top of which is frequently exhibited the horrid spectacle of public executions!! the Marshalsea prison, the Borough Clink (as it is called, for small debts from the Court of Requests), and that recent, but very famous *House of Correction* in Cold Bath-fields, of which so much has been so properly said, in and out of parliament. This prison was originally built on Mr. Howard's plan of solitary confinement, *for reclaiming and reforming hardened and convicted villains;* but, persons *only suspected,* and confined merely for *security* not for *punishment,* have, by some strange accident, been sent there, and detained, without trial, like the most abandoned felons! a measure which actually was no part of Mr. Howard's plan! *Nothing is more certain, than that the keeper of a prison* UPON SUCH A PLAN AS THIS, *ought to be a man of liberal education, possessed of enlightened views, and of unimpeached integrity and humanity.* MAY THE MAGISTRATES OF MIDDLESEX CONSULT THEIR OWN HONOUR AND THAT OF THEIR COUNTRY, BY KEEPING THIS TRUTH STEADILY IN THEIR VIEW!

Spunging Houses

BESIDES THE PUBLIC prisons belonging to the country, there are numerous provisional prisons, kept by the sheriff's officers, called lock-up houses, where, for twelve or fourteen shillings a-day, a debtor may remain, either till he has found means of paying his debt, or finds it necessary to go to a public prison, when the writ against him becomes returnable. We have heard that great abuses prevail in these spunging-houses, and that many of the impositions practised in them ought to be rectified.

GENERAL OBSERVATIONS

IT WOULD BE wrong to quit the melancholy subject of prisons, without observing, that such is the bad arrangement of the laws between debtor and creditor, that ruin to both is greatly accelerated by the expensiveness of every step in the proceedings, insomuch, that not one debtor in ten ever pays his debt after he enters a prison.

If abuses ever exist in prisons, the fault is less in the keeper than in his superior officer, whose duty it is scrupulously to visit prisons subject to his cognizance, to redress all grievances, and to prevent the employment of improper persons. Nothing can be more absurd, than for superior officers or magistrates, to visit the cells and yards of a prison, in company with the keeper or his turnkeys: the fear of the future vengeance of these persons, always deters the injured prisoner from stating his grievances, and these sort of public visitations are a most ridiculous mockery of duty in those who hold the supreme jurisprudence of prisons. In performing this important duty, to apply Scriptural language, the officers, or magistrates, should exchange characters with their prisoners, and visit the prison which is under their superintendence, 'Like a *thief* in the night, and in an hour when no man expecteth them.'

No stranger who visits London should omit to view these mansions of misery, and it would be an interesting employment to the opulent and humane if they were occasionally to seek unfortunate objects in these prisons, upon whom to bestow their superfluous wealth. It has occasionally happened, that a single twenty pounds, judiciously disposed, has set at liberty ten fathers of families. Even the trifle thrown into the poor's-box, from its being properly distributed, gladdens the hearts of hundreds of distressed men, women, and children.

Magdalen Hospital, in St. George's-fields

THE OBJECT of this charity is the relief and reformation of wretched outcasts from society; and the principle on which it is founded, gives it a strong title to the countenance and favour of the public, and particularly of the female sex. No object can possibly be more worthy of *their* care, than the rescuing from the deepest woe and distress, the most miserable of their fellow-creatures, leading them back from vice to virtue and happiness, reconciling the deluded and betrayed daughter to her offended mother, and restoring hundreds of unfortunate young women to industry, again to become useful members of the community.

The Magdalen Hospital was opened in the year 1758. During the period that it has subsisted more than two-thirds of the women who have been admitted, have been reconciled to their friends, or placed in honest employments, or reputable services. A very considerable number are since married, and are, at this moment, respectable members of society; and could their names and situations be disclosed, (which for the most obvious reasons would be highly improper) the very great utility of this charity would appear in the strongest light.

A probationary ward is instituted for the young women on their first admission; and a separation of those of different descriptions and qualifications, is established. Each class is entrusted to its particular assistant, and the whole is under the inspection of a matron. This separation, useful on many accounts, is peculiarly so to a numerous class of women, who are much to be pitied, and to whom this charity has been very beneficial: viz. *young women who have been seduced from their friends under promise of marriage, and have been deserted by their seducers.* They have never been in public prostitution, but fly to the Magdalen to avoid it. Their relations in the first moments of resentment, refuse to receive, protect, or acknowledge them; they are abandoned by the world, without character, without friends, without money, without resource; and wretched, indeed, is their situation! To such especially, this house of refuge opens wide its doors; and, instead of being driven by despair to lay violent hands on themselves, and to superadd the crime of self-murder to that guilt which is the cause of their distress, or of being forced by the strong call of hunger into prostitution, they find a safe and quiet retreat, in this abode of peace and reflection.

The method of proceeding for the admission of women into this hospital, is as follows: The first Thursday in every month is an admission-day; when, sometimes from twenty to thirty petitioners appear, who, without any recommendation whatever, on applying at the door to the clerk, receive a printed form of petition, gratis, which is properly filled up. Each petition is numbered, and a corresponding number is given to the petitioner herself. They are called in singly before the Board, and such questions are put to them, as may enable the committee to judge of the sincerity of their professions, and to ascertain the truth of their assertions.

The treatment of the women is of the gentlest kind. They are instructed in the principles of the Christian religion, in reading, and in several kinds of work, and the various branches of household employment, to qualify them for service, or other situations wherein they may honestly earn their living. The chaplain attends them daily, to promote and encourage their good resolutions, and to exhort them to religion and virtue.

The time they remain in the house varies, according to circumstances. The greatest pains are taken to find out their relations and friends, to bring about a reconciliation with them; and, if they be people of character, to put them under their protection: if, however, the young women are destitute of such friends, they are retained in the house, till an opportunity offers of placing them in a reputable service, or of procuring them the means of obtaining an honest livelihood. No young woman, who has behaved well during her stay in the house, is discharged unprovided for. When discharged, they are for the most part UNDER TWENTY!

Phillips, THE MIRROR OF LONDON, 1804

OUR ASSOCIATION FOR IMPROVING the condition of the female prisoners in Newgate, was established in the fourth month of 1817, since which period we have had several hundred women under our care. The object which we have in view, is to provide for the clothing, the instruction, and the employment of these females, to introduce them to a knowledge of the Holy Scriptures, and to form in them, as much as lies in our power, those habits of order, sobriety, and industry, which may render them docile and peaceable whilst in prison, and respectable when they leave it. We may acknowledge, that when we commenced our undertaking, by instituting on the female side of Newgate, a school for the children, the reformation of these women, lost as they were in every species of depravity, was scarcely an object of consideration, much less of expectation. When we considered the innumerable disadvantages which stood in our way, the utmost we could hope for, was to prevent these miserable creatures from becoming worse and worse; – the inevitable consequence of their continuing in that unchecked condition of idleness, drunkenness, riot, and vice of every description. But, through the blessing of the Almighty, the result of even our earliest efforts exceeded our most sanguine hopes. We found in the prisoners, depraved and abandoned as they were, an ear open to hear us, and a heart still alive to every act of kindness. They felt the wretchedness of their lawless and dissolute mode of living, and they eagerly embraced the remedy.

The regulations proposed to them for bringing them into a state of order, sobriety, and good discipline, were unanimously accepted; and thus an easy way was opened for the commencement of the committee's labours.

Those labours indeed were pursued under great disadvantages. Ready as the prisoners were to receive the committee, they were nevertheless of the lowest and worst description, the very scum both of the city and country, filthy in their persons, disgusting in their habits, obscene in their conversation, and ignorant to the greatest degree, not only of religious truth, but of the most familiar duty and business of common life. Frequent communication was allowed them in the prison through an iron grating, with visitors of both sexes, many of whom were as vile and desperate as themselves. There was no possibility of general inspection, nor of any other separation of classes, than that of the tried from the untried; – and they were obliged to sleep promiscuously in large companies. To these difficulties, most of which still continue, may be added the dreadfully hardening effect of occasional executions, and the perpetual removal and change of prisoners.

Notwithstanding these evident disadvantages, the efforts of the committee soon began to produce a visible effect. It was truly surprising to observe how quickly these abandoned criminals conformed themselves to the standard held out to them by their visitors, and quietly submitted to the restraints of the new system. The scene is now totally changed. The prisoners are for the most part quiet and gentle in their demeanour, orderly and industrious in their habits, comparatively neat and clean in their persons; their very countenances changed and softened. We have often the satisfaction of continuing for hours together in their company, without witnessing any thing in their conduct or conversation which can offend our most delicate feelings. Many of them have acquired the art of reading, and have become adepts in knitting and needlework; and almost all, by some means or other, are busily employed.

The prison is visited daily by some of the committee; mostly by two members of it at once; and the visitors devote such a portion of their time to the object, as enables them to become intimately acquainted with the individual prisoners, and to gain a beneficial ascendency over their minds.

The women frequently come into Newgate covered only with rags, and in a state of deplorable nakedness. They are now plainly and decently clad, partly by the aid of their own earnings, and partly at the expense of the Association.

They are employed in patchwork, coarse needlework, spinning, and knitting. They receive a fair price for their work; and although their earnings are small, they are strongly recommended to reserve a part of them to accumulate for their benefit, against the period when they may leave the prison. Some of the women willingly adopt the plan: upon others, in consequence of their extremely destitute condition, we find it neither easy nor advisable to enforce a compliance with the recommendation.

We have two schools in the prison; one for children, with the formation of which the labours of the committee commenced; and another, established within the last few months, for grown-up women. Both schools are in an orderly, and therefore prosperous condition; and considerable numbers of women as well as children have already derived from them the benefit of some useful education. The governesses of these schools are prisoners, who, by their steadiness and perseverance in the work, have justified the confidence placed in them.

A complete system of superintendence, independently of that exercised by the committee, we deem to be of indispensable importance. Over every twelve or thirteen women we place a monitor, who is answerable for the women's work, and renders an account of their conduct. We have also ward's-women, who are responsible for the cleanliness of the wards; a yard-woman, whose business it is to maintain good order in the yard; and a nurse and assistant in the sick-room. These officers are all selected from the most orderly and respectable of the prisoners; and they receive, of course, some extra emolument. Thus the situations of monitors, school-mistresses, yard-women, &c. become objects of desire; and as changes frequently take place, they operate on the whole society as an excitement to good behaviour.

Besides these officers, there is a matron, paid partly by the Corporation of London, and partly by our Association, who superintends the whole arrangement, and constantly resides in the prison. The constant care and inspection exercised by this officer is quite necessary to the success of the system; and few can be better suited to the duties of the situation, than the person who was appointed to it at the first formation of the Association, and who still continues to fill it. We have lately appointed a sub-matron also, who assists in the duties of inspection, and keeps a little shop, furnished chiefly with groceries, for the use of the prisoners.

The women are assembled together in the committee-room, at a certain hour every morning, when the Scriptures are read to them, sometimes by the matron, but mostly by one of the visitors. After the reading is over, the company sits for a few minutes in perfect silence. These occasions are very often interesting and affecting: a striking solemnity prevails in them, and the feelings as well as understandings of these poor criminals are, through the divine blessing, open, much beyond our expectation, to the reception of religious truth. The words of Scripture, and the prayer or exhortation by which they are at times accompanied, appear to excite in the prisoners much tenderness of mind; and we have sometimes observed, during these periods of serious thought, that almost every eye in the room is wet with tears. It is very gratifying also to observe the order and quietness with which the women, on being dismissed, withdraw to their respective employments. We have only one thing further to mention in connection with this part of our subject: namely, that the inculcation of all peculiar tenets is strictly avoided. The essential doctrines and moral precepts of the

175

Gospel are alone held up to view. The Ordinary of Newgate, from whom we receive much kind and useful assistance, is frequently present at our readings; and the Bishop of London, when he visited the prison, expressed his entire approbation of the simple mode thus adopted of communicating religious instruction.

On the subject of the reformation actually effected amongst these once abandoned females, we feel much difficulty in making a precise statement. When we reflect on the deceitfulness of the human heart, and consider how generally these poor creatures have been strengthened in their natural corruptions, and habituated to every kind of depravity, we cannot be surprised at the disappointments which, in this respect, we often meet with; and we are thoroughly convinced, that nothing less powerful than the grace of the Supreme Being can produce in the objects of our care, a *radical* change.

We entertain a hope, grounded on frequent observation, that the truths conveyed to their understandings, by the daily reading of the Bible amongst them, are so impressed upon the hearts of many of them, that they will never be forgotten, but will influence the conduct of these individuals during the remainder of their lives. There are also certain broad and conspicuous facts connected with our institution, from which the committee may certainly derive substantial encouragement.

The first is, the change of manners and habits which has taken place amongst the prisoners *generally;* a change from drunkenness to sobriety, from riot to order, from clamour to quietness, from obscenity to decency. The second is, the honesty of these females, as it regards the property of any of the Ladies or of the Association. There cannot have been less than one hundred thousand articles of work manufactured in the prison since the formation of the Association; *and it does not appear that any one of these articles has been stolen.* Some time since, one of the visitors lost her purse in the prison; it was truly interesting to observe the gloom which this circumstance spread over our community of criminals, until, on the following morning, the purse, which had only been mislaid, was recovered by its owner. The third fact is, the small number of re-commitments; for out of the whole number of women, who have been placed under our care, *only four* have as yet returned to us, convicted of fresh offences. On being seen by us a second time, these criminals evinced a strong sense of uneasiness and shame.

Those who leave the prison and return to common life, are mostly more or less superintended by some one member of our committee. By too many of these persons, a continued good conduct has not been maintained; but of many others we have received very satisfactory accounts. Some are earning an honest livelihood in the bosom of their own families; others have obtained places as servants, and maintain the character of industry and respectability. There are several of the women, who, on their leaving the prison, have received small loans of money, and nothing can exceed the punctuality with which some of them make their weekly payments, in order gradually to discharge the debt.

We may conclude the statement of our case, with three general observations.

We wish to remark, in the first place, that in all our plans to promote the reformation of these females, it has been our constant endeavour to associate them with ourselves in the object. It is on this principle, that all the regulations which have been fixed upon for the management of the women, have first been submitted to their own consideration, and received their voluntary consent. Thus a useful principle of independence has been excited in their minds, and they have been stimulated by their natural feelings, to promote a work which they know to be in part their own undertaking.

We may observe, in the second place, that the change which has been wrought in the women, and which has excited so much surprise in the minds of some persons, may be attributed, under the blessing of a gracious Providence, not only to the system of employment and discipline to which these women are gradually accustomed, but more particularly to the effect of *kindness* upon those reprobates amongst mankind, to whom, alas! that kindness is altogether a novelty.

Thirdly, let it be noticed, that the means which are in the power of this Association, are also in the power of other persons in every part of the kingdom; and we venture to express our conviction, that the formation of similar Committees of Visitors, in connection with all our various prisons, would probably lead to results equally striking and equally satisfactory.

THE BRITISH MAGAZINE, 1819

A REFUGE FOR THE HOUSELESS

IT NOT BEING known on Monday that the Refuge for the houseless had been opened, few presented themselves for admission at the Workhouse. On Tuesday, however, placards announcing that the Institution had commenced operations were posted up in various parts of the Metropolis, and in the evening 70 wretched individuals, principally labouring men, were admitted.

MORNING HERALD, 4 *January*, 1821

WHAT IS EDUCATION? is a question we may not unfitly pause a moment to ask, in passing from the scholastic establishments – originated in an earlier – to those of the present time; for never before did the spirit of improvement, as now exhibited on all sides, promise to work more radical changes of principle, as well as of detail, in all our educational arrangements, because never before did the necessity of improvement appear to be so vitally connected with all the best interests of society. Education, then, is the art of drawing out or developing the faculties – of training human beings for the functions for which they are destined. 'Now,' we are told, 'in order to the perfection of an art, it must be founded on a corresponding science; and of nothing is this more true than of education. Before we can hope to mould a human being in a desired way, the nature of that being must be well known. The knowledge of man's nature is usually comprehended under three divisions: the constitution of his body (physiology); the constitution of his mind (psychology); his moral and religious nature (ethics and religion). If we suppose these branches of knowledge thoroughly investigated, they would furnish the solution of the two main points on which all questions of education turn: first, what are the dispositions and acquirements which it is most desirable to implant and foster? in other words, what is the end or aim that the educator ought to pursue? and second, what are the best means to attain that end.' Had the question, What is Education? been asked a quarter of a century ago, the enquirer might have been referred for an answer to one of the lowest class of schools, such as were to be found in all parts of the metropolis, from Westminster to Bethnal Green, the Dame Schools; there it might have been seen that education meant the keeping out of the streets the children of those who were not able, or who were unwilling, to take care of them at home, and that the educator was a person who, being utterly unfit for anything in the world else of any importance, naturally resorted to this. It is true that at such intervals of time as the mistress could spare from her needle-work, her washing-tub, or her culinary operations – perhaps even during these avocations – she taught reading and spelling; but her labours were more meritorious than successful. 'I have not,' said the Inspector of the British and Foreign Metropolitan Schools some few years ago, 'met with any of these children who could read.' Religious

178

instruction fared no better in their hands than secular.

'Of 540 schoolmasters and schoolmistresses (in Westminster and Finsbury),' says the Report of the Committee of the Statistical Society on Popular Education in London, 'who were asked whether they had any other occupation than their schools, 260 (or 48.1 per cent) answered that they kept a shop, or took in washing or needle-work, or had other laborious employment: the rest answered that they had no other occupation than their schools. But although they might not have any other ostensible occupation, it can hardly be supposed that they were in a condition to devote their whole energies to their scholastic duties. On the contrary, the mistresses of the common day-schools were sometimes young persons unable to go to service from ill-health, or desirous of staying at home with a sick or aged parent, and glad to add something to their means of maintenance: some, again, were mothers of large families; and, in all cases, even the most favourable, the female teachers, had their own household work to attend to. A very large portion of the masters of common day-schools, and still more of middling day-schools, were men in distressed circumstances, or who had, at some time or another, failed in trade, and seemed to have taken up the profession of schoolmaster as a last resource. The little estimation in which the proprietors, and more especially the mistresses, of schools held their profession, some quarter of a century ago, is shown by the circumstance, that whenever they had any other trade or calling, they entered that other trade by preference in the census schedules. Thus a woman who took in needle-work would be almost certain to describe herself as "dress-maker," not as "schoolmistress." On a reference to the census of 1841, it will probably be found that the figures under the head of "School-masters, &c." bear a very small proportion to the real number. An inspection of the census schedules of the above date leads us to believe that the same kind of prejudice holds good for and against many other professions also.' We need not ask what is education in the better order of day-schools, or in those old foundations which engaged our attention in the preceding chapter, since the views of their supporters and directors are those generally held, or at least acted upon, by society at large, that education means a certain amount of knowledge simply, which the schools in question, no doubt, give.

The incidental notices contained in the foregoing passages will have given our readers some slight notion of the general quality of the education formerly afforded for the children of the poor in the metropolis, as well as in all the other great towns of England;

the quantity demands a few words of direct notice. In 1837, an inquiry was instituted by the Statistical Society of London into the state of the parishes of St. Martin-in-the-Fields, St. Clement Danes, St. Mary-le-Strand, St. Paul, Covent Garden, and the Savoy; when the result showed that but one in fourteen of the population received any education at all; and that of those who did nominally receive instruction, one-fourth were the attendants merely of the dame and common day-schools. If we turn from the western to the eastern part of the metropolis, we find matters, as we might expect, worse. About one in twenty-one of the population seems there to be the average number of those who attended any sort of school. The Inspector of the British and Foreign Schools once remarked to the Committee for Education- 'I know a gentleman who recently visited the parish of Bethnal Green on Sunday; and he walked about the neighbourhood, and counted in different groups about three hundred boys, who were gambling on the Sabbath-day; and on inquiring of many of these youths, he ascertained that they could not read, and their appearance was very rough and degraded.' But really this is a trifle to speak of in connexion with the locality. A committee of its inhabitants[1] state that, 'after making allowance for such as must at all times be prevented from attending school, there are at this moment from 8,000 to 10,000 children in Bethnal Green alone, not only without daily instruction, but for whom no means of daily instruction are provided.' Spitalfields, Shoreditch, Whitechapel, Wapping, Newington, Bermondsey, St. George-in-the East, Christchurch (Surrey), – the same state of things characterized them all. Omitting from the returns for these parishes laid before the Committee the number of children attending the dame and common day-schools, which are intrinsically worthless, the result is that one in twenty-seven of the population alone was instructed.

J. Saunders, KNIGHT'S LONDON, 1842

PROGRESS OF THE LONDON REFORMER

IT IS A BLESSING that we have now no such street sights as bear-baiting. Bull-baiting, too, is gone: cock-fighting is no more seen. Pugilism has made a faint attempt at revival but we can part with that too. Are the people, then, to have no amusements accessible to all? We answer, let a wise government double and treble the class of healthful exercises and of intellectual gratifications. Give us new parks if possible.

C. Knight, KNIGHT'S LONDON, 1842

[1] Referred to in the Report of the Committee on Education, 1838.

180

NEW PIE-STREET, WESTMINSTER. – This school for the destitute was opened in January, 1840. It is designed for the children of persons inhabiting the most wretched parts of Westminster, many of whom are professionally beggars; others get their bread by selling various articles about the streets, and it may be stated, that three-fourths of them are probably deeply engaged in crime.[1] It was opened originally as a Sunday-school, but it was found 'that the good effects of the Sunday's teaching were done away by the mischievous influence of domestic habits and example during the week. With a view to remedy this, a day-school was formed in addition to the Sunday-school. A few persons hired a stable, by way of experiment, for three months; this was rudely fitted up as a school-room, when, to their surprise, no less than to their gratification, they had in a few weeks 120 children. For some time past there have been 170 in constant attendance, and at the present time the names of 200 and upwards are upon the books.' The accommodation afforded in this building is of the humblest kind. The tiled roof remains without a ceiling; the floor is only partially boarded; no ventilation could carry off the exhalations inseparable from such a spot. Nevertheless, it has satisfactorily served the purpose of the experiment that has been tried in it, and the attendance being steady and increasing, the influential persons who have interested themselves about the formation of this school, and contributed to its support, now contemplate an attempt to provide funds for a proper building.

The appearance of the children sufficiently denoted the class to which they belonged. Many were without shoes or stockings; almost all were of English parents; some were so ill-clad, that their naked skin appeared through many parts of their tattered clothing; all were equally dirty, the effect of extreme poverty or domestic depravity, and therefore its correction was very properly left to time. They were ranged on forms for want of desks, of which the confined space does not admit of a sufficient number. The master stated, that 'by talking kindly to the new-comers, they became after a little time willing to learn.' Eighteen out of seventy boys present could read fairly; thirty could write a word on their slates; six wrote on paper. They were classed in three divisions, by which the master was able to give his personal attention to each for

[1] Printed prospectus of the school.

nearly an hour during every school time, in addition to the scriptural lesson addressed to them all. They expressed pleasure when they found themselves learning something, and in some instances, when they were able to read, they were glad to be allowed to take home a book to read to their parents. Some good results are said to have been traced to occasions of this kind. It caused evident and very natural satisfaction to them to perceive that the darkness and confusion of ignorance was giving place in their minds to new ideas, and that instead of the neglect, perhaps aversion, to which their poverty had made them familiar elsewhere in the school, they met with nothing but kind treatment, and consideration for their deficiencies. No prizes or rewards, no gifts of clothing, or bribes in any shape for attendance, were allowed, neither were punishments, except of the slightest kind, and those seldom found necessary. The apparatus is scanty, consisting only of twelve Bibles, six copybooks, a few lesson-boards, and three slates. They had learnt to sing by ear a few songs and hymns. The school is dismissed daily with a short, impressive, and appropriate prayer. On passing out of the school many seemed pleased to exchange salutations with the master, and some advanced to him for a friendly shake of the hand. 'Christian instruction and Christian benevolence' had awakened their sympathies, and led them to feel that 'the world and the world's law' was not altogether against them. Some were the children of known thieves; some had themselves been habituated to thieving; others were orphans; and all belong to the poorest and most destitute grade of life. The instruction was of course gratuitous, and care was said to be taken not to abstract any from schools where payment was enforced, and also not to admit those whose parents could afford to send them elsewhere. It was found, indeed, that very few of the latter would, under any circumstances, allow their children to mix with the class of which this school is composed. It is stated, that before it was opened, no fewer than eighteen children had been transported from families now sending children to it, but that since it has been in operation there has not been one. 'The same benevolent persons[1] who have induced the children to attend the school, endeavour to secure that they do so regularly; they use every argument to persuade the parents to send them, and they call almost daily to satisfy themselves that the children are present; they also go to the residences of the absentees to ascertain the reason of their non-attendance.' A part of the stable was fitted up as an infant-school, and contains 100. They are taught in the method of the Infant-school Society,

[1] *Missionaries of the London City Mission.*

DISTRIBUTION OF CLOTHES BY
THE LONDON SAMARITAN SOCIETY

In chill November comes once more the bitter grip of cold and starvation, and then all the charitable agencies begin to be busy in the attempt to cope with the waves of misery that surge up on every side. One of the most valuable of these is the London Samaritan Society and Homerton Mission, which has its head-quarters in one of the poorest parts of the East End, and which provides food, clothes, and assistance of all kinds, besides thinning the ranks of the starving legions by taking troop after troop of them to Canada, and there procuring situations for them. A prominent part of its system of feeding the hungry is the sale of penny breakfasts of hot cocoa and bread throughout the winter, a great boon to those who would otherwise start with empty stomachs on their weary search for the work which too often cannot be obtained, as well as to those others who have work to go to, but no prospect of food till it is done. But the department of the Society's labours which brings the most genuine satisfaction is the feeding and clothing of children. The law which compels these little creatures to go to school does not take account of their bodily necessities, and vast numbers of them stand shivering in their places at nine o'clock in the morning without having tasted a mouthful, and were it not for the 'Samaritans' would starve all day. ILLUSTRATED LONDON NEWS, 1884 by a mistress who has received instruction at that establishment, and who had succeeded in making some progress with the different materials with which she had to deal. Twenty-four had learnt to read the lesson-boards; 8 could read in the Testament, and could repeat texts with accuracy and intelligence; 16 could work with the needle; a few were taught to scour and clean the school-room. They were furnished only with a few slates, on which some had learnt to write, and also a little ciphering. While the eldest class is at needlework, one of the number reads a story to the rest from a book. They were able to repeat hymns and other simple pieces of poetry, and took an interest in the scriptural and other subjects to which their attention was directed.

I made a subsequent visit to this school, with the view of endeavouring to satisfy myself by personal inquiries to what class of society the children attending it belonged; and whether it was probable that they were withdrawn to any extent from other schools, where payments were required and regularity of atten-dance enforced, and attracted to this by the circumstance of its being gratuitous, and by the absence of any attempt to make neatness and cleanliness of dress and person a rule and a character-istic. Sixty boys were present; and of these, taken *seriatim*, I obtained from the master the following particulars:

Seven had been at other schools, 4 of them at National, 3 at British; 2 of the former had been dismissed for irregularity of attendance: the parents of the remaining 5 were said to be too poor to dress them decently, and to provide the weekly payments.

Twenty-five were the children of parents in various grades, of very humble employment, having from 2 to 5 young children each, and subject to be frequently without work altogether. A few of these had 1 child at a school where payments are made, but were unable to afford to pay for more, or to procure proper and decent clothing for them.

Eleven had lost their fathers, and were supported by their mothers, having also from 2 to 4 children each to provide for: the mothers of three sold fruit in the streets; 2 more sold herrings and fire-wood. It was stated that the mother of one was often obliged to earn a trifling sum by her morning's occupation before she could provide a breakfast for her child, which she brought to him to the school; the child of another remained frequently at the school all day without food, the mother bringing some when she was able.

Five had been deserted by their parents, and were dependent on the sympathy of neighbours.

HOW IS LONDON TO BE UNITED?

A RHETORICAL CALL TO THE METROPOLIS

IN VIEW OF CERTAIN CIRCUMSTANCES

LIKELY TO ARISE

THERE MUST ARISE occasions, and that constantly, when London will be expected to speak *in the name of London;* unless our legislators intend the first City of the world to remain dumb in the future. There must arise occasions, and that constantly, when London will be expected to receive, to compliment, perhaps to entertain, some distinguished personage, foreign potentate, or exalted individual whom London may delight to honour. There must arise occasions, and that constantly, when London will desire to express its congratulations on some auspicious occasions; to celebrate some great event, social or political, or to confer a mark of distinction upon some philanthropist, or heroic commander returning home victorious, some benefactor, scientific or otherwise, of his species, some statesman who shall deserve well of his country. Is London, under all such circumstances, to be silent and passive? Is the Capital of the British Empire to be the only space in that Empire in which the nation cannot speak through its local representatives? Or will it be convenient or becoming (assuming that all London shall be incorporated) that a portion shall speak and act in the name of the whole. Either alternative is impossible. If Parliament shall add *ten* Municipalities to that *one* which exists, and no bond of Union be discovered or provided, then London must (assuming that unanimity exists) utter eleven voices, or tender eleven congratulatory addresses, or offer eleven receptions, or provide eleven entertainments; but what becomes of the voice of the Metropolis of England – unless it is intended that an aggregate meeting be held in Hyde Park? What will be the feelings or the perplexity of the unfortunate individual who shall have to make choice under such circumstances, or to run the gauntlet of all this Municipal kindness? Or assuming want of unanimity, what then? Again, is it not likely that occasions will arise when a Board of Works, however fairly constituted, will not be able to supply what aggregate London will need – a Chamber of Commerce, for instance – which must arise out of the organization of the Metropolis, even if it be not constituted at an earlier date? The City will be chiefly, but not by any means exclusively, interested in the questions constantly awaiting solution in such a Chamber.

Benjamin Scott, F.R.A.S.,

STATISTICAL VINDICATION OF THE CITY OF LONDON, 1877

PROPOSAL FOR A HOUSEHOLD SALVAGE BRIGADE

OR HOW TO DEAL WITH LONDON

BY GENERAL BOOTH

WHAT I PROPOSE would be to go to work on something like the following plan: –

London would be divided into districts, beginning with that portion of it most likely to furnish the largest supplies of what would be worth collection. Two men, or a man and a boy, would be told off for this purpose to this district.

Households would be requested to allow a receptacle to be placed in some convenient spot in which the servants could deposit the waste food, and a sack of some description would also be supplied for the paper, rags, &c.

The whole would be collected, say once or twice a week, or more frequently, according to the reason and circumstances, and transferred to depots as central as possible to the different districts.

At present much of this waste is thrown into the dust-bin, there to fester and breed disease. Then there are old newspapers, ragged books, old bottles, tins, canisters, etc. We all know what a number of articles there are which are not quite bad enough to be thrown into the dust heap, and yet are no good to us. We put them on one side, hoping that something may turn up, and as that something very seldom does turn up, there they remain. Crippled musical instruments, for instance, old toys, broken-down perambulators, old clothes, all the things, in short, for which we have no more need, and for which there is no market within our reach, but which we feel it would be a sin and a shame to destroy.

When I get my Household Salvage Brigade properly organized, beginning, as I said, in some district where we should be likely to meet with most material, our uniformed collectors would call every other day or twice a week with their hand barrow or pony cart. As these men would be under strict discipline, and numbered, the householder would have a security against any abuse of which such regular callers might otherwise be the occasion.

At present the rag and bone man who drives a more or less precarious livelihood by intermittent visits, is looked upon askance by prudent housewives. They fear in many cases he takes the refuse in order to have the opportunity of finding something which may be worth while 'picking up' and should he be impudent or negligent there is no authority to whom they can appeal. Under our Brigade, each district would have its numbered officer, who would himself be subordinate to a superior officer, to whom any

186

complaints could be made, and whose duty it would be to see that the officers under his command punctually performed their rounds and discharged their duties without offence.

Of the immense extent to which Food is wasted few people have any notion except those who have made actual experiments. Some years ago, Lady Wolseley established a system of collection from house to house in Mayfair, in order to secure materials for a charitable kitchen which, in concert with Baroness Burdett-Coutts, she had started at Westminster. The amount of the food which she gathered was enormous. Sometimes legs of mutton from which only one or two slices had been cut were thrown into the tub, where they waited for the arrival of the cart on its rounds. It is by no means an excessive estimate to assume that the waste of the kitchens of the West End would provide a sufficient sustenance for all the Out-of-Works who will be employed in our labour sheds at the industrial centres. All that it needs is collection, prompt, systematic, by disciplined men who can be relied upon to discharge their task with punctuality and civility, and whose failure in this duty can be directly brought to the attention of the controlling authority.

Much of the food collected by the Household Salvage Brigade would not be available for human consumption. In this the greatest care would be exercised, and the remainder would be dispatched, if possible, by barges down the river to the Farm Colony, where we shall meet it hereafter.

But food is only one of the materials which we should handle. At our Whitechapel Factory there is one shoemaker whom we picked off the streets destitute and miserable. He is now saved, and happy, and cobbles away at the shoeleather of his mates. That shoemaker, I foresee, is but the pioneer of a whole army of shoe-makers constantly at work in repairing the cast-off boots and shoes of London. Already in some provincial towns a great business is · done by the conversion of old shoes into new. They call the men so employed translators. Boots and shoes, as every wearer of them knows, do not go to pieces all at once or in all parts at once. The sole often wears out utterly, while the upper leather is quite good, or the upper leather bursts while the sole remains practically in a salvable condition; but your individual pair of shoes and boots are no good to you when any section of them is hopelessly gone to the bad. But give our trained artist in leather and his army of assistants a couple of thousand pairs of boots and shoes, and it will go ill with him if out of the couple of thousand pairs of wrecks he cannot construct five hundred pairs, which, if not quite good, will be immeasurably better than the apologies for boots which cover the feet of many a poor tramp, to say nothing of the thousands of poor children who are at the present moment attending our public schools. In some towns they have already established a Boot and Shoe Fund in order to provide the little ones who come to school with shoes warranted not to let in water between the school house and home. When you remember the 43,000 children who are reported by the School Board to attend the schools of London alone unfed and starving, do not you think there are many thousands to whom we could easily dispose, with advantage, the resurrected shoes of our Boot Factory?

This, however, is only one branch of industry. Take old umbrellas. We all know the itinerant umbrella mender, whose appearance in the neighbourhood of the farmhouse leads the good wife to look after her poultry and to see well to it that the watchdog is on the premises. But that gentleman is almost the only agency by which old umbrellas can be rescued from the dust heap. Side by side with our Boot Factory we shall have a great umbrella works. The ironwork of one umbrella will be fitted to the stick of another, and even from those that are too hopelessly gone for any further use as umbrellas we shall find plenty of use for their steels and whalebone.

So I might go on. Bottles are a fertile source of minor domestic worry. When you buy a bottle you have to pay a penny for it; but when you have emptied it you cannot get a penny back; no, nor even a farthing. You throw your empty bottle either into the dust heap, or let it lie about. But if we could collect all the waste bottles of London every day, it would go hardly with us if we could not turn a very pretty penny by washing them, sorting them, and sending them out on a new lease of life. The washing of old bottles alone will keep a considerable number of people going.

There is one material that is continually increasing in quantity, which is the despair of the life of the householder and of the Local Sanitary Authority. I refer to the tins in which provisions are supplied. Nowadays everything comes to us in tins. We have coffee tins, meat tins, salmon tins, and tins *ad nauseum*. Tin is becoming more and more the universal envelope of the rations of man. But when you have extracted the contents of the tin what can you do with it? Huge mountains of empty tins lie about every dust-yard, for as yet no man has discovered a means of utilising them when in great masses. Their market price is about four or five shillings a ton, but they are so light that it would take half a dozen trucks to hold a ton. They formerly burnt them for the sake of the solder, but now, by a new process, they are jointed without solder. The problem of the utilisation of the tins is one to which we would have to address ourselves, and I am by no means desponding as to the result.

I see in the old tins of London at least one means of establishing an industry which is at present almost monopolised by our neighbours. Most of the toys which are sold in France on New Year's Day are almost entirely made of sardine tins collected in the French capital. The toy market of England is at present far from being overstocked, for there are multitudes of children who have no toys worth speaking of with which to amuse themselves. In these empty tins I see a means of employing a large number of people in turning out cheap toys which will add a new joy to the households of the poor – the poor to whom every farthing is important, not the rich – the rich can always get toys – but the children of the poor, who live in one room and have nothing to look out upon but the slum or the street. These desolate little things need our toys, and if supplied cheap enough they will take them in sufficient quantities to make it worth while to manufacture them.

A whole book might be written concerning the utilisation of the waste of London. But I am not going to write one. I hope before long to do something much better than write a book, namely, to establish an organisation to utilise the waste, and then if I describe what is being done it will be much better than by now explaining what I propose to do. But there is one more waste material to which it is necessary to allude. I refer to old newspapers and magazines, and books. Newspapers accumulate in our houses until we sometimes burn them in sheer disgust. Magazines and old books lumber our shelves until we hardly know where to turn to put a new volume. My Brigade will relieve the householder from these difficulties, and thereby become a great distributing agency of cheap literature. After the magazine has done its duty in the middle class household it can be passed on to the reading-rooms, work-houses, and hospitals. Every publication issued from the Press that is of the slightest use to men and women will, by our scheme, acquire a double share of usefulness. It will be read first by its owner, and then by many people who would never otherwise see it.

We shall establish an immense second-hand bookshop. All the best books that come into our hands will be exposed for sale, not merely at our central depots, but on the barrows of our peripatetic colporteurs, who will go from street to street with literature which, I trust, will be somewhat superior to the ordinary pabulum supplied to the poor. After we have sold all we could, and given away all that is needed to public institutions, the remainder will be carried down to our great Paper Mill.

The Household Salvage Brigade will constitute an agency capable of being utilised to any extent for the distribution of parcels newspapers, &c. When once you have your reliable man who will call at every house with the regularity of a postman, and go his beat with the punctuality of a policeman, you can do great things with him. I do not need to elaborate this point. It will be a universal Corps of Commissionaires, created for the service of the public and in the interests of the poor, which will bring us into direct relations with every family in London, and will therefore constitute an unequalled medium for the distribution of advertisements and the collection of information.

One word as to the cost. There are five hundred thousand houses in the Metropolitan Police district. To supply every house with a tub and a sack for the reception of waste would involve an initial expenditure which could not possibly be less than one shilling a house. So huge is London, and so enormous the numbers with which we shall have to deal, that this simple preliminary would require a cost of £25,000. Of course I do not propose to begin on anything like such a vast scale. That sum, which is only one of the many expenditures involved, will serve to illustrate the extent of the operations which the Household Salvage Brigade will necessitate. The enterprise is therefore beyond the reach of any but a great and powerful organisation, commanding capital and able to secure loyalty, discipline, and willing service.

General Booth, IN DARKEST ENGLAND AND THE WAY OUT, 1890

THE LONDON

CRITIC

DURING THE NINETEENTH CENTURY

SELECTED FROM
CONTEMPORARY SOURCES
AND INCLUDING

GENERAL OBSERVATIONS UPON
THE MORALS AND MANNERS OF THE METROPOLIS
FROM PHILLIPS' 'PICTURE OF LONDON' 1804

ADVICE ADDRESSED TO A YOUNG MAN
CONCERNING THE PITFALLS TO BE AVOIDED IN LONDON
FROM 'BENTLEY'S MISCELLANY,' 1844

A DESCRIPTION OF THE ACTIVITIES
AND PERSONALITY
OF THE LONDON HOTEL-KEEPER
FROM 'BENTLEY'S MISCELLANY,' 1844

OBSERVATIONS UPON
THE EXTREME DEPRAVITY OF THE UNLICENSED CAB-DRIVER
FROM GARWOOD'S 'THE MILLION PEOPLED CITY,' 1853

CRIME AND DESTITUTION
IN THE LONDON STREETS
FROM LOUIS BLANC'S 'LETTERS ON ENGLAND,' 1866

AN ATTACK UPON
THE ACTIVITIES OF THE LONDON LANDOWNERS
FROM THE STAR 1888

TOGETHER WITH
OTHER BRIEFER REFERENCES
AND NOTICES

London is the richest of all cities, yet if a woman wishes to drive a mile she must get into a box on wheels, with doors no woman can open from the inside, and with seats which ruin her dress, with draughts which give her the face-ache, and with a floor like that of a badly cleaned stable.

SPECTATOR, 9 *February*, 1867

GENERAL OBSERVATIONS

UPON THE MORALS AND MANNERS

OF THE METROPOLIS

AT THE OPENING OF THE CENTURY

THE VICE OF GAMING seems to have reached its climax at the fashionable end of the metropolis: and though the magistrates have endeavoured to check its progress among the subordinate ranks of society, it is not only winked at, but tolerated, in the higher circles. The petty gambler who opens his shop of iniquity with the puny traffic of silver, is without mercy punished, and held up as an example of depraved manners; while the nobles hold their public clubs, gamble for thousands, out-face the magistrates, and defy the laws, with boldness and impunity! It is at the gaming-tables of the exalted, that our legislators, our nobility, our generals, and our country gentlemen, practice those very vices which the needy and the private individual is punished for attempting. It is at those ennobled midnight scenes of folly and rapacity, that the DEMON OF SUICIDE anticipates his triumphs over the weakness, avarice, and false pride, of mortals.

In an age when literature and the arts are so generally cultivated, when books are known to enlighten all classes of the people, it is singular that authors of acknowledged celebrity should so rarely mingle with the *soi-disant* patrons of the Muses. The cabinets of our statesmen are closed against the aristocracy of genius; the habitations of our nobles are also unfrequented by artists of every description, excepting as they are employed in the labours of their profession. Even in public they are seldom acknowledged; and if by chance they are recognized, it is by a nod of condescension, which mortifies and degrades the person whom it ostentatiously aims to distinguish.

It is not only the custom of the present day to exclude men and women of letters from the society of the high-born; that tyrannical species of oppression is also extended to painters, actors, actresses, and the most distinguished ornaments of science. The pictures of our most celebrated masters are purchased at an inordinate price; and considered as the embellishments of our most magnificent mansions. But the painter is unknown, excepting in his works! The actor, or the actress, is applauded in public, but, in private, they are seldom honoured by the most trivial mark of approbation. Our nobles make music their study; some of them are tolerable performers; they dedicate whole years to the acquirement of a moderate degree of skill; while their masters, who have attained the utmost point of perfection, are considered as unworthy of their friendship and society.

Among the many nuisances which disgrace the metropolis, there is not, perhaps, one which excites more horror than the frequency of public executions. The numbers of unhappy culprits that annually forfeit their existence by a violation of the laws, afford sufficient proofs that an ignominious death is no longer our safeguard. Six, eight, and ten criminals executed in the public streets, even in the heart of the metropolis, in the broad light of day, before the eyes of the multitude, scarcely excite emotion. The populace rather consider the new drop as a *raree-show*, than as the fatal instrument of termination to all earthly offences. Still more odious to the reflecting mind, is the gibbet, which disgraces our most public roads. In a polished nation, in the very sight of the humane and philanthropic traveller, a filthy, offensive example of public justice is displayed at the expence of public decency! The robberies frequently committed within sight of these hideous scarecrows, sufficiently prove that they harden, more than they deter, the thief; while, by exciting the attention of the traveller, they render him less guarded against the peril that awaits him.

A certain but false species of refinement seems now to pervade the various classes of the community. From the stall of the *poissarde* to the *boudoir* of the duchess, the tea-table is the magic circle of busy conversation. The nourishing diet which tended to promote the hardihood of our ancestors, is nearly exploded in the scenes of honest industry; while the enervating plant composes the beverage of men, women, and children. Time is also taught to display a change of his ancient occupation; and domestics are now sleeping, at the west end of the metropolis, at an hour when the courtiers of Harry the Eighth were preparing for their dinner. Novels are also universally read; the female apprentice longs for the hour of shutting shop, that she may indulge her fond imagination in the melting pages of a love-fraught tale; or teach her sensitive heart to palpitate with terror at the mysterious horrors of romantic improbability.

Refinement is also visible in the exterior ornaments of all ranks of people. Veils and parasols are universally adopted, even where the wearers, in other respects, are but meanly dressed. For the same reason opera-glasses, and even spectacles, are used by the clearest-sighted. Carriages are hung on springs which prevent the advantages of wholesome exercise; sedan-chairs convey the buxom woman of fashion through the fatiguing *routine* of morning visits; and, in some great families, annual sums are allowed to the male domestics, for the exclusive provision of powder, perfumes, hair-bags, *bouquets*, and silk-stockings! ·

The same species of eccentricity governs the household decorations. Sofas of down, pillows of perfume, artificial festoons of flowers, iced wines, and fruits out of season, mark the encroachments of elegant luxury. Yet it is to be admired that the bed-furniture of our most splendid mansions is chiefly composed of cotton: which, in a metropolis like that of England, cannot but be conducive both to cleanliness and to comfort. The velvet canopies of our ancestors were the repositories of dust, as well as the nurseries of obnoxious vermin: and the use of worsted hangings, among the lower classes, unquestionably, by harbouring such nuisances, promotes the contagion of diseases; while it forms an apology both for filth and idleness.

The various occupations assigned to the different sexes, in the metropolis, are now so preposterously absurd, that a reformation is become absolutely necessary. It is no uncommon thing to see men employed in the most effeminate branches of art and commerce; the artificial florist and the man-milliner are the most conspicuous in this class of innovators. Who that has feeling can endure the sight of young and artless females employed at all seasons, and in all weathers, to carry the bandbox from morning till night; exposed to the insolence of street libertines, and the perils of vicious example displayed by their abandoned associates, while, with unwet feet, the perfumed coxcomb measures the ribbon at home; or folds the gauze, as he lisps fine phrases to females of distinction! Even in our domestic establishment, the powdered lackey wastes his day in idleness, swings with listless, pampered ease behind the gaudy vehicle, or waits in the halls of ceremony, to usher in the morning visitor; while the laborious female is employed in washing, scrubbing, and other domestic toil! How is man degenerated! How much superior are the women of Britain at this period to the effeminized race of modern *petit-maitres*.

The architecture of the country has been gradually improving during the last sixty years. The heavy fabrics of brick-work, the uniform square mass of building, which were admired in the days of William and Mary, and which had succeeded the uncouth structures that braved both time and proportion since the reign of Elizabeth, now yield to the more light and finished elegance of Italian models. The introduction of Portland stone has tended very considerably to improve the beauty of English architecture; while the balcony window, and the Venetian gallery, by admitting a large body of air into the apartments, greatly contribute to the health of those who inhabit the metropolis. Dress has also been considerably improved by our intercourse with foreign nations. The women of this country now adopt a species of decoration at once easy and graceful. Nature seems to resume her empire, while art is hourly declining. The deformities of stiffened stays, high heels, powder, whalebone petticoats, and unmeaning flounces of many-coloured frippery, now yield to the simple elegance of cambric and muslin drapery; thus health is preserved by an unconstrained motion of the body; and beauty is ascertained by the unequivocal testimonies of symmetry and nature. *Phillips's* PICTURE OF LONDON, 1804

MR COBBETT ON LONDON

IF YOU COULD all of you come to London, and see the fine carriages in Hyde Park of a fine Sunday; if you could see the beautiful horses, the finely-dressed coachmen and footmen, pannels of the carriages shining enough to put your eyes out; if you could come and see all these, how surprised you would be; how little you would seem to yourselves! with silks and cambrics in your eyes, you would be ashamed to look down upon your own bodies, covered with your miserable smock-frocks. If any of the gods or goddesses who sit within the carriages were to condescend to cast a look at you, how ready you would be to snatch off your hats! Now, my good fellows, do see this matter in its true light. Nineteen twentieths, and perhaps ninety-nine hundredths, of all this dazzling finery has been taken out of your labour; for, even those of you who have been making hedges and ditches have been paying the taxes, which, being given to these people, enable them to purchase all these fineries; and, perhaps, one single equipage, amongst the many that you behold, has been the cause of filling a hamlet or a village with beggary and misery.

William Cobbett, TWO-PENNY TRASH, *May*, 1831

THE PURLIEUS OF LONDON

THE PURLIEUS of London are not to be described. The mind sickens in recalling the odious particulars of the immediate neighbourhood of the bridges. The hucksters and Hew furniture-shops, the enormous tawdry gin-palaces, and those awful little by-lanes, of two-storied tenements, where patent mangles are to let, where the street is encumbered by oyster-shells and black puddles, and little children playing in them. All these we passed: likewise grim-looking Methodist chapels, and schools, churches, and asylums innumerable. PUNCH, 1845

NOTES ADDRESSED TO A YOUNG MAN

CONCERNING THE PITFALLS TO BE AVOIDED

IN THE ENDEAVOUR

TO GET ON IN LONDON

IN MANY POINTS of view, London is not a desirable place to dwell; in many more it is positively objectionable; to the young and inexperienced, it is in almost every sense highly dangerous. Let the young man, excited by what he may have heard or read of London, and who finds in this, as in every other case, how greatly

'Distance lends enchantment to the view,'

pause before he swells the full tide of existence struggling in London, and hear what one old and experienced in its ways has to say.

Let him recollect, in the first place, that the London labour-market is always overstocked. We do not refer only to mere mechanic toil; professional skill is supplied in much greater abundance than is required by the demand.

The warfare of London life is a contest in which the raw recruit has all disadvantages to contend with, save youth, activity, and the desire of doing; he has to force a place among thousands, whose places are already settled and made fast; he has before him the difficult *premier pas qui coute*.

In the next place, everything in London is done by CONNEXION. Connexion necessarily implies introduction; not the ordinary letter of introduction which, when young and inexperienced, we carried with us to town by pocketsful, and found to introduce us to just – nothing at all; but the introduction of knowledge, experience, skill applicable in a high degree to some useful, practical purpose of life, for which men are wanted, and for which, when they *are* wanted, they are accustomed to be paid. Of course, if you go to London for the gratification of your vanity, or as an author, or other poor devil of that sort, or because you think yourself a clever fellow, or your parents think so for you, that is another affair. I only recommend you to take plenty of money in your pocket. I am now writing for the information of people who mean to do well, *in a well-doing way*, and not for clever fellows or madmen.

Another word in your ear; if, unhappily, you may be a bit of a scamp, which is not at all unlikely, don't be fool enough to imagine that you can go on with your pranks in London without paying the customary penalty. London is a wide place and a long, but rumour has wider scope and a longer tongue; nor is there any place I have seen (and this I tell you in good time) where *character*, in the most comprehensive sense of the word, is so vital, or where

197

the want of it is so fatal to a man's success as London.

Never imagine that London wraps a man's vices or follies all over like a cloak. It does no such thing. When we told you that there is freedom here from observation and neighbourly gossip, we told the truth; but the truth holds only of those who choose to live alone, and who, perchance, may have reasons for living alone. If you choose to be a recluse, or to lead the life of an outlaw, London is the greatest desert you can find, and a more secluded hermitage than mountains can bestow. So long as you pay your way, annoy nobody, and be not found out, you can go on as you please, and pursue, without interference or observation, your especial vice or dissipation.

If you are a man of any note, or striving to make a name for yourself, you will, of course, have enemies. Nowhere will you have more than in London, because nowhere is competition, not only for fortune, but for that bombastic bladder of wind, *fame*, more active and unremitting. Of course your enemies will have a fling at you; and your friends, if you have any, you may rest assured will be very little behind your enemies, in damning with faint praise, assenting with civil leer, and good-naturedly bringing on the *tapis*, which they are sure to do, whatever defects in your life or conversation their intimacy may have given them an opportunity of becoming acquainted with.

In London, especially among the enterprising and ambitious, we have often sighed over the hollowness and selfishness that exist even among friends. The field being unlimited, and the horizon boundless, each man's desires, each man's ambition, are perpetually extending from the centre of self. Nowhere is commendation less warm, nowhere encouragement less hearty, nowhere does failure or misfortune find less compassion, pity, or relief.

This all-absorbing selfishness is one of the greatest evils attending a London life; it re-acts upon yourself, hardens your heart in your own defence, and renders you incapable of those tender promptings of pity, and those delicate sensibilities of affection, without which, in our estimation, a man is no more than a two-legged rhinoceros.

But never for a moment imagine that without conduct, and its consequent character, you can get on in London. We hear it called a sink of vice, an abiding place of iniquity, and what not. Was it inquity or vice, we might inquire, that raised the stately frame of its social structure, where every gradation in the scale of life is preserved harmoniously and in order? Was it iniquity or vice that filled its streets and squares with spacious buildings, that spread over its face a thousand charitable institutions, that crowd the shipping of nations into its docks, that fill the hand of the artizan with work, and his home with fatness? No, sir, it is industry, enterprize, self-denial, economy, and credit. London is a place of work; and if you have not a turn for that amusement, – if you cannot take your pleasure out of a tough job, – if you cannot begin at the bottom, and fight your way to the top, try Yankee-land, or Australia, or Texas, or some other loose-living place, where you can work one day and sleep six. That will not do here, it *will* not do, sir, I assure you.

Vice hides in holes and corners, lurks about in the clouds of the night, gets transported or hanged, lives miserably on gin, and dies in the hospitals or the workhouses of London, just the same as it does in Little Pedlington; and London being larger than Little Pedlington by several chalks, more vice is concentrated here, and more concentrated is more seen. But it is by industry, and its consequences, not by good luck or accident, that the adventurer in London must stand or fall.

A young man coming here to learn or pursue a trade or profession, is exposed to terrible temptations. Vice is not here, at first sight, a monster of 'so hideous mien' as she appears in places less luxurious and less populous; she is disguised in every seductive form, decked out with every ornament, and apt to excite every passion. Mere moral education or the soundest principles will often fail to preserve youth from ruin. However well and creditably the business of the day may be gone through, there is the vacant evening to be passed, and the gloom of solitude to be dispelled; the theatre, the tavern, the concert-room, parade before his inexperienced eyes their dangerous attractions; he cannot mope in his chamber; he must go somewhere, and he can hardly go anywhere that he will not go wrong.

The want of *a home*, – the escape from the well-governed paternal roof to the chamber or the furnished lodging, is a trial too great for many. Many sink beneath it. If, therefore, we might offer our humble suggestion to the guardians of youth, – if we might be permitted to attempt to do a little good (without which twopence-halfpenny is too much for the best papers ever penned), we would advise, that the first establishment of youth in London should be, if possible, in a well-governed family, where the graces and amenities of life might not be forgotten in its business, and where a refuge might be found in the social circle from low pursuits, mean habits and dangerous dissipations.

Never be seduced into those learned professions by what you hear of poor men's sons rising by dint of naked talent to the highest offices in the state; don't be quoting Lyndhurst, and Brougham, and Johnny Campbell, and two or three more; quote, if you can, the number of poor men's sons, who have followed the profession of these eminent men, and have struggled, and starved, and died, and have left neither name nor money behind them. Do the same in the church, and the army, and then calculate *your chances* like a man of this world; open an account of profit and loss, and determine your choice as the *balance* will direct you.

To those great lotteries–ten thousand blanks, and twenty prizes–are attracted all the clever fellows, the great geniuses, the vanity-struck children of vanity-struck parents; these you have to compete with, and I ask you, is vanity or ambition, a solid, rational ground whereon to determine your aim, that is, your happiness or misery of life?

To the professions also are attracted the sons of wealthy people, who can, as far as money will do, purchase their promotion; these, also, are your competitors, and very formidable ones they are; they can wait; while the grass is growing they are eating their oats, while perhaps you are starved out of your profession just as you may begin to hope to make a living of it.

If your choice is independent, let *utility* determine your choice. London is a commercial place – a place of buying and selling; a big shop, where everything is always wanted, and where everything is always to be had; by going into the shop with a good character, and a good, but not *too* good education, you will get a living; nay, more, if you take advantage of the Londoners in their weak points; if you *live* hard, as well as work hard, you may save money, and in the meanest occupation make yourself more or less independent.

Nobody can beat a Londoner at work; he puts his head, as well as his shoulder to the wheel; like a night cab-horse he is always in harness, never has time to get tired, or fall down; but he is too fond of spending his money, and my hair has often stood on end at the indifference with which he flings down his hard-earned shillings for glasses of brandy and water. Work hard, and save your money.

Another thing – *begin low;* this is a wrinkle worth putting in your eyebrow. London is a place where promotion goes by seniority; by time and patience you succeed to the death-vacancies; but you will find yourself very much mistaken if you think you are to jump over people's heads. John Bull is a fellow who will not let you take him by the horns; your plan, therefore, is to begin by holding on at his tail, and by patience, tact, and courage, you may in time get on his back and ride him anywhere.

John Fisher Murray, BENTLEY'S MISCELLANY, 1844

A DESCRIPTION OF

THE ACTIVITIES AND PERSONALITY

OF THE LONDON HOTEL-KEEPER

A LONDON HOTEL-KEEPER is usually some nobleman's maître d'hôtel, or groom of the chambers, made an honest man of in holy matrimony by her ladyship's confidential maid or consequential housekeeper; who sees fit to invest their united earnings, perquisites, pickings (and no matter for the *last* word of the indictment), in furnishing and burnishing some roomy mansion of the West-end, too much out of repair to serve as a private residence, for 'noblemen and gentlemen,' by dint of showy calico, stained mahogany, and half the brass of a whole Birmingham foundry, thereby entitling themselves to demand, as the rent of every separate suite of apartments, as much as the whole house would have cost, if hired for the season. Prodigious four-post beds, groaning with draperies and fringes, destined to accumulate dust, soot, and their living concomitants, for ten years to come, are erected in the sleeping rooms, with as much labour and ingenuity as are employed to run up a three-storied house in the suburbs; – with rickety wardrobes and washing-stands, picked up at sales, or purchased at cheap and nasty furniture-brokers in the Blackfriars Road – whereof it is hazardous to open a drawer, not only on account of the effluvium of the boots or shoes of antecedent occupants, exhaling therefrom, but from the certainty that three-quarters of an hour must be wasted in shoving, sidling, and swerving the said ill-fitting drawer back into its original position. For the same reason, the prudent frequenter of a London hotel is careful not to draw down a blind, – premonished of the impossibility of ever getting it up again; – or to *un*draw a curtain, from the clouds of dust instantly circulating through the apartment. Moreover, the blind so displaced, or the drawer thus incautiously drawn forth, is sure to be thereafter recalled to his memory by a heavy charge in the bill for repairing the same; such as

			s.	*d.*
To man one day repairing Blind	.	.	17	6
Cords, &c., for	do.	.	.	6	10
Easing Drawer, strained	.	.	.	10	6
&c.	&c.	&c.		

To touch the handle of a China or marble vase is equally rash. Pooloo's cement will not last for ever; and when you find the vase standing handle-less before you, like a door from which the Marquis of Waterford has wrenched off the knocker, but with evident symptoms of the glue of preceding fractures and mending, be assured that you will have to book up the full original cost of the 'handsome vase of Nankin dragon China, finely enamelled,' which was purchased damaged at a sale ten years before, and has been successively paid for by twenty victims, inhabitants of the same unlucky suite.

The first object of the hotel-keeper, after fitting up his rooms with gaudy papers, showy carpets, and trophies and cornices of gilt brass, is to purchase vast services of iron-stone China, and plated dishes and covers, which, on an emergency, when the families under his roof are sufficiently frantic or unfortunate to dine at home, he fills with parsley beds; in the centre of which, by dint of much examination and a powerful glass, are discover-able a thin slice of cod or salmon, or a couple of fried whitings, – a few chips of cutlets, – a starveling cat roasted rabbitwise, or a brace of sparrows deluged in parsley and butter, designated in the bill of fare as pigeons or chickens. The second course will probably be a bread pudding, formed of the crumbs that fall from the rich man's table, or a tart, apparently composed of buff leather and mouldy fruit, having been allowed to mellow for a week in the larder, in company with the Stilton cheese. But then it is served on a lordly dish, and covered with an embossed cover.

Such is the moderate *mem.* of an hotel dinner. Its gaudy days are still harder of digestion. The business of the host is to purchase the worst viands, to be charged at the highest rate; – meagre poultry, – stale vegetables, – doubtful fish. It is not he who has to eat them; and the fashion of the olden time, of allotting to the hotel-keeper his share of the repast, was surely so far advantageous, that it operated like the functions of the carver and taster at a royal banquet, as a security against being poisoned in cold blood.

On the Continent, hotel-keepers are uniformly in the pay of the police: in London they exercise an inquisition of their own, of which the waiters are the familiars. Not a note or letter passing through the hands of these worthies but assumes a rotundiform shape, from the bulging torture to which it has been subjected; and every night when the head-waiter carries in his daily evidence to the book-keeper of the wine, soda-water, and other extras con-sumed by the inmates, he accompanies his account with particulars of visits and visitors, letters, and duns, which, by dint of prying into drawers and loitering on staircases, he has been able to amass, mismatch, and weave into a tissue of scandal. He 'has his sus-picions that the gentleman in black whom Sir Thomas calls his solicitor, and to whom he is never to be denied, is no better than a

THE INSISTENT DUNNER

'I shan't go out of this room till I gets my money!'

Robert Seymour, SCENES IN LONDON, 1834

money-lender; and as to the handsome Colonel, who calls every day at five, being a cousin of the gay widow on the second-floor, – fudge! he knows better!'

A most important branch of consumption in London hotels consists in the potables; whereas during his aristocratic service, the hotel-keeper, when waiting at table as maître d'hôtel, used to hear frequent remarks that nothing was more injurious to wine than the rumbling of carts and carriages over the cellars, he provides against such an injury by laying in no stock to be rumbled over, but contents himself with having in his fresh-brewed port or sherry from an advertising shop in the Strand, per cart, weekly, or per barrow, daily. It is only his soda-water, which, being uninjurable by street rumbling, he keeps by him from year to year. To ask for French wines in the common run of London hotels, is an act of intrepidity only excusable in such as are scientifically curious in chemical compounds.

It is scarcely possible for the frequenter of a London hotel to remain unconscious or insensible to his fellow lodgers. Thanks to the thinness of partitions and a common staircase, he soon becomes painfully and reluctantly participant in their family secrets. A sympathy is inevitably begotten. He not only dines upon their fillet of veal minced, or sends his fillet to them minced in his turn, – he not only resigns himself to their potatoes mashed, or inflicts upon them his drum-sticks of a chicken in a fricassée, but is unpleasantly apprised by oral tradition when the ears of her ladyship's daughters have been boxed, or when her ladyship's self has been subjected to conjugal objurgation for the price of her box at the opera. He is kept awake till daybreak morning after morning, by two charming sisters prattling their mutual confidences in an adjoining room, while curling their hair after their balls, or by the sobbings of the lady's-maid above, after a universal blowing-up. By the scent of the towels placed on his stand, screwed into a dry linen press, instead of being subjected to the washing-tub between service and service, he is able to ascertain whether his fair neighbours prefer eau-de-cologne to lavender-water, or indulge in Barège's baths; and without exercising the baleful scrutiny of the head-waiter, is compelled to know *when* they are waiting for the milliner, or when they are 'at home only to the Captain.'

The Hotel-keeper, meanwhile, snugly ensconced in his private room, like the spider which, retired into a corner of its web, watcheth the simple flies gradually entangling themselves in its meshes, takes care only that the brills which figure on the table shall figure in the ledger as turbots with lobster sauce, and that the heads of the woodcocks and pheasants shall be kept sacred as that of the Baptist, in order to consecrate dishes of hashed mutton, to appear hereafter as *salmis de bécasse* or *de faisan*, – writing down tea*s* for tea, – coffee*s* for coffee; and every Sunday afternoon converting in the standing accounts the every 5s. into 5s. 6d., and every 2s. into 2s. 9d., by the addition of a curly tail above or below zero.

Be it admitted, however, that, with all their penalties on purse and comfort, the London Hotels afford a satisfactory relief from the cares of temporary housekeeping. Deaths, marriages, or baptisms in country families, involving brief and sudden visits to the metropolis, would otherwise be scarcely carried on with decency. The happy wretch relieved from an East India voyage, – the *un*happy one subpœnaed for a Chancery suit, sees in the gas-lamps blazing over the door of a fashionable hotel a beacon of hope. The courteous welcome of the cringing host and bowing waiters appears auspicious; everything comes with a call. In one's own domicile, a ring of the bell is an injury inflicted on one or more members of the establishment, who have nothing to gain by answering the summons. But in an hotel, every ring secures expenditure, varying from twelve-pence to a guinea. Coals, a sandwich, nay, even a candle to seal a letter, becomes an item to swell the amount of the narrow folios arrayed against the peace and purse of the lodger. Satisfy your conscience, therefore, oh ye who sojourn in hotels, that, give as much trouble as ye may, none but yourselves are the worse for it. A hotel-keeper knows how to value a perpetual ringer of bells!

But for this highway and byway robbery during the harvest of the season, how, in fact, could the hotel-keeper enable himself to get through the autumn, when his house might just as well be closed as Her Majesty's theatre, for any moneys taken at the doors? Saving painters and white-washers, not a soul crosses his threshold; unless, now and then, some skinflint of a dowager, on her way through London from Broadstairs to her dower-house in some midland county, who, saving for the sops of her parrot, and the board of her maid, expends not a sixpence in the hotel; – or a brace of tender parents conveying some young hopeful to Eton, and spending four-and-twenty reluctant hours in London, for a preparatory visit to the dentist. For six or eight months, in short, every caravanserai stands empty as the heads of the honourables and lordlings who frequent it in May and July; its kitchen-range rusting; its curtains and hangings being required to 'down with their dust,' instead of its customers. Nevertheless, rent, taxes, and waiters, must be paid as regularly as if the hotel-keeper were not taking his pleasure at Ramsgate, and his customers at three hundred miles distance. And how is this to be effected, we should like to know, unless by charging three-and-sixpence a bottle for soda water while the sun shines, and the town is crowded?

But if there be something unspeakably dolorous and funereal in the autumnal aspect of a fashionable hotel, there are few things pleasanter than its June countenance. When the summer days are at their longest, the hall is thronged with liveries of every dye, and a perpetual discharge of milliners' baskets and jewellers' cases encumber the lobby. The landed gentry who arrive in town from their country seats at an hotel, come for the express purpose of spending and enjoying. The business of their visit to the metropolis, is pleasure. They come to present their daughters, attend levees and drawing-rooms, get invited to the Court balls, if they can; and if not, content themselves with Almack's and the Caledonian. Such people take wondrous delight in a new bonnet, are much addicted to fine feathers and French ribbons; frequenting the Zoological Gardens on Sundays, and the Horticultural for every fête. Not over-choice in their diversions, they amuse themselves without intermission. Operas, plays, balls, parties, dinners, déjeûnérs, exhibitions, fill up the round of every merry, busy, bustling day. Carriages stand at the doors of the hotels for shopping, at an hour when the doorways of private mansions are fast asleep. There are pretty sure to be children in the house, and Punch or the Fantocini to be stopping before it: not an itinerant band but strikes up its Strauss and Labitsky under the windows of the London Hotel. There caper the dancing dogs – there stalk the conjurors on stilts – there tumble the tumblers! Small change is never wanting at the receipt of custom of an hotel; and of these itinerant showmen, some secure retaining fees from the nursery, others gratuity of dismissal from the drawing-room. Throughout the morning, one mountebank succeeds to another; and the moment the lamps are lighted for dinner, the *cornet-à-piston* and his fellow conspirators against public comfort, commence their clangour; while, clustered before the door, stand family coaches, chariots, and well-appointed cabs, waiting to convey the country-cousin to the opera, or French play. Oh! joyous merry-go-round of pleasure life! Oh! laborious toil and labour of the do-nothings! where are you more actively, or more brilliantly carried on, than in the neighbourhood of the fashionable hostels.

Albany Poyntz
BENTLEY'S MISCELLANY, 1844

A COMPARISON OF THE REALITY
OF MONEY-GETTING
AND THE IDEALITY OF EMPTY BELLIES

LONDON HAS LONG been familiar with wealth; it is not a new thing, and therefore it is not either too closely hoarded, or too recklessly speculated upon. There is a judicious enterprise in the use of it here, unknown to poorer places recently made rich. The employment of wealth in London is eminently an employment of action, a turning of it from one thing to another; a system of golden irrigation, where the speculator directs his current in whatever direction he sees a reasonable probability of increased production through its fertilizing agency.

To trace the origin and growth of the enormous wealth of London would be to write a history of the progress of civilization over the world. But it is to nature, or, to speak more properly, to the inscrutable wisdom and bounty of Providence, that we must come at last for the true explanation of *real* wealth before enterprize, industry, and commerce diffuse it, and before *credit*, like a magician, enables its ready, secure, and uninterrupted transfer from place to place, and from hand to hand.

Yet how seldom does the pride of artificial wealth condescend to fix its speculation upon its humble origin!

We talk magniloquently of our enterprize, our industry, our trade, our commerce, our national faith, our commercial credit; yet, after all, whence comes our *real* wealth, our *means* of money, our *great first cause* of commercial life? Buried i' th' earth, after all, is our Bank of England; silks, satins, gold, jewels, wines, spices, – whence are they but dug out o' th' earth, disguised as iron, coal, copper, lead, tin? Who made these things, or what is man, that he should pride himself on what the God of nature has bounteously been pleased to bestow upon him, and to withhold from others? Natural wealth is at the root of our grand superstructure of riches; it is the stone-and-lime foundation of our lath-and-plaster opulence. All that we have done is but the inevitable consequence of our inexhaustible resources, and is as little subject for the exultation of pride as if a man, whose careful father bequeathed him a strong box well filled with uncoined gold, should regard himself as its creator, because he deposits his gold at a banking-house, taking in exchange portable, marketable, and convenient securities.

Truly it is no wonder that, as we go on and see these things, and wonder, our favourite exclamation should have become a cuckoo

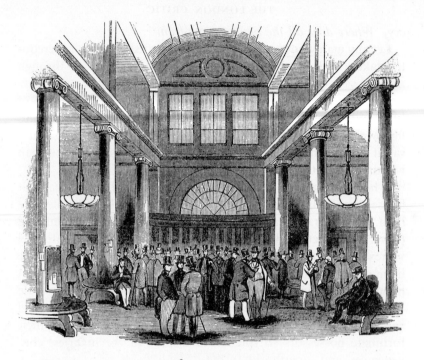

THE STOCK EXCHANGE

The House was bound to draw a distinction between business and gambling, and he held that the practices of the London Stock Exchange constituted the most mischievous form of gambling known upon the earth. Speculators, it was said, ought to be responsible for the consequences of their own acts, but if it was true —and it had been shown to be—that they had not fair play, a strong case had been made out for Government interference. But it was urged that such interference would cast a gloom over the parties which were the subject of it. So also would the capture of banditti in Calabria cast a gloom over banditti in Sicily. But it would not, therefore, be regretted by honest people. Another argument used in opposition to the motion was that if the Committee were appointed, a great deal of distressing evidence would be adduced; but that was in his view an argument in favour of inquiry. His hon. friend the Secretary to the Board of Trade said that the fault lay with the class known as promoters; but was it not a fact that a fictitious value was too often given to loans and shares by the Stock Exchange? The practice of gambling in stocks was by courtesy called specula- tion, but in fact it was gambling, and that of the very worst description.

Report of a speech made by Mr. Bentinck in the House of Commons, March 1877, on the motion of Mr. Yorke for the appointment of a Royal Commission to inquire into the origins, objects, present constitution, customs and usages of the London Stock Exchange, and the mode of transacting business therein.

208

cry, '*Where does all the money come from?*'

Let any man who thinks we are drawing at sight upon his credulity take a walk to the westward of the Edgware Road, through HYDE PARK GARDENS, SUSSEX GARDENS, and all the other gardens of great houses, as far as Westbourne, where the deluge of brick and mortar pauses, arrested by winter's icy hand, only to flow with accumulating westward force in spring and summer, and say if this extension of the habitations of men is not more than wondrous – if it is not *miraculous*.

When we consider that each and every one of the myriads of houses that spring up, mushroom-like, are let as soon as they are built, or sooner, we cannot but be astonished at the accumulated power of attraction drawing so many human creatures into one vortex of busy life. When we reflect, moreover, that each of these habitations presupposes an income and an expenditure, from hundreds of thousands a-year, downwards in the descending scale of wealth to hundreds without the thousands, we cannot but feel bewildered at the magnitude of resources, permitting to their fortunate possessors so splendid a display of the luxuries, conveniences, and superfluities of life.

Yet this, which everybody sees, this exterior distant view of magnificence to which our vision is confined, is the least of that which sets us wondering. External show is not only not desired by almost every class in London, but it is really as much as possible avoided. They have that within these crowded palaces that passeth show; their luxuries are domestic, their pleasures self-contained, their splendour secluded; yet even that which they cannot hide, that which is all that we are permitted to behold, that which peeps from their doors and windows is enough to bewilder us and to confound.

London is a world of money-getting; we have long since scouted the romance of naked toes, the ideality of empty bellies, and the dignity of the philosopher without twopence; we have established a standard of respect altogether different from that of monarchies, autocracies, and republics; Rothschild is a Crœsus, a Midas, who turns everything he touches into gold; our 'merchant princes' swarm like honey-bees on May Day; we boast every gradation of marquis, earl, viscount, baron, in our commercial world, only we represent their rank by substantial things, not shadowy sounds; we have great men, good men, responsible men, all measured by a thermometer inserted in the breeches-pocket.

John Fisher Murray
BENTLEY'S MISCELLANY, 1844

A CIRCUMSTANCE which has given a very evil name to cabmen in general, on the part of the public, is a class of men, who, though dismissed from their body, are yet much mixed up with it. These are cabmen who have been deprived of their licenses for drunkenness or bad conduct. The law, in kindness to the licensed cabdriver, allows him, in case of need, to employ an unlicensed substitute for a period not longer than 24 hours, and by this means these discharged men get to drive licensed cabs. This is especially the case with the cabs of what are called 'long-day men,' – for the cab-drivers are divided into several distinct classes, according to the number and character of the hours during which they ply for hire, and there are, consequently, the long-day men; the morning men, who are out from 7 a.m. to 6 p.m.; the long-night men, who are out from 6 p.m. to 10 a.m.; and the short-night men, who are out from 6 p.m. to 6 a.m. The long-day men (and it is they chiefly who are employed by the contractors) leave the stables at 9 or 10 in the morning, and do not return home till 12 or 1, or, in some cases, till 4 or 5, or even later, the next morning. These hours are more than one man can well endure, and he is therefore glad to avail himself of the help of the unlicensed driver towards the end of the day, or while he is at his meals. There is also employment for these discarded men on the stands, and the licensed driver is ordinarily glad to give them the sixpence they expect from each driver for cleaning up the cab and harness, which otherwise he would have to do himself. Their mode of life is correctly sketched in the following extract: – 'They usually loiter about the wateringhouses (as the public-houses are called) of the cab-stands, and pass most of their time in the tap-rooms. They are mostly of intemperate habits, being usually "confirmed sots." Very few of them are married men. They have been what is termed fancy men in their prime, but, to use the words of one of the craft, "got turned up." They seldom sleep in a bed. Some few have a bed-room in some obscure part of the town, but the most of them loll about and doze in the tap-rooms by day, and sleep in cabs by night. When the watering-house closes they resort to the night coffee-shops, and pass the time there till they are wanted as "bucks."[1] When they take a job for a man they have no regular agreement with the drivers, but the rule is that they shall do the best they can. If they take 2s., they give the driver 1s., and keep 1s. If 1s. 6d., they

[1] Name given to cab-drivers deprived of their licenses.

usually keep only 6*d*. . . . The regular driver has no check upon these men, but unless they do well they never employ them again. . . . In the season some of them will make 2*s*. or 2*s*. 6*d*. a-day by rubbing up, and it is difficult to say what they make by driving. They are the most extortionate of all cab-drivers. For 1*s*. fare they will usually demand 2*s*., and for a 3*s*. fare they will get 5*s*. or 6*s*. If the number of the cab is taken, and the legitimate driver summoned, the party overcharged is unable to swear that the legitimate driver was the individual who defrauded him, and so the case is dismissed. It is supposed that the "bucks" make quite as much money as the drivers, for they are not at all particular how they make their money. The great majority – 99 out of 100 – have been in prison, and many more than once, and they consequently do not mind about re-visiting gaol. It is calculated that there are about 800 or 1,000 bucks hanging about the London cab-stands, and these are mostly regular thieves. If they catch any person asleep or drunk in a cab, they are sure to have a dive into his pockets; nor are they particular if the party belong to their own class, for I am assured that they steal from one another while dozing in the cabs or taprooms.'[1] The number of these unlicensed men has since materially increased, about 700 cab-drivers having been deprived of their licenses last June (1852), on the ground of character. These are now added to the 'bucks.' And it illustrates how many even of the licensed cab-drivers were little or nothing better than the others. A class has always existed of a very profligate character, chiefly those employed in night work, although some *respectable* contractors employ a portion of their cabs at night, simply because they have not room in their stables for all their stock during the same hours. The bad class are willing to 'sign' for a higher amount than others, and they resort to every discreditable purpose to make it answer, especially seeking for fares from swell-mobsmen, drunken, and profligate persons. They also ordinarily live with bad women, who by their sin assist in their support.   *Rev. J. Garwood*, THE MILLION PEOPLED CITY, 1853

WEALTH AND POVERTY

THE NATION is accustomed to the instantaneous creation of wealth. It is the maxim of their economists, 'that the greater part in value of the wealth now existing in England, has been produced by human hands within the last twelve months.' Meantime, three or four days' rain will reduce hundreds to starving in London.

R. W. Emerson, ENGLISH TRAITS

[1] *Labour and the Poor*. Letter lxxii, *Morning Chronicle*, 3 October, 1850.

AN ATTACK UPON
LONDON GIN PALACES

IN LONDON, IT IS WELL KNOWN, that such is the external splendour of a great number of the houses, in which ardent spirits, chiefly, are retailed, as to have obtained for them the appellation of gin-palaces. These, by continually striking the eye of the passenger, remind him that within them is to be obtained every variety of intoxicating liquor; and if he should have acquired an appetite for such liquor, they thus keep it in such a state of continual excitement, as nothing can allay, but such oft repeated indulgencies, as necessarily end in actual drunkenness. It may be said that the decorations of such houses are only calculated to draw customers to them in particular, and not to increase the general sale of intoxicating drinks; but whatever may be the design of the owners or occupiers of gin-shops, in expending large sums of money on their external embellishments, the effect of such attractions is an awful increase of drunkenness; for they can do no otherwise than operate as a continual stimulus to an intemperate appetite; and many instances have been recorded, in which, both men and women, have been known to be enticed by them into one den of pollution after another, until, overcome by the poison they have taken, they have sunk down in a state of helplessness and insensibility.

But the decorations of the gin-palace are not the only enticements, by which the wretched victims of intemperance are lured onwards to their utter destruction. In many public houses, both in town and country, clubs are established by their landlords, professedly to promote good fellowship, or to advance some political, or benevolent object, but in reality to ensure the sale of a certain quantity of liquor; and thousands of labourers and mechanics, as well as of individuals in superior situations, have found the day, when they first became members of such clubs, to be the commencement of a career of intemperance, which was marked throughout by misery, and which ended in everlasting death.

In some public houses are to be found the attractions of music and dancing, and in others is the charm which draws the gambler. – The former enticements have the greatest influence upon the young; and many, who in the unsuspicious days of youth, have been lured to such houses by the sound of the viol, the merry song, and the lightsome dance, have at last found them to be the habitations of demons, and the highways which lead to ruin and despair.

But there is another class of persons, interested in the drinking

THE LURE OF THE GIN PALACE

'I want a small glass of Gin.'
'Old Tom, Sir?'

Robert Seymour, SCENES IN LONDON, 1834

of these liquors, whose influence must not be overlooked. It is well known to be the practice of many tradesmen, to calculate on securing the favour of their customers, by presenting them with bottles of wine, glasses of spirits, or cups of beer, rather than by their own honourable conduct, and business-like demeanour. All such persons will be likely to regard an interference with the artificial drinking usages of society, as aiming a blow at the profits, by which they subsist; and therefore, should they not present an attitude of bold defiance to such interference, they will, in all probability, be found on the side of those, who are for things remaining as they are, which is nothing better than maintaining a position, so far unfriendly to the cause of temperance, as to be, in reality, opposed to it.

From a temperance tract published circa 1855

OBSERVATION BY A FRENCH WRITER
ON CRIME AND DESTITUTION
IN LONDON STREETS IN 1862

IN SPITE OF ITS so much vaunted police, London has ceased to be a city which one can traverse at night, with mind at rest and the hands in the pockets. For some days past, nothing has been talked of but of men being suddenly half strangled and robbed in the streets. This is what happened about a week ago, at eleven o'clock at night, quite close to my own house; and the case might be cited of a member of the House of Commons who, only a short time since, had reason to think himself fortunate that he was not killed outright in Pall Mall, a very fashionable quarter, and, what is more to the point, exceedingly well lighted at night. Is it the Exhibition that is answerable for this revival of ugly adventures? It might be thought so, did not the provinces furnish to paragraphists their contingent of lugubrious stories. But there, also, the slime very frequently rises to the surface. News have in succession reached us of unaccountable deaths, of mysterious crimes. Suicide, too, is on the increase.

In the newspapers 'The Suicide Mania' has become a stereotyped heading! For some months past, it has fallen to the lot of Baron Lionel Rothschild to receive, day after day, letters of the most threatening character. 'We must have £500. If you are of opinion that your life is worth more than a miserable sum of £500, let us know it through the newspapers. If not – a word to the wise. A. B.' The chapter of misdemeanours would be a long one, were I to enter into details and omit nothing; which proves, be it parenthetically observed, that even in England one does not live in the best of possible worlds – much less elsewhere.

From crime to indigence, the transition is as natural as that from effect to cause. Now, England, which is the land of extreme wealth, is also the land of extreme poverty. I doubt if there be anywhere on the globe a spot where one is exposed to see poverty under a more hideous aspect, or in a state of more profound degradation.

I was going one day, in company with a friend, a Frenchman like myself, along that magnificent road which is bordered on one side by a row of houses that are palaces, and on the other by Kensington Park, to my thinking, the finest in the world. It was Sunday. At that hour there were few persons about, and, where we were walking, not a soul. I am wrong; for we observed at a short distance, dragging himself on in front of us, a man – was it a man? Yes, it was a man, a being who, as we are told, was made in the image of God! He was half-naked, and his feet were quite bare. He was evidently not aware that we were following him. Suddenly he stopped, his eyes fixed upon something that was there, not far from him, on the ground, in the dust. He was moving towards that something, when we overtook him.

On seeing us, he sat down on the edge of the pathway, as if he were tired, and we passed him. 'Did you notice that poor wretch with the haggard countenance?' asked my friend. 'Yes,' I replied, 'it is the spectre of hunger.' – 'Do you know why he stopped?' – 'Why?' – 'He stopped to pick up and eat a piece of orange peel.' – 'Nonsense!' – 'You shall see.' We turned sharp round. My friend was right. You guess the rest.

'A beggar's comedy!' will, perhaps, be the exclamation of people who think themselves strong-minded. And if it were so? What a state must that be which could force a human being to act such a comedy, under such circumstances, with the frame of a skeleton and a face – that face will never fade from my memory; I see it now.

Nor is this, one of those exceptional cases the import of which may well be questioned. Of course, such encounters are rare in the handsome and wealthy quarters of the town. But to surprise want in its squalid undress, it is by no means necessary to beat it up in its lowest haunts. At certain periods of the year it takes care to come before you, as if in a hurry to meet your eye.

Louis Blanc
LETTERS ON ENGLAND, 1866

HOW VENTURE OUT IN THE EVENING? Such is the strange question which everyone asks himself here, so much do nocturnal violences multiply! When I say everyone, I mean those who have neither carriages nor lackeys, I mean the unfortunate foot passengers, doubly unfortunate if they wear on their backs a decent coat and are suspected of carrying a watch.

In truth, the evil has now attained the limits which raise the fact of street robberies to the importance of a State question. London is becoming in the middle of the nineteenth century what the forest of Bondy has ceased to be. Is not that an incredible thing? Nevertheless, it is so. Yes, in this city full of life, full of men; in this city, in which, more than in any other place in the world, civilisation has accumulated its resources and means of defence; in this city which has hitherto been usually regarded as one that had solved, by a skilful and admirable police organization, the problem of public security, every one has come to ask himself, at nightfall – and Heaven knows that it falls soon enough at this season of the year! – if he shall venture upon this great enterprise. Go out a-night! Farewell to theatres! Farewell to clubs! Farewell to pleasure! Farewell to business! as soon as daylight has ceased to illumine the streets and render them safe.

And yet – would you believe it? – quite recently, at two o'clock in the afternoon, a woman passing along one of the most thronged and most fashionable quarters of London was stopped at the entrance of a livery-stable yard, by a wretch who, in spite of the piercing shrieks of his intended victim, dragged her into a corner where two other individuals were waiting – the one a male, the other a female! They were engaged in tearing from this poor woman her earrings and were preparing, for want of something better, to cut off her hair in order to sell it, when some passers-by came up. This, I repeat, took place in the heart of London at two in the afternoon. What think you of such an incident? Will you have a further example of audacity? A Frenchman was walking in Hyde Park a little before four in the afternoon, when four of the amiable individuals known as garrotters threw themselves upon him. But see what it is to have to do with a Zouave! Our friend happened, fortunately, to be one, and also a thorough master of the science of the *savate*. In the twinkling of an eye he stretched on the ground, bruised and stunned, two of his assailants, while the other two took to flight. So far, so well. But not everybody has served in the Zouaves. It is a curious circumstance, too, that when, on coming out of the Park, the conqueror related to the first policeman he saw, what had happened to him, the latter exclaimed: 'But how imprudent of you to cross the Park at four in the evening!' Just as one would say to a traveller robbed in Germany: 'But how imprudent of you to pass through the Black Forest at night-time!'

You may well think after all this, that gas-lamps are a useless luxury. The old saying, 'The wicked fear the light,' has decidedly ceased to be true in London. I do not know if these garotters aim at heroism and get up an enthusiasm in braving the gallows; but it is very clear that in warring upon the passers-by, they appear to choose in preference the battlefields where they are perfectly in sight. They afraid of gas! Bah! It is in Oxford-street, – ay, in Regent-street, if it be necessary, that they will show us what they can do, by taking our purses after they have broken our heads.

For, one point especially worthy of note, is the peremptory fashion in which they go to work. Formerly, they cried to you, 'Your money or your life!' and that was something, because, by offering the one you could save the other. But it is now that Sganarelle would exclaim, if he had to speak of these gentry: '*Nous avons change tout cela.*' Their line of reasoning is: 'Let us try to take the life, the purse will come of itself.' And in order to have both in this order of succession these disagreeable wags make use of a weapon, which is called in English a 'life preserver!' The traditions of politeness attached to the names of Cartouche and Jose-Maria are, you see, either lost, or judged out of harmony with the progress of modern ideas. They begin by knocking you on the head, content to despoil you afterwards.

But do not imagine that these crimes proceed from solitary, individual inspirations. No. The cases brought every day before the Police Courts prove that the robbers and murderers who, at this moment, are desolating and terrifying London, are massed in regiments, obey the rules of discipline, act in troops and in virtue of skilful combinations. The principle of association is at the bottom of it all.

Superfluous to add, that there is a general and profound sensation. These successive outrages are the subject of every conversation; the papers are black with narratives which reveal their number and abominable character; journalists write upon this gloomy subject endless tirades; every morning the authorities are interrogated as to the measures they have taken, or intend to take, and as they make no reply, the public anxiety becomes more and more lively.

On the other hand, far from being alarmed by the noise that is made about their atrocious achievements, the malefactors seem to derive from it twofold audacity. The more they are denounced, the more are murderous assaults multiplied. Nor is this all. A sort of fearful contagion appears to be spreading abroad. Crime is developing itself into a mania. The other day two little girls of eleven years of age were taken up for having essayed the art of garotting upon an old woman – alluding to which, *The Times* exclaims with bitterness: – 'An infant Roscius may be a very interesting object on the stage; but it is a sort of phenomenon which it is not good to encourage in criminal matters.'

Where will the development of this moral pestilence be stayed? The newspapers, not feeling themselves bound to any sort of circumlocution, call upon the citizens to provide for their own safety, by furnishing themselves with good firearms, and by taking the firm resolution of making use of them on the first opportunity. They record, with much eulogium, all that attaches to the right of legitimate defence energetically exercised. They encourage every one to dispense justice on his own account, until society finds means of defending itself collectively. There are thus individuals in whom apprehension has at last turned into fury. Yesterday, an Englishman of my acquaintance, a man of great courage, but also very eccentric, confessed to me that being tormented by a morbid impatience to prove to these daring ruffians that honest men did not fear them, he had purchased a revolver with which he wandered about at night along the streets reputed the most dangerous, in the hope of being attacked, and of being able to make an example. To such a pass have things come!

Louis Blanc, LETTERS ON ENGLAND, 1866

A JOURNALISTIC ATTACK
UPON THE LONDON LANDOWNER

THE POOR OF London are robbed by the Corporation and the Companies of the education and the food which were left to them by the pious and the humane of past generations. The other boards of London are in no way representative; and are besides incompetent, extravagant, in many cases corrupt. To rich and poor alike, the present system of government is inimical leaving the greatest and wealthiest city in the world the most helpless and impotent

ROBBERY WITHOUT VIOLENCE

'I say Old Boy, lend us a sovereign will ye? I'm rather short tonight. I'll give it you again.'

Robert Seymour, SCENES IN LONDON, 1834

before any emergency. One fall of snow, a single fog reduces London to chaos. Recently the want of proper control, especially over the police, has encouraged on the part of the Government and of the police authorities, a system of violent suppression of popular rights which should be impossible in a self-governed city.

Nor are public bodies the only ones from which the Londoner demands and requires relief. The gas companies and the water companies, the market monopolists – all find in the Londoner a helpless victim. Against all these things we proclaim war. We hope to bring before the people and the representatives of London, a policy that shall form a distinct radical policy for London itself. It will mean the election of all public bodies by adult suffrage, the diversion again to the poor of every single penny left to them; cheap water, cheap gas, cheap meat, cheap fish, the exposure, conviction and punishment of every thief of the public funds.

No measure of Radical reform for London can be complete which does not provide for the taxation of ground rents. It is as flagitious as it is absurd that while two millions worth of house property should bear all the heavy taxation of a city, as huge and therefore as expensive to govern as a nation, four millions worth of ground rents should remain free from one penny of this vast expenditure. It will be our duty to rouse the London householder and lodger from the perilous apathy on this great question; to show them how the fierce and desperate struggle they have to wage for life and bread in the terrible rush of this crowded city is rendered still fiercer and still more desperate by needlessly heavy rents and needlessly heavy taxation – to direct their anger from the visible taxpayer to the invisible landlord who skulks and robs behind – and to bring home to their imaginations the great fact that the spectre of land monopoly does not stop short at the house of the farmer or the agricultural labourer, but penetrates to the inmost recesses of their own dingy streets and their own wretched attics. For of the pounds that the small tradesman pays for his house, of the shillings the seamstress pays for her room, at least a quarter goes to the idle and opulent landowner that lives in luxury and ease in the West-end of London. Cheap houses for the tradesman, cheap rooms for the artisan of London, is, then, another plank in our platform.

Extract from the editorial in the first number of the STAR
17 *January*, 1888

THE LONDON

CELEBRITY

DURING THE NINETEENTH CENTURY

SELECTED FROM

CONTEMPORARY SOURCES

AND INCLUDING

PEN-PORTRAITS AND ANECDOTES

LITERARY, MUSICAL, THEATRICAL AND SOCIAL

REMINISCENCES

BY

JULIAN CHARLES YOUNG A.M.

FROM 'A MEMOIR OF CHARLES MAYNE YOUNG, TRAGEDIAN,' 1871

JAMES ROBINSON PLANCHÉ

FROM 'RECOLLECTIONS AND REFLECTIONS,' 1872

HENRY FOTHERGILL CHORLEY

FROM 'AUTOBIOGRAPHY, MEMOIR AND LETTERS,' 1873

ALSO

POLITICAL REMINISCENCES AND PORTRAITS

BY GEORGE SMALLEY

LONDON CORRESPONDENT, 'NEW YORK HERALD'

FROM 'LONDON LETTERS,' 1890

TOGETHER WITH

OTHER BRIEFER REFERENCES

AND NOTICES

But great as was the confidence of Mr. Brunel, and the resources which he must have felt he had within himself, ready for every difficulty, it is impossible that he could ever have anticipated the all but overwhelming amount of obstacles that he actually experienced, principally from the character of the soil, and the extraordinary influence which the tides exerted even at the Tunnel's depth.

T. *Saunders*, KNIGHT'S LONDON, 1842

IN 1812, KEMBLE revived and adapted, with a splendour, in those days unparalleled, the play of 'Julius Cæsar.' No piece was ever more effectively cast: Brutus had for its representative, John Kemble; Cassius, Young; Anthony, Charles Kemble; Casca, Terry; First Citizen, Simmons; and Portia, Mrs. Siddons. I have never spoken with any one fortunate enough to have seen that play rendered, as it then was, who has not admitted it to have been the greatest intellectual recreation he ever enjoyed.

It was really difficult to believe that one had not been transported while in a state of unconsciousness, from the purlieus of Bow Street and the vicinity of Covent Garden Market, to the glories of the Capitol, and the very heart of the Julian Forum; so complete, in all its parts, was the illusion of the scene. When but six years old, I saw the play on the first night of its representation; and I was allowed to see it again in 1817, with the same cast, minus Mrs. Siddons. And, although I was then but eleven, the impression left upon my mind has never been effaced. If it appear a thing incredible, that any play, however well put on the stage, however gorgeous its accessories, and however spirited the acting, should have left definite and durable traces on the brain of a child of such tender years, it must be mentioned that he had not only inherited a turn for the stage, but had read and re-read the play in question over and over again, had committed its chief speeches to memory, had rehearsed them by heart, and often represented the characters before small but select audiences, composed of all the squabs, bolsters and pillows available in the house. The consequence was, that when I saw 'Julius Cæsar' for the second time, I attended to the stage-business. and more particularly to the by-play, with an intentness and inquiring interest, which it amuses me, even now, to recall. Owing to my reproductions, in the privacy of my little bedroom, of the effects I had seen and heard on the boards of the great theatre, I was tolerably qualified, in my own opinion at least, to distinguish between the comparative merits of each actor. And there was, perhaps, nothing which elicited more of my boyish admiration, than the fidelity with which the players of prominent parts indirectly indicated the peculiar idiosyncrasies of each (and this too before they had opened their lips) by their very mien and movement. Ordinary actors, on first making their entrance in the second scene of the first act, march in procession towards the course, with all the precision of the Grenadier Guards, stepping

223

in time to the martial music which accompanies them. And, even on the part of leading actors, I have noted a tameness of deportment (as stilted as if they were automata) until speech has stirred them into action.

In the play I am writing of, as then enacted, one would have imagined that the invariable white toga, beautiful as it is when properly worn and tastefully adjusted, would have rendered it difficult, at first, for any but frequenters of the theatre to distinguish, in the large number of the *dramatis personæ* on the stage, John Kemble from Daniel Terry, or Charles Young from Charles Kemble. Whereas, I feel persuaded that any intelligent observer, though he had never entered the walls of a theatre before, if he had studied the play in his closet, would have had no difficulty in recognizing in the calm, cold, self-contained stoical dignity of John Kemble's *walk*, the very ideal of Marcus Brutus; or in the pale, wan, austere, 'lean and hungry look' of Young, and in his quick and nervous *pace*, the irritability and restless impetuosity of Caius Cassius; or, in the handsome, joyous face, and graceful tread of Charles Kemble, – his pliant body bending forward in courtly adulation of 'Great Cæsar,' – Mark Antony himself; while Terry's sour, sarcastic countenance would not more aptly portray 'quick-mettled' Casca, than his abrupt and hasty *stamp* upon the ground, when Brutus asked him 'What had chanced that Cæsar was so sad?' In support of my theory of the mute eloquence of gait and movement, Charles Young was wont to speak in terms of almost wanton admiration, of a bold point he saw Mrs. Siddons once make, while playing the comparatively inferior part of Volumnia for her brother's benefit.

In the second scene of the second act of 'Coriolanus,' after the victory of the battle of Corioli, an ovation in honour of the victor was introduced with great and imposing effect by John Kemble. On reference to the stage directions of my father's interleaved copy, I find that no fewer than 240 persons marched, in stately procession, across the stage. In addition to the recognized *dramatis personæ*, thirty-five in number, there were vestals, and lictors with their fasces, and soldiers with the spolia opima, and sword-bearers, and standard-bearers, and cup-bearers, and senators, and silver eagle-bearers, with the S.P.Q.R. upon them, and trumpeters, and drummers, and priests, and dancing-girls, etc., etc.

Now, in this procession, and as one of the central figures in it, Mrs. Siddons had to walk. Had she been content to follow in the beaten track of those who had gone before her, she would have marched across the stage, from right to left, with the solemn,

224

stately, almost funereal, step conventional. But, at the time, as she often did, she forgot her own identity. She was no longer Sarah Siddons, tied down to the directions of the prompter's book: she broke through old traditions – she recollected that, for the nonce she was Volumnia, the proud mother of a proud son and conquering hero. So that, when it was time for her to come on, instead of dropping each foot at equi-distance in its place, with mechanical exactitude, and in cadence subservient to the orchestra; deaf to the guidance of her woman's ear, but sensitive to the throbbings of her haughty mother's heart, with flashing eye and proudest smile, and head erect, and hands pressed firmly on her bosom, as if to repress by manual force its triumphant swellings, she towered above all around, and rolled, and almost reeled across the stage; her very soul, as it were, dilating, and rioting in its exultation; until her action lost all grace, and, yet, became so true to nature, so picturesque, and so descriptive, that pit and gallery sprang to their feet, electrified by the transcendent execution of the conception.

Young

DR CHALMERS, THE EMINENT PREACHER

IN HEIGHT AND breadth, and in general configuration, he was not unlike Samuel Taylor Coleridge. I have, since I knew Coleridge, sometimes thought, that if Chalmers' head had been hidden from sight, I could easily have mistaken him for that remarkable man. His face was pallid and pasty; and, I rather think, showed slight traces of small-pox. His features were ordinary; his hair was scanty, and generally roughed, as if his fingers had been often passed through it; his brow was not high, but very broad and well developed.

There was one feature in his face which struck me as so very peculiar, and I may say, anomalous, that I have often wondered never to have heard or read any comment upon it from others: I allude to his eye. The eye by its mobility, its power of expressing the passions, and the spirit it imparts to the features, is usually considered as the index of the mind. Now, I never beheld so mute, impassive, inexpressive an eye as that of Chalmers. It was small, gray, cold, and fishy. When, either in preaching from the pulpit or lecturing in the class-room, he was excited by his subject; when his heart grew hot within him, and the fire burned; when the brilliancy of his imagery and the power of his phraseology carried the feelings of his auditory away with all the impetuosity of a torrent; – *his* eye remained as tame and lustreless as if it had been but the pale reflex of a mind indifferent and half asleep! *Young*

FOR MANY YEARS the combined attractions of John and Charles Kemble, Mrs. Siddons, Miss O'Neil, Charles Young, and William Macready, had rendered Covent Garden the favourite resort of the lovers of the legitimate drama. To so low an ebb indeed was the exchequer of the rival house reduced, that its committee gravely entertained the idea of closing, till 'the tide in their affairs' should turn and propel them on to better fortune, when Edmund Kean's sudden and unparalleled success revived their hopes and refilled their coffers. Of course, in proportion, as the star of one house was in the ascendant, that of the other began to wane. A great part, therefore, of the receipts of Covent Garden were diverted from their ordinary channel, and, in consequence, its managers, on purely financial grounds and in self-defense, felt constrained to reduce the salaries of the principal actors on their staff. It was in the prosecution of this intention that in 1822 they proposed to reduce Young's salary from £25 a week to £20, and from three months' vacation for provincial tours to two. If one cannot blame the managers for consulting their own interests, neither can one wonder that the actor, in the prime of life, and in the zenith of his fame, should have refused to accept diminished remuneration for his labour. This questionable economy proved eventually as detrimental to its authors as it was beneficial to its subject; for no sooner was it known that Charles Young's connèction with Covent Garden was at an end than the manager of Drury Lane waited on him and offered him £50 a night for nine months (three nights a week); three months' leave for country work, and a clear benefit, provided that he would consent to play with Kean, in certain stipulated pieces, exchanging parts with him on alternate nights. Thus Kean was to play Othello, and Young Iago; and the next night Young Othello, Kean Iago. The same rule was to hold good with regard to every piece in which their joint talents were to be exercised. One hundred and fifty pounds per week was a wonderful rise from twenty-five; and proved a bait too alluring to resist. Bills were posted all over London, advertising the early appearance on the same boards of the two men who had long been regarded as the representatives of two opposite schools of art. The widespread excitement produced, few but the *habitués* of the theatre in those times could believe. Places were secured at the box-office five and six weeks beforehand, and the comparative merits of the two histrionic athletes were canvassed at fashionable tables with as

226

much vivacity and warmth of temper as the far more important political questions of the hour. Kean was the Coryphæus of a new school, Young of the old. Kean was supposed to have had the mantle of George Frederick Cooke descend upon him, Young was looked on as the disciple of Kemble. Kean's forte was known to be the vigorous delineation of the stronger passions – jealousy, malignity, revenge. Young's *specialité* was allowed to be dignity, pathos, and declamation.

On the very first night of their appearance in the same play I was present; on the very last night of their playing together I was present; and in every piece in which they acted together I have seen them. On each and every one of these occasions I should find it difficult to determine which carried off the palm. The writer of the last published life of Edmund Kean has been pleased to write in terms of measureless contempt of Charles Young's powers as an artist. He has a perfect right to his opinion; but I doubt if his hero, had he been alive, would have indorsed it, or admitted either the justice or the good taste of his criticism. And I venture to think so for this reason. Both the rival candidates for histrionic fame were engaged on terms of perfect equality. Each received exactly the same salary, each was in turn to play the same parts: and had the manager thought there was such vast disparity between the qualifications of the two candidates, he would never have given both the same terms. If Kean had considered himself so far superior to Young in public estimation, he would have been indignant at his receiving the same salary as himself, and would have expected his name to be printed in the bills in larger characters than his rival's. To show that Kean did not think as meanly of Young as his secretary-biographer seems to have done, I may mention that on the first night of their playing together, while Young was in his dressing-room receiving congratulations on his success from 'troops of friends,' Kean was storming about in search of Price, the manager, and vowing that he would not give up Othello the next night to Young. On Price's telling him that he was bound by the terms of his agreement to do so, he exclaimed, in violent anger, 'I don't care! if he plays after me the same part I have just played, I will throw up my engagement, and you may seek your redress in a court of law.' On Price's trying to pacify him, and asking him what had caused him to think so differently in the evening from what he had done in the morning, he said, 'I had never seen Young act. Every one about me for several years has told me he could not hold a farthing rushlight to me; but he can! He *is* an actor; and though I flatter myself he

227

could not act Othello as I do, yet what chance should I have in Iago after him, with his personal advantages and his d——d musical voice? I don't believe he could play Jaffier as well as I can, but fancy me in Pierre after him; I tell you what,' said he, 'Young is not only an actor, such as I did not dream him to have been, but he is a gentleman. Go to him, then, from me, and say that, if he will allow me to retain Othello, and to keep to Jaffier, if I succeed in it, I shall esteem it as a personal obligation conferred upon me. Tell him he has just made as great a hit in Iago as I ever did in Othello.'

Young was anxious to oblige Price, knowing how seriously refusal on his part would affect the interests of the treasury, and unhesitatingly complied with Kean's request.

The great effects which Kean produced upon his audience were the spontaneous effusions of real genius. Young's happiest hits were the result of natural sensibility, quickness of apprehension, and study. Kean dazzled his audience by coruscations of fancy, and the vivid light which he shed on passages of which the meaning was obscure. Young hardly ever astonished; but, with the un-prejudiced, rarely failed to please.   *Young*

WORDSWORTH IN LONDON

WHEN WORDSWORTH was in London, during the height of the season, he was aware it would be expected, after his appointment to the laureateship, that he should present himself at one of the *levées* of the sovereign. As his means had never been large, Samuel Rogers told him that, as he should never go to court again, he was welcome to make what use he could of his clothes, bag-wig, sword, buckles, etc. By the help of a little tailoring he was enabled to attend the *levée*. When it was over and they were walking together up the footway (under the gardens of the Arlington Street houses) which leads into Piccadilly, and is directly opposite to Stratton Street, Wordsworth's attention was arrested by the prepossessing looks of a little girl, who was sitting on the grass alone. He stopped and talked to her, and being well pleased with the ingenuous answers that she gave him, he put one hand on her head, and with the other dived down into the recesses of his coat-pocket, and drew forth a little copy of his minor poems, telling her to look at him well, and note his person; to be sure also to observe well the time of day, and the spot; and to recollect that that little book had been given to her by the author, the celebrated William Wordsworth!

N.B. – The narrator of the story was Rogers himself.

                    Young

AN ANECDOTE CONCERNING

PAGANINI

AND THE DENTIST, CARTWRIGHT

I HEARD PAGANINI. The *furore* there has been about this man has bordered on fatuity. The prices paid for seats to see and hear him have been fabulous.

On the principle, I presume, of 'omne ignotum pro magnifico' the great violinist has shut himself up in close confinement since his arrival in this country, and refused to receive any one but his *entrepreneur* and his dentist. In both cases the relaxation of his rule was a matter of necessity, and not of choice. With the gentleman who had engaged him he could not avoid making certain pre-liminary engagements for his *début*. Still less could he dispense with the help of the dentist; for, as nature had failed him in her sup-plies, art was called in to aid him. Sorely discomfited, on arriving in London, by the state of his teeth, and hearing that among the brethren of the profession, Cartwright was *facile princeps*, he sent for him; and after having such teeth as he had filed and scraped, he asked him if he could undertake to supply him with such as he had not by the following Thursday. The commission was unhesi-tatingly accepted, and faithfully executed. On Paganini's asking Cartwright what he owed for the service he had rendered him, the dentist assured him that he felt honoured by having had it in his power to administer to the comfort of such a man; and that the only remuneration he could think of claiming at his hands would be his giving him the pleasure of his company at dinner the next day.

After such extraordinary liberality, Paganini felt that he had no alternative but to accept the invitation so gracefully given. It happened that ten minutes after the great lion of the hour had left the door in Burlington Street, the Duke of Devonshire entered it, by appointment, to have his teeth looked at. Cartwright asked his noble patient in the course of his manipulations if he had yet been fortunate enough to hear Paganini. The Duke said that he had tried to get him at Devonshire House, but had been unable to induce him to go, his reason for refusal being that it would not suit him to play in private till after his appearance in public. 'Well,' said Cartwright, 'there is no rule that has not its exception, and I shall be very much surprised, my Lord Duke, if I do not hear him to-morrow.' 'How so!' exclaimed his Grace. 'Because he dines here; and I feel sure will bring his instrument with him.' 'Good gracious,' said the Duke, 'I wish you would ask me to meet

229

him.' Of course Cartwright immediately did so. The Duke told every one he called on in the afternoon that he was going to meet the great lion next day, and where. By a curious coincidence the Duke of ——, and the Duke of ——, and the Duke of ——, and the Duke of ——, instantly discovered that their teeth were much out of order; and the next morning between ten o'clock and one, four dukes had been under Cartwright's hands, and received invitations to his table for the same day. The consequence was, that when Paganini arrived at seven P.M. to dinner, in a hackney-coach, expecting to meet a professional friend or two of his host, he found himself sitting down with the most aristocratic party he had ever met in his life, and among them the very magnate whom he had refused to honour with his fiddle.   *Young*

ANECDOTE OF
CONSTABLE THE ARTIST

I SAT A LONG time with Constable the artist, and watched him paint. He is a most gentle and amiable man. His works will have greater justice done them by posterity, when they have become mellowed and toned down by time. His theories of art are original and instructive. I was surprised to see the free and frequent use he makes of his palette-knife in painting; often, where he wants to impart force and breadth to his subject, preferring it to his brush. He told me that, if he lived in the country, and could afford it, he would never paint a landscape anywhere but in the open air. He told me that he believed most artists sketched their subjects out of doors, and finished them in; and that he could always distinguish the parts of a picture which had been painted *al fresco* from those which had been elaborated in the studio.

My uncle, George Young, mentioned to me a beautiful instance of Constable's imperturbable sweetness of temper. He called on him one day, and was received by him in his front room. After half an hour's chat, the artist proposed to repair to the back, to show him a large picture on which he was engaged. On walking up to his easel, he found that one of his little boys, in his absence, had dashed the handle of the hearth-broom through the canvas, and made so large a rent in it as to render its restoration impossible. He called the child up to him, and asked him gently if he had done it. When the boy admitted his delinquency, he took him on his knee, and rebuked him in these unmeasured terns : – 'Oh, my dear pet! See what we have done! Dear, dear! What shall we do to mend it? I can't think – can you?'   *Young*

PAGANINI

JOHN WILSON CROKER was a faithful public servant, and a passionate partisan. For one-and-twenty years he sat at the Admiralty Board, its influential and indefatigable secretary. For five-and-twenty years he was an active member of the senate; prompt and effective in debate; a master of detail; one of the pillars of the Tory party. For forty years he filled a prominent position, if not an elevated one, in the world of letters in which, if he had the reputation of meting hard measure to others, it was certainly measured to him again. Perhaps few men, who lived within the last half century, contrived to provoke a greater amount of personal hostility than Croker. He was a man of vast and versatile ability, of singular astuteness, of great powers of application, of a high sense of duty; but possessed an asperity of temperament which caused him to take a pessimist view of everything which came within his keen but narrow scrutiny.

Against the consistency of his political career I doubt if anything could be advanced by his bitterest antagonists;

> 'He was constant as the Northern Star,
> Of whose true, fixt, and resting quality
> There was no fellow in the firmament'

of St. Stephen's. During a transition period, when even such men as the Iron Duke were forced to sacrifice their convictions, and bend to the pressure of imperious necessity, Croker stood firm as a rock. Believing, as he honestly did, that reform, if carried, would be the inevitable precursor of revolution, he adhered doggedly to the old traditional policy to which he had been attached; and opposed, with might and main, the doctrines of progress, which he felt persuaded would tend to the subversion of the monarchy, and the undermining of our most venerable institutions – especially the Church. I remember, in speaking of the perils of the Establishment, his saying,

> 'C'est un vieux batiment, si on y touche, il crulera.'

The virulence with which he assailed political opponents, and the merciless energy with which he slashed and tomahawked the writings both of friends and foes in the pages of the 'Quarterly,' begot an accumulation of antipathy to him which would have crushed a man of ordinary sensibility; but made only a transitory impression on his hardy and impenetrable nature.

The majority of the present generation, who have derived their impression of him either from Mr. Disraeli's able but sarcastic delineation of him under the character of Rigby, or else from the reports of those who have writhed under the lash of his incisive invective – will naturally think of him as one of the least lovable of men. But, however he may have abused his critical acumen to the pain and prejudice of others, in private life he exhibited qualities deserving of respect and admiration. To the poor and friendless he was generous: when not blinded by party feeling, he was conscientious; in the face of perpetual opposition, he was courageous. He was a tender husband, and an indulgent father. He had stuff enough in him for the making of a great statesman, though he hardly ever attained to that rank in public estimation. It is a notorious fact, that during the debates on the reform question, he took the wind out of Peel's sails. The fact was, that shortly before the bill came into committee, Croker had been confined to his bed for many days by serious indisposition. During that time, as he lay on his back, he studied the contents of every schedule, dissected them with anatomical precision, and sniffed out every unsavory clause that could be objected to. The consequence was, that when he had arisen from his bed, and found himself again on the floor of the House of Commons, he displayed such intimate knowledge of his subject, that Peel, who, from the multiplicity of his avocations, had not had leisure to devote the same study to the question, gladly gave to him the *pas*, and allowed him not only to bear the burden and the heat, but to win the honours of the battle. He so signalized himself on this occasion by his adroitness, that he astonished the most rancorous of his opponents, and greatly enhanced his reputation with the leaders of his party. From that time Peel never neglected to consult him on every great question that came before him. I told him that I had heard as much, and asked him if it were true. 'Yes,' said he, 'he always asks my advice, and never takes it.' From that time the Duke of Wellington gave him more and more of his confidence; and on his coming to power, offered him high place in his administration; but his health had been so shattered by the extraordinary excitement and exertion which he had undergone during the Reform agitation, that his wife exacted a promise from him that he would never accept office, or sit in a reformed House of Commons. His dread of the consequences to the country through the admission of the Reform Bill was quite genuine, though, as the event has proved, greatly exaggerated.

Young

OF ALL MY LITERARY acquaintances, dear Leigh Hunt was, I think, the most delightful, as assuredly he was the most affectionate. Living within a short walk of us, his disengaged evenings were usually passed in Brompton Crescent, and most charming evenings he made them by the brightness, the originality, and loving-kindliness of his nature. Suffering severely from the *res angusti domus*, there was no repining, no bitterness, no censoriousness in his conversation. He bore his own privations with cheerful resignation, and unaffectedly rejoiced in the better fortune of others. He was greatly delighted with the success of his play, and began another, the scenes of which he brought to us as he wrote, and read as only he could read. He had the wildest ideas of dramatic effect, and calculated in the most utopian spirit upon the intelligence of the British public. As I often told him, if he read them himself, the magic of his voice, the marvellous intonation and variety of expression in his delivery, would probably enchain and enchant a general audience as it did us; but the hope of being so interpreted was not to be entertained for a moment. As an example of the playfulness of his fancy, take the following: I was on my way to the theatre one morning with Charles Mathews in his carriage. We had not spoken for some minutes, when, as we were passing a wholesale stationer's at the west end of the Strand, Mathews, in his whimsical way, suddenly said to me, 'Planché, which would you rather be? Roake or Varty?' such being the names painted over the shop-windows. I laughed at the absurdity of the question, and declined hazarding an opinion, as I had not the advantage of knowing either of the persons mentioned. On my return home in the evening, for I usually dined at the theatre, I found Hunt at tea with my family, and told him the ridiculous question that had been put to me. 'Now, do you know,' he said, 'I consider that anything but a ridiculous question. I should say it was an exceedingly serious one, and which might have very alarming – nay, fatal consequences under certain mental or physical conditions. You might have become impressed by the notion that it was absolutely necessary for you to come to some decision on the question, and so absorbed in its consideration that you could think of nothing else. All business, public or private, would be neglected. Perpetual pondering on one problem, which daily became more difficult of solution, would result in monomania. Your health undermined, your brain overwrought, in the last moments of fleeting existence, only a few seconds left you in which to make your selection, you might rashly utter "Roake!" then, suddenly repenting, gasp out "Var," and die before you could say "ty." '

He had a most amusing habit of coining words. Having paid my poor invalid wife, what she considered a great complinent, she said, 'Oh, Mr. Hunt, you make me really begin to fear that you are – pardon me the epithet – a humbug.' 'Good gracious!' he exclaimed, 'that a man who has been imprisoned for speaking the truth should be accused of *humbugeism!*' – the softening of the *g* adding elegance to the novelty of the expression. He had familiar names – *noms d'amitié* – for us all, made to rhyme according to an Oriental custom. My two daughters, Kate and Matilda, were, of course, 'Katty and Matty.' My wife's name, Elizabeth, instead of Betty, became 'Batty.' Her sister, Fanny, was transmuted to 'Fatty,' which she indignantly objected to as personal. 'And what is papa's name to be?' asked one of my girls. 'Papa's? oh, James must obviously be "Jatty," ' and so we remained to the end of the chapter.   *Planché*

WILLIAM MAKEPEACE THACKERAY

MY ACQUAINTANCE WITH Thackeray commenced some time before he joined 'The Garrick,' and while I was the guest of his cousin, Captain Thomas James Thackeray, in the Rue du Faubourg St. Honoré, during one of my many visits to Paris. He was at that time a slim young man, rather taciturn, and not displaying any particular love or talent for literature. Drawing appeared to be his favourite amusement; and he often sat by my side while I was reading, or writing, covering any scrap of paper lying about with the most spirited sketches and amusing caricatures. A member of 'The Garrick,' who was specially unpopular with the majority of the members, was literally *drawn* out of the club by Thackeray. His figure, being very peculiar, was sketched in pen and ink by his implacable persecutor. On every pad on the writing-tables, or whatever paper he could venture to appropriate, he represented him in the most ridiculous and derogatory situations that could be imagined, always with his back towards you: but unmistakable. His victim, it must be admitted, bore this desecration of his 'lively effigies,' with great equanimity for a considerable period; but at length, one very strong – perhaps too strong – example of the artist's graphic and satirical abilities, combined with the conviction that he was generally objectionable, induced him to retire from the club, and leave the pungent pen of Michael Angelo Titmarsh to punish more serious offenders than bores and toadies.   *Planché*

IT WAS AT THE table of the Duchess-Countess of Sutherland that I had the gratification of meeting Mr. Samuel Rogers ('that anomalous personage, a rich poet,' as Leigh Hunt used to call him), and that brilliant conversationalist, Mr. Luttrell, with both of whom I remained on terms of the greatest friendship to the end of their lives. The latter was at that period my near neighbour, residing in Brompton Square; and shortly after our dining together in Hamilton Place, I asked Mr. Rogers, with whom I had breakfasted the following morning, to favor Mrs. Planché and myself by breakfasting with us in Brompton Crescent. I had just previously been subpœnaed as a witness in the case of Jerrold *v* Morris, which was tried in the Court of Common Pleas; and instead of writing a note to Mr. Luttrell, to ask him to meet Mr. Rogers, I sent him over-night the subpœna altered to suit the circumstances, with which in his hand he punctually made his appearance at ten in the morning. These two celebrated men, without whom few dinner parties in high life were considered complete, were very differently gifted. Rogers had an inexhaustible fund of anecdote of the most interesting, as well as amusing description, and told his stories in the fewest words possible, so that not only did they never weary you, but they might have been printed without the slightest verbal alteration. Luttrell rarely recounted anything he had heard or seen, but charmed you by the sparkle of his language, and the felicity of his epithets. One evening at a party, having accepted a verbal invitation to dinner, under the idea that his son, who was present, would also be asked, and finding subsequently that he was not, he said, 'Then who is going to dine there?' 'I really don't know, but I believe the Bishop of —— for one'. 'The Bishop of ——!' exclaimed Luttrell. 'Mercy upon me! I don't mix well with the Dean, and I shall positively effervesce with the Bishop.'

Though great friends, for many years, and almost constant companions, they would occasionally comment on each other's peculiarities with humorous freedom. At an assembly at Grosvenor House Mr. Luttrell informed me Mr. Rogers had hurt his foot. On expressing my regret at the cause of his absence, 'Oh!' said Luttrell, 'he'll be here to-night for all that; that old man would go out with the rattles in his throat!' I don't think Rogers was five years his senior.

Rogers had the reputation of being very ill-natured, and many instances have been given to me by others. I am bound to declare that during all the time I knew him I never heard him say a really ill-natured thing of any one; but he by no means denied the accusation. 'When I was young,' he observed to me, 'I used to say good-natured things, and nobody listened to me. Now that I am old I say ill-natured things and everybody listens to me.'

Rogers had very peculiar notions respecting poetry. The highly imaginative had no charm for him. He could not appreciate the grandeur of oriental language of the Old Testament, and constantly contrasted it with the simple pathos of the New. He would quote the celebrated description of the Horse in the Book of Job, 'His neck is clothed with thunder, and he crieth Ha! ha! to the lightning.' 'That's nonsense,' he said to me – then turning to the 11th chapter of St. John, he pointed to the two words which form the thirty-fifth verse, 'Jesus wept.' '*That's* poetry!'

The same taste induced him, whilst he admired the plays of Shakespeare, to speak contemptuously of his sonnets. At breakfast one morning, Mr. Procter and I undertook their defence. Rogers challenged us to repeat a line of them, and to his infinite amusement neither of us were able. I got as far as 'Oh how much more doth beauty,' and there I stuck. Procter could not remember a word. He who had sung the 'Pleasures of Memory' chuckled triumphantly. We whom it had treacherously deserted sat humiliated, but 'of the same opinion still.'

It was much the same with respect to music. Simplicity and brevity alone had charms for him. 'Is not that delightful,' I asked him one evening at Mrs. Sartoris's. It was an air by Sebastian Bach. 'Yes, and so short,' was the reply. With Dr. Johnson, he wished that everything 'wonderful' in the way of execution or ornamentation was 'impossible.' During the performance of a 'grand scena,' no matter who was the singer, it was his custom to ask any one who sat near him, 'If you heard those sounds in a hospital wouldn't you suppose some horrible operation was going on?'

The jokes on his personal appearance never seemed to disturb his tranquillity. 'Rogers, you're rich enough, why don't you keep your hearse?' is a well-known question addressed to him by some wicked wag – I think Lord Alvanley; but he was as hard upon himself. He tried to cheer my wife, who was becoming a confirmed invalid, by assuring her that he never knew what health was till he was fifty, and that when he was a young man he wore a yellow coat, and was called the Dead Dandy. Singularly enough, after the accident which deprived him of the power of walking, it might truly have been said he kept his hearse, for he was carried in his chair and put into his carriage by a door made at the back of it. *Planché*

EXCEPT IN CONNEXION with his great work in Hyde-Park, there is little in the life of Joseph Paxton of more than passing interest to the reader. A self-made man, he owes his proud position to his own indomitable energy and untiring perseverance; and he whose portrait now graces a page of our book – he whom the world delighteth to honour – he who has won for himself a name imperishable and of high reputation as a benefactor of his time and country – makes it his proudest boast that he comes of, and belongs to, the People. It is ever so; genius and talent exist in the mass, and rise from out its bosom as circumstances call forth their manifestation. The greatest of Britain's Sons are of the People; and if they rise, they owe their elevation to the assiduous cultivation of their own minds and the tireless industry of their own hands.

What matters it to tell the precise spot which gave him birth, or the exact hour which ushered him into the world? Suffice it, that the mind which could conceive a Crystal Palace is yet healthy and vigorous, and fit for the work prepared for it to accomplish. And there is little fear that the man who could master such a grand idea as that we see realised in Hyde-Park, will sit idly down by his laurels and strive no more to enrich the world by contributions to its arts, its science, and its literature. Whether, in the words of a contemporary, we consider the noble and humanising purposes to which the building is consecrated, the appropriateness, elegance, vastness, and beauty of the design, or its simple but most admirable novelty, we must acknowledge its designer's high claims to the grateful appreciation of his fellow-men, and to that enduring place in the national annals which is the best reward of true greatness in any and every department of public usefulness.

Mr. Paxton, whose original profession, as is well known, was that of a landscape gardener, was first employed in a responsible capacity by the Duke of Somerset, at his seat at Wimbledon. From thence he passed, we are told, into the service of the Duke of Devonshire, at Chatsworth. But that nobleman was not slow to perceive that his gardener possessed administrative faculties, and a knowledge and skill in financial arrangement, of a high order, in which capacities, we believe, he has been of essential service in the management of the Duke's estates, both in England and Ireland.

There are few instances of scientific application which present so many points of interest as the circumstances by which this gentleman has earned his present fame as the architect of the

Great Exhibition Building. With the name of Mr. Paxton have long been associated the glories of Chatsworth, and the sole contrivance of the vast conservatory which the King of Saxony graphically compared to 'a tropical scene with a glass sky.' In 1848 Mr. Paxton erected an ornamental glass structure for the reception of the new and splendid plant called the 'Victoria Regia.' This building, as may be seen, was of a light and airy appearance, and was in fact the parent of the Crystal Palace. It is 60 feet 6 inches in length, 49 feet 9 inches broad, and proportionably high. It is built entirely of glass and iron, with a roof on the ridge and row principle, and is in other respects similar to the Great Exhibition Building. Several designs for the latter structure had already been prepared, but they had all failed to impress the public with their fitness for the purpose; and Mr. Paxton, apprehensive that an irreparable blunder would be committed in the intended building, proposed to the Executive Committee another plan. Certain difficulties lay in the way, but Mr. Paxton was not to be deterred – his mind was made up; 'and,' said the Duke of Devonshire at a public meeting held at Bakewell, 'I never knew Mr. Paxton resolve to undertake anything he did not fully accomplish.' On the morning of the 18th June, whilst presiding at a railway committee, he sketched upon a sheet of blotting-paper his idea for the Great Industrial Building. He sat up all that night until he had worked out the design to his satisfaction, and the elevations, sections, working details, and specifications, were completed in ten days. Next morning Mr. Paxton started from Derby by railway for the Metropolis; and in the same train and carriage was Mr. Robert Stephenson, the engineer, a member moreover of the Royal Commission, and who, at Mr. Paxton's request, examined the plans.

'Wonderful! (exclaimed the engineer) – worthy of the magnificence of Chatsworth! – a thousand times better than anything that has been brought before us! What a pity they were not prepared earlier!'

'Will you lay them before the Royal Commission?' – 'I will,' was the reply.

Next day the Royal Commission met; but Mr. Stephenson had not the opportunity of submitting Mr. Paxton's plan to his colleagues and Prince Albert; the office was, however, delegated to an able hand, Mr. Scott Russell, one of the secretaries of the Commission. Mr. Paxton next waited upon Prince Albert at Buckingham-Palace, to explain the details. The scheme was referred to the Building Committee, who could not entertain it, as they had already devised a plan of their own. However, Mr. Paxton

MR (AFTERWARDS SIR) JOSEPH PAXTON

But yesterday a naked sod,
    The dandies sneered from Rotten Row,
    And cantered o'er it to and fro;
        And see 'tis done!
As though 'twere by a wizard's rod,
    A blazing arch of lucid glass
    Leaps like a fountain from the grass
        To meet the sun!

Whilst the plan of the Building Committee was still under discussion, Mr. Paxton was led by the hostility which it had incurred, to submit a plan for a structure chiefly of glass and iron . . . whatever objections were entertained originally against the use of the site have gradually disappeared during the progress of the present building and have become changed into positive approval and admiration of the building itself and assent to the particular location of it.

THE OFFICIAL CATALOGUE TO THE EXHIBITION, 1851

240

appealed to public judgment, and the practicability, simplicity, and beauty of the scheme became instantly popular. Thus encouraged, he lost no time in sending in a tender for his design, prepared, under his direction, by Messrs. Fox & Henderson; and at length Mr. Paxton's plan was tendered by them as an 'improvement' on the Committee's design, and their offer proved to be the lowest. It will be recollected what followed: the Crystal Palace was eventually chosen unanimously, not only by the Building Committee, but by the Royal Commission; and the many thousands who assembled with their Queen and her husband within the fairy-like structure at its inauguration, on May-Day last, must have been impressed with the soundness of this decision.

Such is a brief *résumé* of the circumstances which led to this fortunate adoption of Mr. Paxton's design; a more fitting temple for the world's industrial treasures could not be devised; and it was but a just recognition of its author's great share in contributing to the success of the Exhibition, that he led the inauguration pageant in which the Queen of Great Britain took so prominent a part.

Mr. Paxton is a distinguished Fellow of the Linnæan and Horticultural Societies, and has produced a Botanical Dictionary of accredited worth, besides editing the 'Flower Garden,' and other botanical and horticultural works. The gardens at Chatsworth form an excellent finishing school for botanical students; and many foreigners having received from Mr. Paxton instructions in horticulture and ornamental landscape gardening, his name has come to have, as it well deserves, an European reputation for both taste and skill.

THE UNIVERSAL EXHIBITOR, 1851

ISAAC DISRAELI

AN OLD GENTLEMAN, *strictly*, in his appearance; a countenance which at first glance (owing, perhaps, to the mouth, which hangs) I fancied slightly chargeable with stolidity of expression, but which developed strong sense as it talked; a rather *soigné* style of dress for so old a man, and a manner good-humored, complimentary (to Gebir), discursive and prosy, bespeaking that engrossment and interest in his own pursuits which might be expected to be found in a person so patient in research and collection. But there is a tone of the *philosophe* (or I fancied it), which I did not quite like; and that tone (addressing the instinct rather than the judgment) which is felt or imagined to bespeak (how shall it be?) absence of high principle.   *Chorley*

LADY BLESSINGTON WAS then gathering about her a circle of the younger literary men of London, in addition to the older and more distinguished friends made by her before her widowhood. I went to the studio of Mr. Rothwell, who was engaged on a half-length portrait of her, which he never, I believe, completed, and was introduced to her. She said a few kind words in that winning and gracious manner which no woman's welcome can have ever surpassed; and from that moment till the day of her death in Paris, I experienced only a long course of kind constructions and good offices. She was a steady friend, through good report and evil report, for those to whom she professed friendship. Such faults as she had belonged to her position, to her past history, and to the disloyalty of many who paid court to her by paying court to her faults, and who then carried into the outer world depreciating reports of the wit, the banter, the sarcasm, and the epigram, which but for their urgings and incitements would have been always kindly, however mirthful.

She must have had originally the most sunny of sunny natures. As it was, I have never seen anything like her vivacity and sweet cheerfulness during the early years when I knew her. She had a singular power of entertaining herself by her own stories; the keenness of an Irishwoman in relishing fun and repartee, strange turns of language, and bright touches of character. A fairer, kinder, more universal recipient of everything that came within the possibilities of her mind, I have never known. I think the only genuine author whose merits she was averse to admit was Hood; and yet she knew Rabelais, and delighted in *Elia*. It was her real disposition to dwell on beauties rather than faults. Critical she could be, and as judiciously critical as any woman I have ever known, but she never seemed to be so willingly. When a poem was read to her, or a book given to her, she could always touch on the best passage, the bright point; and rarely missed the purpose of the work, if purpose it had. When I think of the myriads I have known who, on such occasions, betwixt a desire to show sagacity, slowness to appreciate, or want of tact in expression, flounder on betwixt commonplace which is not complimentary, and disquisitions that are rather hard to bear, I return to her powers and ways of accepting as among the lost graces, which have been replaced (say the optimists) by something truer and more solid. I doubt it.

Her taste in everything was towards the gay, the superb, the luxurious; but, on the whole, excellently good.   *Chorley*

It was a pleasure to note his firm, swift stride. His pace was such as few men of past seventy would have cared to set; and he maintained it to the end. The stream of talk ran not less swiftly. I have no notes of what was said, and should not use them if I had, but I remember clearly the subject and scope of his strange outpourings. Kindly and friendly as he was to me, out of the depth of his regard for the friend whose letter I had brought, he was then, and often afterward when I saw him, in a despairing and hostile mood with reference to the world in general. He discoursed on London and all Londoners, storming against the sordid and hollow life by which he was surrounded; complaining of the very houses amid which he took his devious way. They were built, he said, to tumble down in ninety years. The tenant had only a ninety-nine years' lease from the landlord who owned the ground; he could not afford to build solidly and honestly; his architect had learned how to run up a wall which would stand just long enough not to become the property of the landlord; computing that the wall should fall down before the lease fell in. Yes, it was more the fault of the landlord than the tenant, but it was a devil's system all through, and the devil had a sure grip on tenant and landlord both. And what did it matter? 'They are just a parcel of pigs rooting in the mire'; and so on. With all this were mingled flashes of kindly humour and human sympathy which lit up the gloom and almost savage hopelessness of his temper at the moment. This lasted for perhaps half an hour. It was past nine when we returned. The candles had been lighted. The fire – for though it was August a fire had been kindled – blazed cheerfully. The table was spread: the tea was made and keeping hot under its Scotch cosey; and by the time he had laid aside his wraps and reappeared in his ragged red dressing-gown, the stern, strong, sad face reflected the pleasant light which shone on it, and his mood changed with the changing circumstances.

Without any question or hint of mine he began to talk of America. 'They think,' he cried sharply, – 'some of you think, I am no friend to America. But I love America, – not everybody's America, but the true America; the country which has given birth to Emerson and to Emerson's friends; the country of honest toilers and brave thinkers. Never shall I forget,' he went on with kindling eye and a deeper tone, 'that the first money which ever came to me for a printed book came from America. When your people reprinted *Sartor Resartus* out of *Fraser* they sent me a good sum for it. They need not have sent it. I had no claim on it or on them; but they sent it, and I did and do thank them for that. By and by they republished my *French Revolution*. Do you know,

I had not had a penny for that book from the English public till a good while after American friends remitted to me a pretty sum for it? Twice over, twice, my first money came to me from your country. And do they think I forget it, and am not grateful for it, and don't love the country which showed its love for me?' Then, breaking off suddenly, with one of his explosions of wild laughter, half pathetic, half sneering, he exclaimed: 'Yes, I angered you all with my *Ilias in Nuce*, but who shall say I was not right; or right *then?* But you were the stronger at last; you conquered, and you know people will have it I have said might is right. Suppose I did say it? I knew what I meant by it – not what they think I meant, – there is a real, true meaning under it. A man is an atheist who believes that in the long run what God allows to triumph is not the right.'

And again turning the talk not less suddenly, with a quite indescribable inflection of voice which masked an odd mixture of good-humour and contempt, which the phrase also masked, he said, 'You went up and down the country, did you not, with your fighting parties?' He had clearly imbibed from some of his German friends a none too high idea of the military quality of our armies and commanders.

There was no detail of a life strange to him which had not some interest for him. He put all sorts of questions as he sat behind his teapot and took huge sips from his cup and munched his bread and butter and plum-cake. He asked about the law in the United States, the schools of law, and the practice of it, and whether it much differed from English law, and how; and had I got here soon enough to visit the English courts and compare them with the American courts, and in which did I think a man had the better chance of getting justice done him, – 'supposing it was justice he wanted'; at which the loud, bitter laugh broke out again.

Answering as well as I could this volley of questions, I sat watching the old man and trying to make the Carlyle of my guesses and fancy match the Carlyle in the flesh, on whom I looked for the first time. There is little need to describe a face so well known as his; known by countless photographs and many prints of every degree of merit. It is so marked a face that I never saw a likeness of him which had not some unmistakable look of the man himself. No sign of decay was there about him. The eye was full, the glance swift, sure, penetrating. The hollowness of the socket, the deep shadow beneath the eye, were the traces, not of illness, except such as was chronic, but of lifelong vigil and study. 'Writer of books,' as he described himself in his famous petition, was stamped on

245

every feature. A sad, stern face I called it just now, and I know not whether it was more sad or stern, nor whether the sadness of it was not deepest when he laughed. He had still a florid complexion, and the ruddy hue stood out strongly against the iron-gray hair which fell in shaggy clumps about his forehead, while the eyes, naturally deep-set, seemed lost beneath the thicket of eyebrow which overshadowed them. The moustache and beard he wore full; wrinkled and gnarled rather than curled. When he laughed, the grim squareness of the jaw showed itself. It was a portentous laugh; open-mouthed and deep-lunged, and prolonged; ending mostly in a shout of triumph, and seldom quite glad or kindly. The bony hands clutched the table meanwhile with a muscular grip, and the laugh was likely to be followed by a torrent of speech that bore down everything before it. Woe to the man who ventured to gainsay him when in that humour; as I more than once saw proof of afterward.

Tea and questions over, the strung fibres relaxed a little. He sat himself down by the fireside, on the floor, his back against the jamb of the chimneypiece, took a comb out of his pocket and combed down his tangled bushy hair till it hid his forehead altogether, and you could no longer see where the hair ended and the eyebrows began. This done, he filled and lighted his pipe; a long clay pipe quite new, known, I think, as a churchwarden; quite two feet from bowl to mouthpiece. As the perfume of the tobacco filled the room and the clouds of smoke rolled about him, he began to talk again. It was no longer talk in the common sense of the word; there were no more questions, no pauses. It was a monologue, and no small part of it sounded strangely familiar, as if I had sat in that little parlour before and heard the same voice pouring out the same words and ideas. He had, in fact, by that time fallen into the habit of repeating orally what in days long gone he had written, – not consciously or purposely, but as if the same trains of thought came back to him; and he was content to have a listener while he thought over the old problems that had vexed him, and once more offered his solution of them. Page after page of *Sartor* did he repeat, not *verbatim*, but in substance, and of that deep study called *Characteristics*, diverging then into *Past and Present*, and again into one or another of the *Latter Day Pamphlets*. I was fresh from reading most of these; all of them were at that time pretty well known to me, and I never had a stranger sensation than in thus hearing from the mouth of the philosopher the oral repetition of his written and printed wisdom. With intervals of silence or conversation of a more familiar kind, he

246

went on thus for quite two hours. When it seemed to have come to an end I rose to take leave, and upon my telling him I was going to Berlin he asked me to come again on my return and bring him all the news of the Prussian capital.

Smalley

LORD RANDOLPH CHURCHILL IN DEBATE

THE NERVOUSNESS, IF IT be nervousness, which is denoted by the continuing movement of the forefinger to the upper lip, has ceased. If you have studied him in Mr. Tenniel's cartoons only, and have never seen him in the flesh, you may be surprised to note that this slender, carefully dressed figure is rather above the average height. There is not a trace of embarrassment; the stranger would never guess that he stood alone, surrounded by enemies, or at least by opponents; by men once his supporters, now angry, suspicious, resentful.

If he were still Leader of the House he could not be more at his ease, more sure of himself, more ready to meet all comers. The foes at his back seem to give him no concern, and if he has friends in front, their friendship is not of a kind which calls for expressions of gratitude. Slight as the figure is, the stamp of energy on it is as impressive as the stamp of elegance; and both are impressive. It is a Democratic age, but the story of all ages, or of many ages, is the same; the Democrat prefers the Patrician for leader. The voice has the ring of authority in it. The House is silent as death. The faces on the Treasury Bench are the faces of men who wonder what is coming, and are getting ready to meet it. The scene, like so many scenes in the House, is dramatic, and the yellow light that floods the chamber from the ceiling adds to the illusion, and to the theatrical character of it. Mr. Gladstone looks eagerly across the table, Mr. Morley, Sir George Trevelyan, Sir William Harcourt, are all alert. The one unmoved personage in the Liberal phalanx is Lord Hartington.

Almost the first sentence that Lord Randolph utters is a debating sentence: 'When I recall the language in which I attacked the Government of the right honourable gentleman opposite (Mr. Gladstone) for engaging British military forces in the Soudan, I cannot refrain from expressing regret and alarm at what appears to be a recommencement of a course which I then so strongly denounced, and still at the present moment denounce.' I quote it not because I am going to follow the speaker in his argument, for I am not, but as a good specimen of the right way of saying things

247

to the House of Commons. The truth is, the two men most unlike each other are the two men who have taken almost identical views on the Soudan business – Lord Randolph and Mr. John Morley. This single sentence is a reminder to the House of all the disasters that befell Mr. Gladstone's policy in Egypt, and a warning to the present Ministry that they are entering upon the same road. That is what I call a debating manner, and a House of Commons manner.

Smalley

MR CHAMBERLAIN

MR GLADSTONE ONCE said that in his time he had known three men in the House of Commons who always said exactly what they meant and no more. The three were Lord Palmerston, Mr. Parnell, and Mr. Chamberlain. He can take blows as well as give them. Mr. Gladstone's attack on him in the closing speech of the Home Rule debate last year was borne with a stoicism that Mr. Gladstone himself might have envied, and perhaps did. You would never have guessed from his placid face and unruffled composure of manner that he was the object of all that elaborate invective. On the platform as in the House he meets a running fire of questions, taunts, objurgations, insults even, with a tranquillity which enables him to frame a retort before the storm is over. There are greater orators. There is no better debater – no man in England who surpasses him in the power of effective speaking. It is now many years since he passed out of the second rank into the front rank.

He has nothing to do with the aristocracy or with the Established Church. Birth gave him no privileges. Professor Huxley once said of himself that by birth he was a plebeian, and that he stood by his order. Mr. Chamberlain comes of that great middle class which is, in this country, a plebeian class, and is justly proud of being. He was born in it and married in it, and has said more than once that he is never so happy as when among his own friends and people at Birmingham.

The cockney would call him a provincial. He won his first celebrity as Mayor – thrice Mayor – of Birmingham, which he reformed and swept clean, and lighted and set in order throughout. And because he showed himself master of local administration, critics who were masters of nothing but adjectives sometimes called his politics parochial. He still lives at Birmingham, or rather near it, having a place with some acres of land about it, so that this land reformer is also a landowner. Mr. Chamberlain when forty

GLADSTONE IN 1884

But you will deceive yourself if you think you have any real conception of Mr. Gladstone's genius till you sit beneath him or beside him, till that voice speaks to you, till you look into the face of the orator, till you feel the influence of a personality as persuasive as it is powerful; till, in one word, you are in his presence and subject to his sway.

George Smalley, LONDON LETTERS, 1890

years old save one retired from business. He has been able to devote himself since 1874 exclusively to public affairs. London gossip long since fixed the exact figure of his yearly income.

He has, beside his place in Warwickshire, a house in London and a place in London society. Mr. Gladstone not long since thought fit to jest at his social position. There was a sentence about cushioned ease, meant apparently to bring him into disrepute with the poorer members of the part of reform. Mr. Gladstone's known respect for rank might have kept him silent on such a topic, but since it did not there is this to be said: No man in England reaches Mr. Chamberlain's position, or anything like it, without becoming an object of attraction to society. But society sought him, not he society. His opinions have survived the contact, and society itself has laughed at the failure of one or two of its leaders who thought they could 'lionise' the great Radical. His safeguard against that process was like that of the Dutchman who escaped drowning: he did not go in the boat. He stayed away from houses where he thought people wanted to make a show of him. Not even Royalty made an impression on his Radicalism; neither Marlborough House nor Windsor Castle has won him over from any one of his convictions. The officials of the royal household will tell you that Mr. Chamberlain came to Windsor an object of royal aversion, and left it almost a favourite. The Queen liked him. Like the sensible woman she is she can bear plain truths, when told in low tones. One promising courtier ruined his chances by a loud voice which he could not subdue to the conventional pitch. I might add something about one or two other personal traits, but it is quite time for these indiscretions to come to an end.

Smalley

LORD BEACONSFIELD

LAST OF ALL Lord Beaconsfield came. It is three-quarters past the dinner hour; but that delay and the long succession of dignitaries who have preceded him seem to have been contrived to render his entry the more impressive. And impressive it is in all ways. I verily believe the guests would rather have gone without their dinner than without this sauce to it. The whole hall rises for him; the applause is deafening; the greeting such as he is rightly proud of. It was a common remark that Lord Beaconsfield was looking uncommonly well. So he was; so long as he thought people were looking at him. The condition of this great man's health is an affair of State, and is discussed very much as Louis XIV's bodily welfare was discussed when he changed his shirts in public. Lord Beaconsfield does not change his shirts in public. He finds it less embarrassing to effect from time to time an exchange of what are sometimes called his principles. He has, however, his physical peculiarities, and one who sees him from time to time is able to guess near enough at his actual health. When he made his entry into the Library of the Guildhall, I stood near the door. I could see him pull himself together and compose the muscles of his face till the desired expression was attained. All resemblances, says a great physiognomist, lie in the eyes and mouth. Individual expression lies there too, and the brief space during which Lord Beaconsfield was advancing up the aisle was not too brief for a good look at these features. They quite confirmed the food reports from Hatfield which I recently mentioned. A strange fire burned in his eyes. The jaw and lips were set fast. For those two minutes no man's face was more full of energy, no step firmer than his, septuagenarian as he is, with four years added to the seventy. He wore his Windsor uniform of dark blue with embroideries in gold, with pendent sword, and on his breast that matchless and priceless star of diamonds, including the ruby cross of the Garter which fills all meaner breasts with envy. To the Lord Mayor he bowed low; and again to the Mayoress, accomplishing the double obeisance without any too perceptible stiffness or audible creaking of the joints.

As the procession from the Library to the Banqueting Hall slowly made its way about the tables there was no fault to find with his bearing. There are few actors who make up better, or who play their parts, more perfectly so long as they are on the stage. When he stood up to speak and the cheers of the nine hundred guests greeted him, he received the applause with quite admirable dignity. He was too great a man to be moved by these natural expressions of respect. Not even a bow acknowledged them; he stood as upright as the inveterate stoop of his shoulders permitted. No more did he acknowledge by a single word the overdone panegyrics of the Lord Mayor, but began at once what he had to say, which, nevertheless, was so little that it would not have suffered from a brief exordium of politeness. In his contempt for commonplace civilities there was a touch of almost regal manner. It is of the essence of royal good breeding to show, and I presume to feel, a certain indifference to the feelings or comfort of all lesser persons; not because a king may not be kind-hearted but because the distance which separates him from his greatest subject is simply infinite. Had Lady Beaconsfield been living it would hardly have surprised anybody to see her husband give her his arm to dinner, as a king does to his wife. In her absence he took in the Lady Mayoress, as required by Guildhall etiquette. It seems to be Guildhall etiquette, also, that the guest of the evening should not be placed on the Lord Mayor's right hand, nor even next to the host on the left. Lady Salisbury was on the Lord Mayor's right. The Lady Mayoress sat next to the Lord Mayor, and on her left sat the Prime Minister. He did not finally settle himself in his chair till after some fumbling with the cards that lay on his plate and the plates near by, as if perplexed by his position.

During dinner he sat for the most part silent. During his speech he had recourse at intervals to the glass of claret, or it may have been port, which was in front of him, which was full when he began and empty when he finished. His voice was strong enough to reach through the hall, with the help of a singularly elaborate and patient articulation of each syllable that he uttered. But it was hollow; it seemed to be fetched by a succession of calculated efforts from somewhere in his throat, and was husbanded as if he had only a limited supply which might run out if not used with economy. He has very much the trick of mouthing his words which Mr. Irving has in his least happy moments. It is as if the muscles of the tongue were weak and did not invariably respond to the will of the speaker; as if at times it required two distinct exertions, or even more, to bring that unruly member in contact with the palate. If you had heard him for the first time you would not have said this man is a great orator. But you could not listen to a sentence without perceiving that he had a consummate knowledge of the art of speaking in public, and consummate cleverness in making the most of his knowledge.

Later in the evening Lord Beaconsfield paid Sir Stafford Northcote the compliment of supposing that his speech on finance was occupying the attention of the audience. He leaned back in his chair, his mask slipped off for a moment, the light from the great chandelier above streamed full on his face, and you saw what he was like when not posing for the gallery. The cheeks grew hollow, the tint of his skin waxlike, the lips relaxed, the cavernous jaws fell slightly apart, the carefully trained curls on the left of the brow slid out of place, the fire sank low in his eyes, the whole face aged painfully in a minute. If ever a human countenance looked weary and bored and scornful, Lord Beaconsfield's was that countenance at that moment. Perhaps he felt that his speech had fallen flat, in spite of the cheers; perhaps he did not care whether it had or not, but was simply tired and sleepy and wanted to have done with this pageantry and get home. This state did not last; as soon as Sir Stafford gave signs of ending his heavy speech, his chief was once more aware of his public, and alert. He resumed his war paint as nimbly as he had quitted it. When you once begin to study a remarkable face the study soon becomes a fascination. There was nothing else to interest one, unless Lord Salisbury's acid civilities to the Lady Mayoress might be called interesting; but I stayed on to the last.

And to the last the weary old man preserved his air of fresh serenity. He followed the Lady Mayoress dutifully out to the drawing-room. He endured without any show of resentment the congratulations of a few pushing admirers. The ever-faithful Montague Corry presently brought him his cloak, a romantic garment of cloth, very short and lined with fur; then the two put their backs to the wall as if to defy all comers till the Prime Minister's carriage should be announced. He had not long to wait before the far cry from outside the door, 'Lord Beaconsfield's carriage coming up!' was passed on to him by a dozen clamorous yet reverential voices. With a last salute to the company he put on his cocked hat – a laced and plumed piece of headgear of the kind known as a fore-and-aft hat – and limped away between a double hedge of liveried attendants and spectators of every degree. Not even his brougham is like an ordinary man's brougham; it is not a brougham at all but a single coach of ancient fashion, swung high in the air on C springs; carriage, horses, and servants all very smartly turned out. The ever-faithful followed his chief into the coffee-coloured interior. The footman closed the door and climbed up behind, but, his foot catching, came down headlong faster than he went up. There was a cry among the crowd, for it looked as if the man would be drawn under the wheels, and there was a rush to rescue him, but he was already in the arms of a big policeman and presently was righted and thrust up into his perch. All this took a minute or two; during which Lord Beaconsfield sat immovable and uninterested. Then carriage and horses and footman and coachman and Prime Minister and private secretary vanished into the darkness. The play was played out and not for another twelvemonth will the curtain be rung up again on this stage. Lord Beaconsfield was good enough to assure the company that he should in all probability again be the chief performer at the twelvemonth's end. Perhaps this was only an oracular pleasantry; perhaps his lordship had never read that sound maxim of Mr. Hosea Biglow, 'Don't never prophesy onless ye know.'

IN 1862 George Peabody placed in the hands of trustees £150,000, to be so expended as 'to ameliorate the condition of the poor and needy of this great metropolis, and to promote their comfort and happiness'; and suggested that the best way of carrying out his intentions would be 'to apply the fund, or a portion of it, in the construction of such improved dwellings for the poor as may combine, in the utmost possible degree, the essentials of healthfulness, comfort, social enjoyment, and economy.' That suggestion being adopted, commodious buildings have been set up, or are still being erected, at Spitalfields, and at Chelsea, with accommodation for about two hundred persons in each; at Bermondsey, large enough for about four hundred; at Islington, adapted for six hundred and fifty; and at Shadwell, for a yet larger number of inmates. In continuance of this good work, the benefactor applied a further sum of £100,000 in 1866, and a second sum of like amount on the 5th of December 1868.

The modest, manly letter to the trustees announcing this fresh act of munificence, is worth quoting entire:

'MY LORD AND GENTLEMEN,—I beg to acquaint you, who have so kindly undertaken the management of the fund set apart under my second deed of gift, of the 19th of April 1866, for the benefit of the poor of London and its vicinity, that, in pursuance of an intention which I have entertained since the creation of that fund, I am desirous now of adding to it a further sum of £100,000.

'In contemplation of this, I purchased, about three years ago, a tract of freehold building land, of about fifteen acres in extent, at Brixton, near the City of London School, easily accessible, and within a few minutes' walk of frequent trains to and from London. This land has increased in value, and can now be let, on building leases of eighty years, at rents producing about 8 per cent per annum on the cost, which is £16,285 17s. 3d. This land I propose to convey to you with the same powers as are conferred by the deed over the other property of this trust, and with discretion to you either to deal with it as a source of income by letting it, or any portion of it, on lease; or, should you deem it expedient, to retain it in your own hands as sites for dwellings to be erected by the trust.

254

GEORGE PEABODY

Where'er that honoured name is heard
  The tears will gleam in woman's eyes;
The hearts of men will stir and creep,
  And blessings to their lips will rise.
Though Science join'd the sunder'd worlds,
  It needed yet what he has done,—
A noble action, meekly wrought,
  Has knit the hearts of both in one.

LONDON SOCIETY, OCTOBER 1866

'Pursuant to my letter of the 29th January 1866, I transferred to you, subject to a contingency therein explained, 5,000 shares in the Hudson's Bay Company, which accordingly stand in your names, together with 642 additional shares purchased by the reinvestment of the accruing income of the previous 5,000. These 5,642 shares I have since redeemed, conformably to the deed of the 19th April 1866, by the payment of £100,000 on the 1st February last. I have now to acquaint you that it is my intention, so soon as the necessary deeds can be prepared, to hand the shares over to you to be retained or dealt with, according to your best judgment and discretion. The price of these shares shall be fixed on the 17th inst. by the Stock Exchange sales on that day, when I will hand to you a cheque for the balance to make the gift a cash value of £100,000. This amount will increase my former donation of the second trust to £200,000, and, including my gift under the first trust in March 1862, of £150,000, a total of £350,000.

'I trust you will see manifested in this further donation an expression of my entire satisfaction with the manner in which you have conducted the affairs of the trusts.—I am, with great respect, your humble servant,   'GEORGE PEABODY.'

It is not strange that a man so generous as this should be publicly thanked for his benefactions by the United States Congress and the Queen of England; or that spontaneous praises of him should rise from the hearts of millions on both sides of the Atlantic.

H. R. Fox Bourne, FAMOUS LONDON MERCHANTS, 1869